THE INVENTION OF PETER

Apostolic Discourse
and Papal Authority
in Late Antiquity

George E. Demacopoulos

PENN

UNIVERSITY OF PENNSYLVANIA PRESS

PHILADELPHIA

Published by
University of Pennsylvania Press
Philadelphia, Pennsylvania 19104-4112
www.upenn.edu/pennpress

Printed in the United States of America on acid-free paper
10 9 8 7 6 5 4 3 2 1

Library of Congress Cataloging-in-Publication Data
Demacopoulos, George E.
    The invention of Peter : apostolic discourse and papal
authority in late antiquity / George E. Demacopoulos, —
1st ed.
        p.   cm. — (Divinations: rereading late ancient
religion)
    Includes bibliographical references and index.
    ISBN 978-0-8122-4517-2 (hardcover : alk. paper)
    1. Popes—Primacy—History of doctrines—Early
church, ca. 30–600. 2. Petrine office—History of
doctrines—Early church, ca. 30–600. I. Title.
II. Series: Divinations.
BX1805.D377   2013
262′.1309015—dc23   2012041494

CONTENTS

Introduction

On June 29, 2007, Pope Benedict XVI ratified a document prepared by the Congregation for the Doctrine of the Faith that sought to clarify the Roman Catholic Church's position on certain contemporary ecclesiological questions rooted in the proclamations of Vatican II. Among other things, the document defined other Christian traditions as "defective" because "communion with the Catholic Church, the visible head of which is the Bishop of Rome and the Successor of Peter, is not some external complement to a particular Church but rather one of its internal constitutive principles."[1] In other words, membership in the "one Church of Christ" is actualized, according to this text, by solidarity with the bishop of Rome, and this assertion is justified on the basis of the biblical Peter's link to the ancient see.

However contentious such a declaration may be, all students of Christian history are familiar with papal claims to ecclesiastical authority. Equally familiar is the justification for this authority on the basis of the special connection between Peter the apostle and the bishops of Rome who are said to "inherit" his primatial authority. And while there is certainly no shortage of historical studies that have sought to chronicle the so-called rise of the papacy from late antiquity into the Middle Ages, there seems to be a surprising dearth of investigations into the circumstances under which this Petrine connection was initially promoted, how those proclamations evolved, and how they were perceived by other Christians at the time.

What differentiates the present study from previous histories of the papacy is that it is not so much concerned with chronicling the acts of any particular pope or ecclesiastical conflict as it is devoted to understanding the emergence of a particular kind of discourse, the Petrine discourse, which helped to make possible what we might now call a papal theory. As such, the current project is not a history of the early papacy per se so much as it is a study of how the literary and ritualistic embellishment of a link between the historic Peter and the papal see of subsequent centuries functioned within a series of existent and interconnected late ancient discourses of authority and exclusion.

With that goal in mind, this book offers three overlapping levels of investigation and analysis. First, it seeks to identify the content, shape, and shifting parameters of what I call the "Petrine discourse" between the two most creative and dynamic popes of late antiquity—Leo the "Great" (bishop of Rome 440–461) and Gregory the "Great" (bishop of Rome 590–604).[2] Second, this book offers a historical narrative that emphasizes the ways multiple actors employed, extended, transformed, and/or resisted the Petrine discourse for their own purposes. Third, this project provides a revisionist history of the papacy, particularly as it relates to the escalations in its rhetorical claims to ecclesiastical authority in this period. This revisionist history challenges the dominant narrative of an inevitable and unbroken rise in papal power from late antiquity through the Middle Ages. Resisting the temptation to interpret late ancient papal claims to authority as representing actualized or actualizable power and international respect, I argue that the escalations of papal rhetoric, almost always linked directly to a Petrine claim, were often born in moments of papal anxiety or weakness. In other words, whenever a Roman bishop in this period claimed to be the primary or sole arbiter in dogmatic, moral, or judicial conflicts, especially if that claim was rhetorically bolder than those that preceded it, we would be well served to consider whether or not such a statement was uttered in response to the same bishop's authority having been threatened, challenged, or simply ignored by a particular audience.[3] As we will see, those humiliations came in many forms and from many places, both domestic and international, lay and ecclesiastical.

Employing this three-pronged analysis, I will argue that specific features of the Petrine discourse contributed to the survival and, ultimately, the exceptional status of the bishop of Rome. We will see, for example, that the elasticity of the Petrine topos in papal hands was of fundamental importance to the discursive presentation of the papacy's hegemonic claims and the ultimate willingness of other Christians to authenticate those claims through their own use of them.[4] Despite (or perhaps because of) the malleable character of the Petrine topos, however, we will also notice that the papal presentation of Petrine authority was often "totalizing" in its scope—not only in terms of the completeness of the apostle's personal authority but also in the sense that all Christian meaning is said to flow from Peter and, significantly, from his heirs.[5] Finally, we will see that the most creative Roman bishops were able to combine the literary and ritualistic traditions of the Petrine topos (particularly as they related to Peter's shrine and relics) to further the connections between Peter's spiritual authority and their own ability to access and distribute that authority.

Why Discourse Analysis?

To the extent that this study employs discourse analysis alongside other, more traditional, historical methods, it is appropriate to say at least a few words about what I hope to achieve from this approach. In his *Archaeology of Knowledge*, Michel Foucault offered an alternative model for the study of the past not by emphasizing the particular events or actors of history (seeking in them a continuity or a discontinuity with that which comes before or after), but by exploring the conditions that unite what he called a collection of discursive events (i.e., statements, whether oral or written) made in history. In other words, Foucault proposed that there was much to learn from the past (and present) by investigating the "knowledge structures" that both make possible and hold together a particular realm of discourse, be it the discourse of medicine, of economics, or of theology and religion. For Foucault, discourse entails more than words and texts, it also involves actions, institutions, and rituals.[6] Following in this line of thought, we can understand any discourse as offering its own epistemological horizon, a framework within which statements or practices are offered, understood, measured, embraced, and/or resisted.[7]

Scholars of Christian antiquity have increasingly drawn on the intellectual resources provided by Foucault and other literary and cultural theorists (an approach sometimes collectively denoted as the "linguistic turn") to think anew about the development of early Christianity and the ideologies that are often lurking underneath more traditional historical narratives about it. As Elizabeth Clark has argued, early Christianity is an especially rich field for theoretical analysis precisely because its surviving documents are characterized by an unusually high level of literary and philosophical sophistication—stemming, of course, from the fact that they were produced (for the most part) by men steeped in the philosophically and rhetorically rich traditions of the Greco-Roman world.[8] As this study will show, there is little doubt that many of the papal documents of the fifth and sixth centuries offer prime examples of the rhetorical and philosophical sophistication to which Clark refers.

There are a number of reasons, I believe, that it is advantageous to study the papacy through a combination of traditional historical-critical methods and the resources provided from the perspective of discourse analysis. For example, by emphasizing the framework of a Petrine discourse within which papal rhetoric functioned (rather than just chronicling the history of the papal institution itself), one does not need to be unduly concerned with papal figures and statements that lie outside of the historical parameters of the study. Nor does one need to pursue the hopeless quest of recovering and interpreting every historical detail from the period in question.[9] Instead, by engaging the subject from the perspective of discourse rather than seeking a comprehensive institutional history, this investigation is able to focus on a smaller collection of papal exchanges to elicit the epistemological and hermeneutical structures that gave space and meaning to the speech and action linking Peter to Rome and the Roman bishop.

For example, although Pope Leo I may well have been the first to speak of himself as "Peter's unworthy heir," he did so in a language that could be understood by his audience because they shared discursive and epistemological horizons made available by a number of modes of speech (imperial, legal, or Christian). In other words, there were discursive practices in operation that conditioned a great range of things (such as laws of inheritance, significance of the apostles, tradition of episcopal authority, and Christian rhetoric of humility) that preceded and made possible in a very particular way Leo's claim to be Peter's unworthy heir.[10] Those discursive practices had their own regularity, consistency, and operation. By situating Leo's statement in a conceptual horizon made possible by a Petrine discourse, I will not emphasize the claim to be Peter's heir as a pivotal precedent so much as consider the implications of a statement that stretched the possibilities of papal speech and Petrine cult already in existence.[11] Put another way, to the extent that this book investigates the Petrine discourse as discourse, it seeks to understand precisely what the conditions were, the epistemological horizons that enabled such a claim as Leo's to be uttered, heard, embraced, or resisted.

A second reason that it is beneficial to combine discourse analysis with historical-critical methods is that it offers a more comprehensive assessment of otherwise disparate elements of speaking, writing, and doing.[12] Because our documents are of so many genres, contain so many competing interests, and have been in the hands of so many editors, there is a certain advantage in investigating not one author, one text, or one event but the discursive unity that brings those authors, texts, and their editors together.[13] By working from the vantage point of the Petrine discourse, rather than a text, author, or editor, I believe that we find a different prism by which to view the creation, evolution, and subsequent promotion of the papal monopoly through its most effective marketing campaign—the cult of St. Peter.

This approach will also enable us to view the ways in which papal statements about Peter functioned as an exercise in exclusion and prohibition. As we will see, the various actors here examined frequently employ the Petrine topos for exclusionary purposes, whether they do so by means of rhetoric, exegesis, the prosecution of heretics, the promotion of cult, or the act of diplomacy. Indeed, we will see that the rhetorical and ritualistic uses of the Petrine narrative were especially well suited to the construction and naming of difference—those who are and those who are not in agreement with St. Peter. The popes, bishops, and secular officials who invoked Peter often did so to exclude alternative interpretations, alternative ideologies, and alternative authorities.

Finally, the appropriation of discourse analysis further allows, to some small degree, the possibility of avoiding the polemical arena that has so characterized the historical study of the papacy. To the extent that elements of this project are a discourse analysis rather than an intellectual or institutional history,[14] I make no effort to assess whether or not the bishops of Rome were "right" or "honest" or "true" to interpret the Petrine legacy in the way that they did. Similarly, I make no claim as to whether or not the reception of the papal claims by others were "right" or "accurate." Instead, I seek to assess the extent to which the various actors (papal, civil, or ecclesiastical) both operated within and deliberately drew on the Petrine discourse.

Many readers will notice that I have already self-consciously employed the idea of "discourse" in overlapping ways. In the Foucauldian sense, I understand the "Petrine discourse" to refer to a set of conditions (constituted by texts, ideas, rhetoric, practices, institutions, etc.) that make possible the deployment of the Petrine figure in various ways—a discourse that enables papal actors to act, but one that is always shifting and being shaped by their actions. But following another convention for speaking of "discourse," I also employ the phrase "Petrine discourse" to refer to a more stable and tangible set of claims about Peter and his authority—a concept I will refer to most often as the "Petrine topos"—that could be intentionally deployed, or even expanded on and added to, by various individuals to suit their purposes. It is my contention that these two ways of comprehending (and analyzing) the Petrine discourse, while theoretically distinct, are mutually implicated with one another and are not easily separable.[15] The reader should note, therefore, that I typically understand both senses of discourse to be operative (with one simultaneously reinforcing and/or challenging the other), even when my analysis pursues one sense more explicitly than the other.

From the outset, one might ask why I have chosen to narrow my focus to a "Petrine" discourse, rather than, say, a "papal" discourse. While an examination of a papal discourse would certainly be enlightening, I believe that there is something particularly interesting to be learned from an investigation of the ways in which the figure of Peter came to be employed by the bishops of Rome, their supporters, and even their opponents. By sharpening my focus from "papal" to "Petrine," I hope to explore the ways in which the bishops of Rome developed a discursive "Petrine" register to advance a particular knowledge through perceptions, vocabulary, symbols, and rituals. Among other things, I will argue that papal actors and their competitors employed the Petrine topos as an ideological production of theological knowledge for the purpose of spreading power and influence.[16] Interestingly, we will also see that the rhetorical promotion of Peter to papal ends does not convey a universally endorsed Christian belief about who Peter was or what Christians understood his historic role to be—indeed, many papal correspondents rejected or simply ignored the Roman narrative about Peter, precisely because it was so closely linked to papal claims to authority.

Beginning with Chapter 2, one of the features of the Petrine discourse that we will explore the most frequently is the extent to which the biblical Peter came to be interpreted as the undisputed leader, the *primus* and *princeps*, of the apostles. The advocates of papal primacy wove together an embroidery of biblical, imperial, and legal threads to produce a Petrine narrative that, more than anything, accounted for their own ambitions and insecurities. As we will see, Peter's confession of Jesus as "the Christ, the son of God" (cf. Mt 16) was singled out as one of the most important biblical justifications for Petrine and papal authority, not only because it preceded Christ's proclamation of Peter's unique privileges—the ability to bind and loose sin and to be the cornerstone of the Church—but also because it showed Peter to be the most theologically insightful of the apostles.[17] These features of the Petrine narrative came to function as the primary justifications for papal authority in dogmatic questions, particularly in the Christological debates between the Roman Church and its Eastern competitors.

In addition to biblical, exegetical, and dogmatic features of the Petrine discourse, we will also see that Peter's supposed historic presence in the city of

Rome, along with the promotion of his tomb and relics, became increasingly important features of the Petrine discourse. During the period under investigation in this study, the bishops of Rome increasingly linked themselves, physically and symbolically, to Peter's tomb. For the citizens of Rome, they did this through elaborate building and artistic projects at the basilica of St. Peter on Vatican Hill.[18] For their patrons, clients, allies, and enemies around the Mediterranean, Roman bishops promoted this connection in other ways, including the distribution of Petrine relics.

Finally, we will see that the papal reliance on St. Peter also helped to transform the narrative features of papal self-interest in this period. For example, during the tenures of Pope Leo I and Pope Gelasius I, papal correspondence increasingly employed "St. Peter" as the grammatical subject for the pontiffs' own diplomatic interests (a linguistic maneuver that I will refer to as the "Petrine subject"). In other words, when offering their own theological position, both Leo and Gelasius routinely framed their ideas as "St. Peter's teaching." Likewise, when their theological opinions or claims to ecclesiastical sovereignty were being ignored by their rivals, they spoke of this as "an insult to St. Peter" or as a "rejection of St. Peter." It was also in this period that the genre of papal biography first emerged. Not only was this an important step for the eventual fiction of an always existing, always acknowledged papal sovereignty, but we will also see that these biographies initially emerged in the context of internal disputes between rival factions of Roman Christians. As Chapter 4 will detail, it was during the so-called Laurentian schism of the early sixth century that the Symmachian faction used these biographies to outdo its rivals by leveraging Peter's legacy for its own claim to the Petrine throne.

The Changing Face of Papal Scholarship

There has been no shortage of scholars working on the early papacy. Early in the twentieth century, Erich Caspar sought to differentiate himself from previous largely apologetic studies and boldly declared that he would examine only those aspects of papal history that remained within the realm of "scientific research." By this, Caspar meant that he would disentangle the historical progress of the papal institution and its corresponding ideology from a theological conviction in its inherent value.[19] However valuable that move was, Caspar's study of the early papacy, like many that followed it in the twentieth century, shows signs of an anachronistic teleology for the early papacy. In other words, for Caspar, the development of the papal institution was viewed through the lens of what it would eventually become in the later Middle Ages rather than what it was in late antiquity. Thus, he (and especially Walter Ullmann, who follows him) describes the gradual expansion of the Roman See's jurisdiction and ideology as an unbroken ascent that begins with the decline of the Western Roman government in the fourth century and culminates in the papal monarchies of the eleventh and twelfth centuries.[20] In effect, this "rise of the papacy" narrative suggests an uninterrupted move from strength to strength.

The problem, of course, is that there was no unbroken ascent of Roman episcopal authority—the expansion of Rome's hegemony in the Western Church was intermittent and often contested. What is more, the bishops of the late ancient period, whatever their rhetorical claims, simply could not have imagined—and therefore did not call for—the economic and political force that the papacy would enjoy in the later Middle Ages. Even employing the terms "pope" and "papacy" to describe the earliest bishops of Rome and their administrations runs the risk of suggesting a level of institutional development and international recognition that developed only much later— not only is there little evidence to suggest that there was a single presiding bishop of Rome prior to the middle of the second century, the term "pope" was used by other bishops throughout the Christian world in the second and third centuries. Despite the possible anachronisms these terms can imply, the reader should know that I will, for the sake of convenience, repeatedly use "pope" and "papacy" to refer the fifth- and sixth-century Roman bishops and their administrations.

In some ways, the twentieth-century historiographical problem characterized by the "rise of the papacy" narrative was born in the ninth century. Indeed, it was the eighth- and ninth-century papacy and its Carolingian supporters who first "invented" the notion that the popes of late antiquity were powerful and universally respected. Not only do most of our oldest surviving papal manuscripts date to the Carolingian period, but many of the Carolingian editorial choices (such as the decisions about which documents would be preserved and in what sequence those documents would be presented) continue to influence what modern scholars deem most relevant about those sources.[21] For example, as we will note in Chapter 2, editors of Leo I's homilies grouped them according to theme and chose to place those homilies that most identified Leo as Peter's "heir" as the first group in the collection.

Clearly, the editors wanted to emphasize Leo's contribution to papal ideology and did so in their reproduction of his homilies. For now, we will simply note that even though the eighth- and ninth-century story is not the focus of the present study, it is important to bear in mind that later papal advocates turned to the fifth- and sixth-century documents precisely because they believed they could be useful for their own concerns.

What is so intriguing about the later appropriation of this material, and what the present study will demonstrate, is that even though the eighth- and ninth-century editors thought that these documents could be used as a witness to the timelessness of papal authority, these documents in their own day did not represent strength but instead reflect a yearning for it. What is more, we will see that what is so compelling about these particular documents is their discursive linking of Peter to the papacy, a connection that would be continued through cult, pilgrimage, and art well into the ninth century.

An important shift in the study of the papacy came in 1976 when Charles Pietri released his famous *Roma christiana*, a two-volume work that runs nearly eighteen hundred pages.[22] While Pietri's approach suffers from some of the same anachronisms as those of Caspar and Ullmann, he was far more interested than they had been to incorporate the insights of archaeology and ritual studies into his historical narrative. Although Pietri's work focuses on the period 313–440, and therefore only partially overlaps with the present study, it offers one of the few historical assessments of the ways Roman bishops in the late ancient period sought to link themselves to the Apostle Peter. Pietri devotes Book 3, "Idéologie et mentalité dans une église de la tradition," to the ways the idea of Peter and a Petrine tradition of authority developed during the fourth century.[23] In Book 3 of Part II, Pietri returns again to Petrine ideology, this time to emphasize the role of Peter as lawgiver and to link the idea of Peter's primacy to the primacy of the city of Rome itself. In some ways, it would seem that Pietri's goal is to show the continuity between Leo and all that came before him (an approach notably different from that of Caspar or Ullmann, who saw Leo as groundbreaking for the development of the papal ideal).[24]

Building on Pietri's insight that the Petrine idea was produced through objects and rituals as much as through texts, my investigation of the Petrine discourse will encompass a broad range of materials (including texts, images, and rituals) to assess the epistemic horizons that constituted the range of possibilities linking Peter to Rome and the Roman bishop. It will also advance on Pietri's work in the sense that it will carry the investigation into the fifth and sixth centuries, in which the production of Petrine knowledge became an even greater focus for the bishops of Rome.

The challenge to the "rise of the papacy" thesis began in earnest in the latter part of the twentieth century with a series of shorter studies by scholars from multiple disciplinary fields who were able to show that the Roman Church in late antiquity often functioned as a constellation of religious factions rather than as a unified body under the direction of a single bishop. The Symmachian/Laurentian schism, which we will explore in Chapter 4, offers ample evidence of the extent to which the Roman Church was dogged by factionalism and violence several generations after Pope Leo's famous claim that he was the "heir of St. Peter."[25] Near the close of the twentieth century, other studies began to show that individual Roman bishops, once described as integral to the development of the papal ideal, also struggled in their attempts to corral dissenting groups and to compete with lay aristocrats for power and prestige.[26]

In 2012, Kristina Sessa offered an important book-length challenge to the traditional way of investigating the early papacy, by assessing it from the perspective of cultural (rather than institutional, ideological, or theological) history.[27] Specifically, Sessa demonstrates that Roman bishops in the late ancient period sought to exercise moral and material influence in the discourse of estate management (*oikonomia*) and that it was this discourse that opened the door, so to speak, for Roman bishops to assert their authority over a previously autonomous and private space. It was within the complex matrix of aristocratic and clerical households, Sessa argues, that Roman bishops increasingly inserted themselves but did so with only varying degrees of success.

The present study seeks to challenge further the notion that the papacy enjoyed ever-increasing prestige and influence during the late ancient period. Whereas Sessa reevaluated the Roman Church through a study of the late ancient Roman household, I will examine the shifting discursive horizon that made it possible for Roman bishops to assert their authority on the basis of a supposed link between themselves and the Apostle Peter. As we will see in the chapters that follow, the emergence of a distinctive Petrine discourse overlapped with other, familiar forms of privilege in a late ancient, Greco-Roman, and Christian context (such as imperial privilege, paternal privilege, episcopal privilege, and orthodox privilege), all of which coalesce into the assertions of papal privilege. In other words, it is not that statements about Peter's authority were new to the period between Leo and Gregory, nor that statements connecting Peter to the papacy were new. What marks the period between Leo and Gregory as significant, I believe, is that it was in this period that notions of imperial, paternal, episcopal, and dogmatic authority coalesced around the figure of Peter in a way that redefined the nature, scope, and authority of the papacy.

At the same time, I hope to show that many of the rhetorical escalations of Roman privilege, almost always dressed in Petrine robes, emerged at the very time that the authority of the Roman bishop was being challenged by others. Not only was this true in distant regions where individual popes sought to assert themselves (such as Gaul, Illyricum, and North Africa), but it was also true in the city of Rome itself. As we will see, even some of the most important contributors (i.e., Leo, Gelasius, and Gregory) to the ever-expanding narrative of papal primacy through Petrine means faced considerable opposition to their policies among the Roman clergy, the Roman aristocracy, and the ordinary inhabitants of the city of Rome. Viewing the escalations of Petrine claims from this perspective (in other words, exploring the social dimensions that gave rise to an ideology expressed in ever-new literary, rhetorical, and ritualistic forms), I believe, differentiates the current study from previous treatments of the early papacy and its ideology. Indeed, the great paradox of the late ancient claim of papal primacy is that it had to be imposed on the rest of the Christian world because it was not at that time generally accepted. If late ancient Christians had acknowledged the authority that Roman bishops of this period claimed (dogmatic or otherwise), there would have been no reason to develop rhetorical justifications for it, Petrine or otherwise.

A Note on the Sources

For the most part, the textual sources most frequently employed in this study (especially in Chapters 2–5) are the same as those other historians of the early papacy have examined: papal letters, treatises, and biographies. There are, in fact, a great number of papal documents from this period that survive. It was in this period, beginning with Leo, that we have the earliest deliberate collections of papal letters, including more than one hundred from the tenure of Leo and more than eight hundred from Gregory. Between them, Leo, Gelasius, and Gregory also provide us with a vast number of sermons, exegetical works, and dogmatic treatises. As we will discuss in detail in Chapter 4, it was also in this period that the earliest papal biographies began to emerge, both individually and as collections (such as the *Liber Pontificalis*). This is, indeed, a period rich in primary sources.

In the introduction to their edited volume *Religion, Dynasty, and Patronage in Early Christian Rome*, Kate Cooper and Julia Hillner issue a bold directive that we reassess the surviving papal documents, beginning with the very question as to why it is that these texts survive and what it might mean that others did not.[28] Rather than viewing the surviving sources as objective witnesses to the past (as though they were simply archaeological artifacts waiting to be excavated), Cooper and Hillner insist that we scrutinize surviving papal documents as markers and remnants of a struggle (whether by authors or editors) to control the narration of the events they purport to describe. In a similar vein they also suggest that the invention of papal biography (exemplified by the *Liber Pontificalis* and the Symmachian "forgeries") and the emergence of specific collections (selective editions that emphasized certain discursive artifacts and excluded others) of papal documents in this period were "new technologies" designed to establish the Roman episcopacy as an autonomous institution free of control by the emperor or the Senate. These texts and editions are therefore to be understood as remnants of a battle to shape "Roman memory" in the catastrophic years of the Gothic wars during the sixth century.[29]

The following study builds on this premise and applies it to the most potent discursive horizon that enabled and defined papal speech in this period—the Petrine discourse. While I will examine virtually the same texts as other histories of the late ancient papacy, I have decided to employ my own translations of this material as part of my attempt to reconsider these texts from a fresh perspective.[30] More important, I will be asking a modified set of questions about these texts, particularly as they relate to the discursive connections between Peter and Rome, and the authority that one was able to confer on the other. Following Cooper and Hillner, I will operate with the presumption that the surviving documents reflect a deeply invested set of concerns both for the authors who produced them and the subsequent hands that controlled and enabled their transmission. And, with these partisan interests in mind, I will seek to understand more fully the concerns, ambitions, and insecurities that might lie behind the various iterations of Petrine privilege. These iterations, these unmistakably invested and contested statements of authority and exclusion, gave birth to a new Peter—not a new person but a new imagination of the person. It is this process of Petrine invention that this book seeks to understand.

CHAPTER I

Petrine Legends, External Recognition, and the Cult of Peter in Rome

To understand the discursive horizon that made possible the connection between the Apostle Peter, Rome, and the Roman bishop, we must begin by gaining a greater appreciation for the various—sometimes competing— legends, rituals, and material representations of Peter that existed in the religious imagination of Christians in late antiquity. Of key importance, of course, are the ways the traditions surrounding Peter became intertwined with the Roman Church's narratives of its own development and significance and how the two intersected at specific locations across Rome's urban landscape. To that end, this chapter will survey the earliest narratives about Peter and feature those aspects of the Petrine legend that would prove most useful for bridging Petrine and papal authority in subsequent centuries. It will also introduce the contextual settings in which the earliest external affirmations of Roman ecclesiastical privilege occurred. It will conclude with a brief examination of the emergence of Peter's cult in the city of Rome. In particular we will examine the ways the bishops of Rome inserted themselves into that cult and sought to subordinate other martyr cults under a hierarchical structure that placed Peter at the summit. Each of these elements—the Petrine legends, the external recognition of Petrine privilege, and the cultic practices associated with Peter's supposed tomb—contributed to the discursive horizon that was the Petrine discourse.

From Jerusalem to Rome

Given the ancient and widespread association of Peter with the city of Rome, it is important to recall that the New Testament makes no connection between the two in plain speech. The Book of Acts, often regarded as a kind of apostolic history, says nothing of a Petrine mission to Rome. Paul's letters, which offer several historical details of Peter's activity, do not acknowledge a Petrine mission to Rome.[1] Most noticeably, at the conclusion of the Epistle to the Romans (Rom 16.1–15), when Paul sends greetings to Christians he knows to reside in the city (he lists more than two dozen names), there is no mention of Peter ever having been there.[2] Even the two epistles attributed to Peter fail to offer a clear confirmation that Peter journeyed to Rome. For most scholars, the reference in 1 Peter 5.13 (which sends "greetings from your sister church in Babylon") implies that its author was at that moment writing from Rome. But that interpretation has been challenged by Otto Zwierlein, who believes that "Babylon" in this verse can just as easily be taken to mean that the author is writing from exile in general, rather than Rome specifically.[3] Moreover, given the highly questionable nature of Petrine authorship of 1 Peter,[4] a historic connection between the apostle and city appears unfounded.[5]

Although the New Testament does not offer any compelling evidence that the Apostle Peter traveled to Rome, there are other early sources associated with the city that can be interpreted as confirming Peter's connection to the imperial capital. The oldest of these is a letter, known as *First Clement*, that was sent by someone in Rome to the Church of Corinth in the final years of the first century.[6] A brief passage in what is otherwise a long document has led to considerable debate among scholars as to whether or not the letter provides an early witness to the tradition that Peter was martyred in Rome.[7] In chapter 5, the author seeks to encourage the Corinthians to cultivate humility and virtue on the basis of saintly examples, including those of Peter and Paul.[8] The author introduces the apostles shortly after a generic reference to martyrdom as testimony to faith in Christ. Peter is said to have suffered "many hardships," though none are specifically mentioned. By contrast, Paul's sufferings are enumerated with great detail.[9] At issue is whether the example of Peter testifies to the author's knowledge of his martyrdom or simply to his proclamation of the Gospel (the Greek could be interpreted either way).[10] If the former, then it would provide the earliest known witness to the idea that Peter was martyred, and thus it could suggest that the author had this information because the martyrdom had occurred in Rome.[11] But if the passage does not speak to Peter's martyrdom, if it does nothing more than testify to Peter's proclamation of the gospel, then it would seem to suggest that a leader of the Christian community in Rome at the close of the first century does not seem to know anything of a tradition related to Peter's having been martyred, much less having been martyred in Rome.[12] Indeed, there is nothing in *First Clement* that explicitly links Peter to Rome or to a later legend that Peter was martyred during the reign of the emperor Nero.[13]

Another early document linked to the city of Rome that is sometimes interpreted as a witness to a broad Christian understanding of Peter's presence in the imperial capital is the letter of Ignatius of Antioch to the Romans. Likely dated to the first or second decade of the second century, the letter is written to the Christian community of Rome in advance of Ignatius' arrival and martyrdom in the city. Beseeching the Christians of Rome that they not do anything to obstruct his impending death, Ignatius differentiates himself from Peter and Paul in that, whereas they, as apostles, had the authority to issue commands, he must make requests of the Roman community.[14] Like *First Clement*, the passage offers indirect, rather than direct, testimony to the possibility that Peter should be associated with the city of Rome. Does Ignatius mention the authority of Peter and Paul when writing to the Romans because he understood them to have been active in the Roman community, or does he invoke them because they were widely regarded as authorities within the Christian community more broadly?[15] If the former, then this is the oldest surviving testimony that Peter is a leader of the Roman community (*First Clement* may imply martyrdom but does not refer to Peter's active leadership). But there is nothing in Ignatius' *Letter to the Romans* that explicitly links Peter's authority to the Roman community. Moreover, several scholars have challenged the authenticity of the Petrine references within the Ignatius corpus, arguing that they are, in fact, late second-century interpolations.[16]

According to Zwierlein, the earliest testimony to the tradition that Peter was associated with the city of Rome dates to the middle of the second century, beginning with the writing of Justin Martyr, who believed that Simon Magus, the villain of Acts 8, had come to Rome and spread the Gnostic heresy. Peter, as the opponent of Simon and the defender of orthodoxy, came to Rome, it would seem, to confront Simon and protect Roman Christians from false teaching.[17] Thus, for Zwierlein, the impulse for connecting Peter to Rome was inextricably linked to the contest between orthodoxy and heresy in the second-century Church of Rome. Not only did the struggle with Gnosticism lay the foundation for the Petrine Roman narrative; it also provided the context for the emergence of a Roman mono-episcopate that would be retroactively attributed to the first century and confirmed through outside voices like that of Irenaeus of Lyon (an obvious ally in the promotion of an apostolic episcopate).[18]

For the purposes of this study, it does not matter if the Apostle Peter went to Rome. Nor does it matter whether or not the author of *First Clement* or Ignatius of Antioch thought that Peter had been martyred in Rome. What is of significance—and what this chapter will show—is that the traditions associated with the Apostle Peter were multiple, that they changed a great deal over time, and that those changes typically reflected contemporary concerns. While the initial impetus for altering the Petrine narrative so as to "bring Peter to Rome" may have sprung from developments and contests within Rome itself, it would not take long for that story to be embraced and employed by authors throughout the Christian world.[19]

The Apocryphal Legends and Pseudonymous Texts Associated with Peter

Although the earliest documents provide meager resources to link Peter with the city of Rome, the apocryphal *Acts* that were produced in Rome and elsewhere between the late second and late fourth centuries offer ample testimony to a widespread Christian belief that he was martyred in Rome. For the most part, these stories emphasize Peter's ability to perform miracles and his protection of the Christian community from the deceptions of false teachers and prophets (often personified in the figure of Simon Magus). While many of these legends assert specific theological and/or moral positions, they are typically unsophisticated in their theological argumentation and likely reflect popular religious ideas. And, in contrast to later papal narrations of Peter's significance, these accounts do nothing to substantiate Peter's theological authority vis-à-vis the other apostles on the basis of the Petrine privilege of Matthew 16, which granted Peter alone the right to bind and loose sin. They do, however, clearly attest to a pervasive late ancient understanding of Peter as a powerful Christian figure and can be seen to provide an important narrative baseline for subsequent papal appropriations of Peter's legacy.

The Martyrdom of St. Peter the Apostle

The oldest postbiblical account of Peter's deeds of which we have knowledge is a now-lost Greek text known as the *Acts of Peter*, part of which survives in a likely sixth-century Latin translation of the missing Greek original.[20] Scholars typically date the prototype to the late second century—Zwierlein assigns a date of 180–190 C.E.[21] The final quarter of this text, which details Peter's martyrdom, often circulated separately from the larger *Acts of Peter* and survives, on its own, in several manuscripts.[22] It is possible, in fact, that there existed an original *Martyrdom of St. Peter* to which a subsequent author/editor added the pre-martyrdom details of Peter's activity in Rome, which are reflected in the surviving Latin *Acts of Peter*. A resolution to the many textual questions is beyond the scope of the present study, but we will treat the *Martyrdom of Peter* and the surviving *Acts of Peter* as separate documents because the narrative elements that they contain are distinctive.[23] For our purposes, the *Martyrdom of Peter* is significant because it introduces several elements of the apostle's death that became fixtures of the subsequent Petrine legends, including (1) the introduction of Simon Magus as a kind of arch-nemesis to Peter, (2) the assignment of the date of Peter's martyrdom to the reign of the emperor Nero,[24] and (3) the mode of Peter's death as an upside-down crucifixion.[25]

In one manuscript tradition, the *Martyrdom of Peter* opens with a confrontation between St. Peter and Simon Magus, who is presented as corrupting the faith of the Christian community in Rome.[26] At every turn, Peter thwarts Simon's efforts and ultimately shows him to be an imposter. Following Simon's death, the narrative transitions to a cursory review of Peter's missionary success, which is particularly strong among the women of aristocratic Roman households. Those successes draw the ire of two leading men of Rome, who conspire to have Peter killed. Warned of the danger by one of the women, Peter flees the city, only to have a vision in which Christ instructs him to return and face martyrdom bravely.[27] Peter returns, convinces his followers that this is the proper course of action, and is then arrested.[28] He asks his executioners to crucify him upside down and launches into an extemporaneous account of humanity's fallen condition, the salvation offered by faith in Christ, and the necessity that his own death (i.e., being crucified upside down) be a symbol of this faith.[29] After detailing Peter's death, the narrative continues with two vignettes. The first tells a story of how a convert, Marcellus, thinking that he is doing the right thing, takes possession of Peter's body, anoints it liberally with expensive ointments, and places it in his own tomb. On the same evening, Peter visits Marcellus in a dream and scolds him for placing so much emphasis on a dead body.[30] The final portion of the text introduces the emperor Nero, who is said to be upset that Agrippa had killed Peter without Nero's knowledge. Nero had hoped to preside over

Peter's execution himself because the apostle had spread Christianity among the Roman population, and thus it was Nero's desire to see him suffer. In the end, however, Nero is warned in a dream that he has no power over the Christians and that he should refrain from persecuting them further.[31]

More than chronicling the end of Peter's life, the text reveals its author's desire to address questions about martyrdom and death. Peter's initial decision to abandon Rome is "corrected" by a miraculous vision, which must then be explained further so that Peter's disciples can also have the courage to embrace martyrdom for themselves. Interestingly, the text concludes by claiming that once the emperor Nero came to realize that he had no power over Christ, he abandoned his persecution of the Christian community in Rome. The numerous juxtapositions between the physical world and the spiritual world also help to situate the author's theological concerns. The righteous characters in the tale repeatedly promote the spiritual and downplay the physical.[32] The culmination of this apprehension occurs with the censure of Marcellus, who is criticized for concerning himself with Peter's corpse. It is noteworthy that this rejection of Peter's body would need to be amended in future narratives about Peter's activity and death in Rome in order that the legends surrounding the apostle's life could be brought into line with the development of cultic shrines and ritual acts around the supposed relics of St. Peter. Clearly, at this primitive stage in the development of Peter's cult, those considerations either did not exist at all or were secondary to the author's more pressing concerns.[33]

Equally significant for our purposes is the extent to which the narrative is situated so concretely within the city of Rome. Several of the leading figures in the story are Roman noblemen, including the emperor, a friend of the emperor (Albinus), and the urban prefect (Agrippa). Their chief complaint against Peter is that he is disrupting the Roman way of life by separating women (both wives and concubines) from the beds of powerful men. Agrippa, the prefect, is urged to take action on behalf of those Roman men who do not have the authority to put Peter to death for what he has done (i.e., stolen their women).[34] Similarly, as Peter begins his flight, the text states that he "saw the Lord entering Rome." And when Peter questions him, Christ responds that he is "going to Rome to be crucified again."[35] Following Peter's arrest, the "entire multitude," including "rich and poor, orphans and widows, weak and strong," desire to see and rescue Peter.[36] With one voice, we are told, they confront Agrippa and challenge him to "tell the Romans" what Peter has done wrong.[37]

Despite the repeated designations of "Rome" and "Romans," there is only one occasion in which the text marks a specific location within Rome's topography—the final confrontation between Peter and Simon, which occurs on the Via Sacra.[38] While that is a significant venue (and richly symbolic for such an important confrontation between good and evil), the remainder of the *Martyrdom* offers an urban landscape that is notably nondescript. There is no mention of specific locations or shrines, as we will find in later Petrine narratives and in the *Gesta Martyrum*.[39] Nevertheless, the author repeatedly emphasizes that these events occurred in Rome. More important still, the Christians in this narrative are presented as Romans, not as resident aliens or foreigners. Indeed the synthesis of Roman and Christian identity will be a key feature in the subsequent development of religious life in the city.

The Acts of Peter

Turning to the expanded version provided in the surviving account of the *Acts of Peter*, we begin by recalling that we simply do not know the shape of the original narrative.[40] Not only do we not have a surviving Greek text of the *Acts*, but some variations within the manuscript tradition include additional sections that are not included in the Vercelli text.[41] The earliest surviving testimony to the existence of the *Acts of Peter* is a brief mention by Eusebius, who deemed the text spurious because, he claimed, no ecclesiastical authorities made use of it.[42]

Apart from a preliminary section that places St. Paul in Rome prior to Peter's arrival,[43] the majority of the *Acts of Peter* is an expansion on the contest between Peter and Simon Magus with which the *Martyrdom* had begun. Soon after Paul departs for a Spanish mission, Simon Magus arrives in the capital determined to corrupt the faith of true believers. So that the work of God will not be undone, Peter is miraculously instructed by Christ to sail from Jerusalem to Rome and to put an end to Simon's misdeeds.[44] What follows is a series of fantastic encounters between Peter and Simon in which Peter repeatedly performs miracles, exposes Simon's errors, and preaches the gospel. Some of the more fanciful miracles from the *Acts* would be appropriated in later hagiographic accounts, including Peter's making a dog talk, his enabling a smoked fish to swim again, and his bringing the dead back to life.[45] Many of the miracles occur as a contest of signs with Simon, and they

are designed to show the authentic power of Christian faith versus the deception of heresy and magic.

Like the *Martyrdom*, the people and city of Rome feature prominently
in the *Acts of Peter*. Rome's elite are very much a part of this story. Several
Roman aristocrats, including two from the house of Caesar, are named
among those believers who are under St. Paul's direction at the opening of
the story.[46] Peter stays in the home of a wealthy Roman, Narcissus, who has
become a Christian presbyter.[47] The mother of the senator Nicostratus
appeals to St. Peter that he might raise her son from the dead—Peter, of
course, obliges after her confession of faith.[48] What is more, the contest that
serves as the climax of the *Acts* takes place in the Roman Forum in the
presence of "senators, prefects, and officers" who join the "multitude in paying one gold piece to watch the spectacle."[49] Indeed, the contest between
Simon and Peter takes the form of a gladiatorial contest of words and
signs, which is performed for the amusement (and salvation) of the city's
population.

The senator Marcellus and his household serve as a focal point for nearly
half of the *Acts of Peter*.[50] One particularly interesting "Roman" encounter
involving Marcellus occurs shortly after his repudiation of Simon. Through
no fault of Marcellus, a statue he owns of the emperor is broken into several
pieces. Seeing that Marcellus is distraught and not wanting to shake his re-
found faith, Peter enables Marcellus to perform a miracle that makes the
statue whole again.[51] Given the typical aversion to "idols" in early Christian
texts and given the role of imperial statues in the persecution of Christians at
various points in the pre-Constantinian period, it is remarkable that the
author of the *Acts of Peter* would employ a miracle for the restoration of a
statue of the emperor. Clearly, there existed for this author and his immediate
community a desire to present *christianitas* and *romanitas* as compatible
entities.

There are two elements in the *Acts of Peter* that we might say differentiate
it from the *Martyrdom*. The first concerns the "orthodoxy" of its theological
position regarding the Gnostic/orthodox debate over the goodness of creation. Whereas the *Martyrdom* repeatedly expressed a concern for the physical
world in general and bodies in particular, there is no such anxiety in the *Acts*.
In fact, during the contest between Peter and Simon in the Roman Forum,
Simon's heresy is made explicit in his rejection of Christ's incarnation and
crucifixion (i.e., Simon denies Christ's physical condition).[52] Second, whereas
the *Martyrdom* contained little material directly parallel to the canonical

gospels, the *Acts* references several well-known biblical stories, including Peter's presence at the transfiguration, his attempt to walk on water, and his denial of Christ.

The use of the denial story is especially interesting in its attribution of agency. When Peter first arrives in Rome, he asserts his credentials as a true teacher on the basis that he had been a witness to Christ's miracles and remains a steward of his teaching. Peter boldly acknowledges that he denied Christ three times because of the temptation of the devil.[53] Indeed, he reveals this sad story as a testimony to Christ's desire to forgive and as a warning of the power of Satan. As we will see in subsequent chapters, Peter's denial of Christ became an exegetical challenge for the late ancient Roman bishops who were eager to employ the biblical Peter to their own ends. Both Leo and Gregory would spend a good deal of time thinking through how best to adapt the story to their theological, political, and moral needs. Though they developed different strategies for doing so, neither adopted the exegetical impulse of the *Acts of Peter*, which treated the denial as a victory for Satan and a warning of Satan's power to tempt the faith of the weak-willed.

The one allusion to the biblical narrative that we might have expected to find more explicitly in the *Acts of Peter* is the famous assertion of Matthew 16.19 that Peter has the ability to bind and loose sin. In chapter 10, after Peter returns Marcellus to the orthodox fold, he prays on Marcellus' behalf that he be forgiven for his misdeeds. While we are left to assume that Peter's prayer is heard by God, there is no mention at all of the so-called Petrine privilege. As we will see, by the mid-fifth century, Matthew 16 was the most important and repeated biblical proof-text for papal authority. For the fifth- and sixth-century bishops of Rome, however, the link between Peter's authority and their own hinged on the notion that Peter had served as the first bishop of Rome, and that they, as his successors, enjoyed the same privileged status. But for the earliest surviving sources that place Peter in Rome, namely the *Martyrdom of Peter* and the *Acts of Peter*, there is simply no mention that Peter ever functioned as a bishop, let alone as the first bishop of Rome.[54] Indeed, these texts never even mention the existence of a Roman episcopate.

The Pseudo-Clementines

While there are other Petrine *Acta* (such as the *Acts of Peter and Paul* and the *Acts of Peter and the Twelve Disciples*), those texts are largely derivative, date

to a considerably later period, or include few of the narrative elements that
featured prominently in the papal appropriation of the Petrine story.[55] So we
turn now to a body of literature known as the *Pseudo-Clementines*. According
to Irenaeus of Lyon (d. ca. 202), Peter and Paul had jointly established the
Church of Rome. They committed it to the hands of Linus, who served as
Rome's first bishop. After Linus, came Anacletus and then Clement.[56] It is
this man, the supposed third bishop of Rome after Peter, to which the letter
now known as *First Clement* is attributed. And it is with this same man that
the author(s) of the *Pseudo-Clementines* claim their authority.[57]

After generations of scrutiny with wide-ranging theories, scholars now
generally believe that the surviving documents that comprise the *Pseudo-
Clementines* were written in Palestine during the early to mid-fourth century,
possibly by an Arian sympathizer.[58] The *Pseudo-Clementines* include a collection
of discourses (attributed to the Apostle Peter) set within a background narrative
that details the circumstances by which Clement came to be Peter's disciple
and traveling secretary. The surviving corpus contains twenty *Homilies* (in
Greek) and a treatise known as the *Recognitions* (which survives only in Latin
translation and is divided into ten books).[59] An introductory letter (attributed
to Peter) and a concluding letter (by Clement to James of Jerusalem) have been
transmitted with the *Homilies*.[60] With the exception of the concluding letter by
Clement to James, the texts view Jerusalem as the center of the Christian world
and deal exclusively with the churches of Palestine and Syria. Apart from estab-
lishing Clement's identity as a citizen of Rome, the ancient capital is never
mentioned in either the *Homilies* or the *Recognitions*.

At the most basic level, the *Pseudo-Clementines* offer a romanticized
account of Clement's adoption of Christianity and his behind-the-scenes
account of the activity and preaching of Peter in Palestine and Syria.[61] As we
saw in the *Martyrdom of Peter* and the *Acts of Peter*, Simon Magus functions
as a focal point for false teaching, and the *Pseudo-Clementines* often present
Peter's preaching as set in opposition to Simon in the form of public disputa-
tions.[62] Clement serves as an eyewitness to these debates and even confronts
one of Simon's disciples.[63] Later, as a testimony to Peter's power and affection
for his disciple, he reunites Clement with his mother, brothers, and father,
all of whom embrace Christianity through Peter.

Whereas the *Martyrdom* and *Acts* made virtually no reference to the episcopate, the *Pseudo-Clementines* emphasize the hierarchical structure of the
church and seek to establish apostolic foundations for episcopal sees throughout Palestine and Syria. For the author(s) of these texts, a bishop functions
as both a representative of Christ and an apostolic successor.[64] More often

than not, bishops are mentioned briefly as leaders appointed by Peter at the completion of his mission to particular cities and as he prepares his departure.[65] In some ways, we might read the *Pseudo-Clementines* as a prolonged justification for the office of the episcopate, its function, and its authority.[66]

Although Peter appoints many bishops, he is not described as one himself. In fact, the only apostle described as a bishop is James, who was appointed bishop of Jerusalem, we are told, by the Lord himself.[67] The author(s) of the *Pseudo-Clementines* describes James as a "bishop of bishops"[68] and even as the "head of the bishops" (*episcoporum princepem*).[69] Given the extent to which the latter phrase will commonly be employed by fifth- and sixth-century Roman bishops to accentuate Peter's authority, it is intriguing to see the text describe James—and not Peter—as the *princeps*. Indeed, even though Peter's gifts for teaching and healing are the central themes of the *Pseudo-Clementines*, the author(s) seems to view James as undisputed leader of the apostolic community.[70]

For our purposes, one of the most important elements of the *Pseudo-Clementines* is that they testify to Peter's role in the foundation narratives of many local churches. Indeed, long before Peter was associated with the city of Rome, he was described by Christian authors (especially those of the canonical New Testament) as the apostolic founder of the Christian communities throughout Palestine and Syria. While most of the smaller communities identified in the Book of Acts and later by the *Pseudo-Clementines* had little influence on the international stage, one of them, Antioch, would achieve considerable standing—ranking third in preeminence according to the Council of Nicaea in 325 and fourth at the Council of Chalcedon, which also conferred patriarchal status on the Syrian capital. As we will see, the legacy of Peter's sojourn in Antioch was so well known that papal pundits could not ignore it. Instead, they carefully incorporated Peter's association with Antioch into their own Petrine narratives but did so in a way that did not compromise their own claim to his legacy. In fact, as we will explore in subsequent chapters, the Roman bishops of the fifth and sixth centuries exploited Peter's Antiochian connection to their purpose in their never-ending competition with the See of Constantinople.

Pseudo-Clement's Epistle to James

When Rufinus introduced his translation of the *Recognitions* at the beginning of the fifth century, he was quick to address an important inconsistency between the Clementine corpus and the received tradition pertaining to the sequence of apostolic succession in Rome. Assuming that the Clementine treatises were from a single author and that the author, Clement, had been the third bishop of Rome after Peter (following Irenaeus' reconstruction), Rufinus sought to tackle the assertion of Pseudo-Clement's *Letter to James* that Clement was the first—not the third—bishop of Rome. Although Rufinus offers what was likely received as a suitable solution to the inconsistency, he made no apology for the fact that the *Recognitions* themselves provide no connection between Peter and Rome or Peter and the papacy.[71] Indeed, the only text in the *Pseudo-Clementine* corpus that places Peter in Rome or connects him in any way to the papacy is the *Letter to James*.

In many ways the letter is an anomaly with respect to the rest of the *Pseudo-Clementine* collection and almost certainly was inserted at a later point by a different author/editor, who was sympathetic to the Roman Church's Petrine tradition.[72] In short, the letter presents itself as authored by Clement shortly after his elevation to the See of Rome. Much of the letter is a word-for-word account of a speech by Peter in which the apostle validates Clement's qualifications as bishop of Rome. The text also details an elaborate ceremony in which Peter invests Clement with apostolic authority in concert with the entire ecclesial assembly (both the clergy and the laity). Noting the significance of the text in the development of the papal idea, Walter Ullmann suggested that it functioned, in effect, as the first papal decretal.[73] Ullmann also demonstrated that aspects of the letter were appropriated by subsequent papal documents that were largely designed to promote the narrative of Petrine succession.[74]

But even more than authenticate Clement's claim to Petrine succession, the letter also carefully asserts what qualities characterize true Petrine leadership and thus can be viewed as an apology for a specific kind of episcopal leadership that may not have been universally desired.[75] And, perhaps in an attempt to speak to the increasing violence that was occasioned by papal elections, the text also makes explicit the importance of a peaceful and uncontested papal succession and does so through an elaborate and public ritual.[76] In short, what we find in Pseudo-Clement's *Epistle to James* is one of the earliest elaborations of a Petrine legend that brings together the constitutive elements of a Petrine discourse that enabled the bishops of Rome to lay claim to Peter's authority in a way that differentiated the Roman See from other sees and the Roman bishop from other bishops. Indeed, the most striking feature of the *Letter to James* is the extent to which it seeks to link Peter's legacy to the Roman bishop—the greater part of the *Clementine* corpus had placed Peter's activity exclusively within Syria and Palestine.

As we conclude this section, it is important to recall that the production of anonymous biographies of Peter and pseudonymous texts associated with Peter's ministry during the second, third, and fourth centuries introduced important extra-biblical elements of the Petrine legend, but those elements were not always conducive to subsequent papal narratives that linked the apostle to their own authority. The *Martyrdom of Peter* and the *Acts of Peter* placed Peter in Rome and presented the Christians of Rome as true Romans. But the same texts fail to identify Peter as a bishop, make no mention of an institutional organization per se, and offer no basis for Petrine succession. With the exception of Pseudo-Clement's *Epistle to James* (which is certainly of a different origin and authorship than the rest of the corpus), the *Pseudo-Clementines* further elaborate on Peter's authority as a witness and interpreter of Christ's ministry. But unlike the *Martyrdom* and *Acts*, they carefully connect Peter's authority to the episcopal sees of Palestine and Syria, authenticating the apostolic credentials of those sees rather than Rome. Indeed, the *Homilies* and the *Recognitions* make no connection between Peter and the See of Rome. What is perhaps most intriguing, however, is that it was Christians outside Rome who were the first to bring the disparate elements of the Petrine narrative together in a way that enhanced the prestige of the Roman bishop.

Episcopal Recognition of Rome's Petrine Connection

The oldest surviving episcopal testimony linking the Roman Church's prestige to the historic presence of Peter in the imperial capital is to be found in Irenaeus of Lyon's *Against Heresies*, which dates to the late second century. In Book III of this lengthy tome, Irenaeus criticizes the Valentinians of theological novelty because, he claims, they have rejected apostolic teaching. According to Irenaeus, the only way to guarantee the proper theological interpretation of the Christ event is to rely on a specific apostolic confession of faith embedded in the fourfold gospel that is upheld through the unbroken line of apostolic succession. Irenaeus asserts that every city that upholds orthodox belief does so on the basis of these twin criteria and that each of these cities can list the chain of bishops from the current holder to one of the apostles. Because it would be too tedious to catalog each of these successions,

Irenaeus proposes simply to chronicle the list of bishops for a few cities, beginning with the city of Rome. This is, Irenaeus tells us, in part because of the preeminence of Rome among other cities; and it is in part because the Church of Rome was founded by the twin pillars of the apostolic faith—Sts. Peter and Paul.[77] For our purposes, perhaps the most significant of Irenaeus' brief statements concerning Rome is the following: "every church should agree with this Church [i.e., Rome] on account of its preeminent authority."[78] He then offers a quick list of men he claims led the Roman Church, beginning with Linus and continuing to Eleutherios, the current bishop.[79]

Although Irenaeus does not elaborate on the connection in Book III, it is nonetheless significant for understanding the pre-Nicaean discussion of Roman privilege that Irenaeus believed Eleutherios, the current Roman bishop, to share his theological views and to be an ally in the battle against the various heretical groups that are often collectively termed "Gnostics." Indeed, if there is any single explanation for why a pre-Nicaean author (who did not reside in Rome) might affirm or reject Roman ecclesiastical prestige it would simply be that he did so when and if he found himself in the midst of a theological or administrative debate and he could or could not rely on the bishop of Rome to be an ally in his cause. This pattern is nowhere more in evidence than in the career of Cyprian of Carthage.

Cyprian was elected the bishop of Carthage in 249 C.E. and held that position until his martyrdom in 258. Shortly into his tenure as bishop, the Decian persecution took its toll on the community of Carthage, leading a great number of Christians to be regarded by their peers as having "lapsed" (i.e., they denied their faith under the threat of violence). When the persecution subsided, Cyprian chose a middle-road path to reconciliation for these lapsed Christians, allowing them to return to the fold via penance.[80] That position was rejected by a more rigorous faction that wanted to deny readmission. In Rome, a similar situation had occurred. There, the rigorous faction was led by the priest Novatus (d. 258), who established himself as a rival bishop to Cornelius (bishop of Rome, 251–253), arguing that Cornelius had, in effect, forfeited his position when he too agreed to allow the lapsed back into communion via penance. The connection between the problems in Rome and Carthage was more than coincidental because Novatus ordained a Carthaginian deacon to the episcopate as rival bishop to Cyprian. It is not surprising, therefore, that Cyprian and Cornelius shared common cause, both in terms of their pastoral approach to the lapsed and with respect to the threat posed by rigorous factions within their own churches. It was in this context that Cyprian famously defended Pope Cornelius against the schis-matic Novatians, arguing that Cornelius had been duly ordained, and they should obey him in all things.[81]

What is most important for our purposes, however, is that in the midst of the controversy Cyprian offered an abstract thesis of Petrine primacy. The central argument of *De Unitate*, perhaps his most important work, is that Christian unity is maintained through the episcopal office. According to Cyprian, the entire episcopate is mystically united precisely because the epis-copal office is united in its having been established through one man—Peter.[82] To work against a lawfully ordained bishop—any bishop—is to work against Peter and, of course, Christ, who appointed him as the leader of the apostles. It is noteworthy that *De Unitate* does not connect the conceptual significance of Peter for the episcopate to Peter's possible sojourn in Rome. In other words, there is no specific location for this unity—the connection between Peter and the episcopate remains conceptual. But Cyprian's under-standing of this Petrine privilege was to go through a series of modifications following the initial publication of *De Unitate*.

After his condemnation by an African synod, the Novatian bishop of Carthage, Felicissimus, fled to Rome, where he complained to Pope Corne-lius about his condemnation. Cyprian, not to be outdone, issued a lengthy missive rehearsing every detail of the schism in Carthage. It was in this con-text, irritated that Felicissimus had tried to outflank him and in need of Cornelius' continued support, that Cyprian explicitly linked what had been an abstract concept of Petrine primacy to the See of Rome. Specifically, Cyp-rian referred to Felicissimus as having traveled to the "throne of Peter, the chief church in which priestly unity takes its source."[83] Cyprian makes no explicit connection between Cornelius and Peter and says nothing else about a link between Rome and Peter in this lengthy letter. But, as we might expect, the reference has been the source of a great deal of interest among the advo-cates of papal authority (and their detractors), who have typically read *De Unitate* and *Epistle* 59 as though they were the same text and reflect a com-mon ecclesiological thesis.[84]

While a thorough analysis of Cyprian's ecclesiology and diplomacy lies outside the scope of the current study, it is nonetheless fascinating to see the shifts in his narration of Petrine privilege. Whereas it had been advantageous to make an explicit connection between Peter and Rome in *Epistle* 59 (typi-cally dated to 252 or 253), by 255 Cyprian found himself in an open conflict with Cornelius' successor, Stephen, who had adopted a new approach to the pastoral challenge created by the lapsed. While both Stephen and Cyprian wished to readmit former Novatians to the Catholic fold, they disagreed over the terms of that readmission. Whereas Cyprian refused to acknowledge that the baptisms performed by Novatian clerics were valid, Stephen preferred a less rigorous policy and accepted them.[85]

It is now believed that Cyprian actually modified the text of *De Unitate* during the subsequent dispute with Stephen to prevent anyone from misunderstanding his previous point about St. Peter. Cyprian did not want his readers to assume that he had suggested that the bishop of Rome had carte blanche to interpret the Scriptures as he saw fit.[86] Cyprian's correspondence from these later years also reflects a scaling back of Peter's primacy and a resistance to Roman interference in the African Church.[87] Whatever Cyprian's ultimate reservations about the authority of the See of Rome in the African Church, the bishop of Carthage serves as one of the earliest and most important sources for our understanding of the early dimensions of (and range of applications for) the Petrine legacy.

Moving from the pre-Constantinian to the post-Constantinian evidence, we turn now to an important connection between Athanasius of Alexandria and the See of Rome that was forged in the middle of the fourth century. Indeed, among all of the intricate theological and political maneuvers that took place during the Arian controversies, the one sequence of events that most helped to advance the articulation of a papal privilege was the interaction between Athanasius of Alexandria and Julius of Rome and the way in which the Council of Serdica, in seeking to defend that interaction *post eventum*, established the See of Rome as an appellate authority for bishops condemned elsewhere.

As is well known, Athanasius (ca. 296–373) was the most ardent of the Nicaean defenders in the decades after the historic council of 325. And, as a consequence of his loyalty to that council, he was frequently at odds with the majority of Eastern bishops, who tended to favor the semi-Arian policies advanced by imperial authorities. Athanasius was repeatedly condemned by Eastern synods and often forced from his episcopal see in Alexandria. In 339, his enemies installed Gregory of Cappadocia as bishop of Alexandria, sending Athanasius into the second of his eventual five exiles, this time to Rome, where he was favorably received by Julius I (bishop of Rome 337–352).

In January 341, approximately ninety Eastern bishops gathered in Antioch under the direction of Eusebius of Nicomedia, then the leader of the Arian cause. They sent a joint letter to Julius expressing their alarm that he

had given shelter to a condemned heretic.[88] Among other things, the Euse-
bian party claimed that Julius had insulted their deliberations at the Council
of Tyre (held in 335) and violated its canons.[89] While it is not known if the
Eusebians made explicit use of the precedent in their letter to Julian (the
letter is not extant), Canon 5 of the Council of Nicaea would have supported
their critique of Julius' reception of Athanasius.[90] That canon had stipulated
that all disciplinary matters were to be resolved within one's province—a
condemned cleric was not to go to another see seeking redress (which is what
Arius had done when he was condemned by his bishop in the years prior to
Nicaea). Whereas the canon had been initially instituted to isolate and censure Arius, by 341 it could be used by the neo-Arians against Athanasius to
deny him a means of Western appeal.

     In the summer of 341, Julius responded by convening a synod of approxi-
mately fifty Italian bishops that exonerated Athanasius of his condemnation
at Tyre and acknowledged him as the rightful bishop of Alexandria.[91] Following the Roman synod, Julius wrote to the Eusebians informing them of the
Italian consensus. In addition to defending Athanasius and criticizing his
opponents, the letter contains a brief assertion of Julius' own authority as it
relates to his status as the bishop of Rome. Referring to the decision of the
Eastern bishops to intervene in the affairs of the Alexandrian Church (i.e.,
the Council of Tyre) without first consulting Rome, Julius opines: "Do you
not know that it is customary first to write to us that a just judgment may be
given from here?"[92] Julius offers a few past examples of this practice before
noting: "for what we have received from the Apostle Peter, this I [write for
your benefit]."[93] For Charles Pietri, Julius' intervention on Athanasius' behalf
was the first significant occasion on which the Church of Rome asserted its
authority abroad.[94]

     Whatever the theological and personal conflicts undergirding the broader
controversy, what we find in the twin episcopal gatherings of 341 is a self-
interested distinction in the protocol for resolving a theological conflict.
According to the Eusebians, Athanasius had been rightly condemned by a
synod of his Eastern peers, and that verdict should be respected by other
Christian bishops, including the bishop of Rome. For Athanasius and Julius,
however, the Alexandrian bishop had been unjustly condemned at Tyre, and
he therefore had the right to appeal his case to an external and objective
authority—in this case, the bishop of Rome. It was against this backdrop
that the pro-Athanasian/pro-Nicaean/pro-papal Council of Serdica convened
in 343 and issued a series of canons authorizing Rome's appellate jurisdiction.

Here too we find a brief connection between Peter and Rome. In a single sentence in the third canon of Serdica, the text offers a justification for Rome's appellate jurisdiction based, in part, on the historic link between St. Peter and the See of Rome.[95] As we will see in the course of our study, this so-called Serdican privilege became one of the most employed and contested of the papal claims in subsequent centuries: whenever a cleric found himself in need of papal assistance, he would ask for an appellate hearing; whenever a bishop or synod of bishops had their own opinion overturned by the Roman bishop, they would object to Roman interference and the papal claim of appellate jurisdiction.

In his exhaustive study of the council and its subsequent interpretation, Hamilton Hess notes that there is a real difference in the way that the Serdican canons authorizing Roman appellate jurisdiction were designed and understood in the fourth century (what he believes to have been exclusively a "moral" jurisdiction), and the way that they came to be advanced by papal propagandists in the fifth and sixth centuries (defining the privilege as a "legal" jurisdiction).[96] It is, in fact, noteworthy that there is no surviving evidence of a pope involving himself in non-Italian matters on the basis of the so-called Serdican privilege until Pope Innocent I (bishop of Rome 401–417). But perhaps even more significant than that is the fact that when Innocent did apply the canon, he justified his intervention not on the basis of the Council of Serdica but on that of the hallowed Council of Nicaea. Indeed, by the fifth century, whether accidentally or deliberately, the Roman archives had already conflated the canons from Serdica with those of Nicaea. It was for this reason that all subsequent popes would claim that a unique attribute of their primatial office was the right to serve as an appellate court for any cleric condemned anywhere in Christendom and to do so on the basis of the canons of Nicaea.

From Irenaeus to Cyprian to Serdica, a series of dogmatic concerns, regional disputes, and pure circumstance helped to constitute a discursive horizon that made possible a series of statements connecting the biblical Peter's presumed authority vis-à-vis the apostles to the bishop of Rome's desired authority vis-à-vis other bishops. Even within the brief snapshots offered in the previous pages, we see that this connection between Peter and Rome could be as advantageous for episcopal authorities outside of Rome as it was for the bishops of Rome themselves. Our objective in this section has not been to provide an exhaustive narrative of Petrine precedents so much as it has been to sample the complex set of circumstances by which a Christian authority outside of Rome might leverage the connection between Peter, Rome, and the Roman bishop for his own purposes. It has also been our goal to show how various aspects of the Petrine narrative (drawn in varying degrees from biblical, apocryphal, and pseudonymous sources) gained a certain momentum of cohesion between the second and fourth centuries.

In the earliest extra-Roman episcopal statements connecting Peter to Rome, we find a series of elements in play, though often in isolation. For example, the city of Rome is acknowledged as important not only because it is the center of the Roman world, but because the two figures most connected to the "faith of the apostles," Peter and Paul, established the Church in that city. Rome is a model church, in part because of its fidelity to the apostolic teaching of Peter and Paul and in part because of the witness of the martyrs to that truth. With Cyprian, however, we find the very notion of episcopal authority being tied to the historic Peter—both because of his confession of faith that Jesus is the Christ, the Son of God (cf. Mt 16) and because the subsequent authority to bind and loose sin was understood to be the foundation for the entire episcopate.[97] When it served his purpose to do so, Cyprian made explicit the connection between Peter's personal primacy and a primacy for the bishop of Rome; when it did not serve his purpose to do so (specifically when he found himself at odds with Pope Stephen), Cyprian isolated Peter's foundational role for the episcopacy from his historic link to the See of Rome, insisting instead that Peter's authority was transmitted to all rightfully ordained bishops.

It was not until the fourth century, however, that these conceptual formulations of a Petrine or papal privilege were deployed to justify any kind of jurisdictional or appellate authority for the Roman bishop. In its most explicit form, the appellate canons of the Council of Serdica, this privilege was the direct result of the collaboration between Julius and the exiled Athanasius, whose sanctuary in Rome was perceived by his enemies to have been contrary to the traditional authority of a provincial council. It was within this context that the pro-Roman/pro-Nicaean Council of Serdica authorized, *post eventum*, the procedural process by which Julius and Athanasius had collaborated—a process that was at odds with the canons of Nicaea and was a sticking point with the Eastern bishops who were opposed to all things Athanasian. It is important to note that, despite the importance that the canons of Serdica would hold in subsequent centuries, the canons themselves make only a slight reference to Peter or justification of papal appellate jurisdiction on the basis of Peter's link to the See of Rome.

Perhaps even more importantly, we must stress the fact that even though
the Serdica canons privilege the bishop of Rome among his peers, that recognition in itself should not be misconstrued as evidence that all Christians
shared the same point of view. Nor should we be misled into thinking that
this external episcopal recognition of the Roman See's authority in any way
indicates that the actual bishops of Rome had the universal support of all
Roman Christians. Indeed, our earliest sources describing the cult of Peter—
and the cult of the martyrs more broadly—indicate that religious observance
in Rome was quite varied and often operated outside of the bishop's control.
As we will see, episcopal patronage for the cult of Peter in the city of Rome
was, at least in part, driven by a desire to legitimize papal authority among
ecclesiastic rivals who did not acknowledge it. It also provided a means for
the Roman bishop to compete with aristocratic patrons, who could easily
outspend him.

The Cult of Peter in Rome

Although the connections between Peter, Rome, and the Roman bishop are
attested as early as the late second century, it was not until the middle of the
fourth century that the bishops of Rome themselves sought to link their
authority to Peter in any kind of concerted way. It is significant that when
they did so, they often appropriated a popular form of Christian devotional
practice in Rome—the cult of the martyrs.[98]

Scholars have been working diligently on the cult of Roman martyrs for
more than a century, and their efforts have been both helped and hindered
by an abundance of literary and archaeological evidence.[99] Although many
aspects of Roman martyr cult are still debated (its patrons, its locations, and
the coalitions it forged), it is clear that the cult of martyrs in Rome was
prominent and well funded, and that it often occasioned or reflected rival
factions among Roman Christians.[100]

Devotion to Roman martyrs had both private and public dimensions.
Just as pre-Christian Roman religious practice incorporated private, domestic
rituals, so too the transition to Christianity included household worship.[101]
In some aristocratic households, private worship was largely dominated by
devotion to the martyrs, which could include private collections of martyr
relics and the creation of household shrines dedicated to the martyrs.[102] In
her recent work on private worship in late antiquity, Kimberly Bowes details

the remarkable and varied practice of martyr devotion in the aristocratic households and imperial palaces within Rome.[103] The most famous example of an urban domestic martyr shrine is the complex surrounding the church of Santi Giovanni e Paolo, two Roman martyrs, on the Caelian Hill.[104] Although scholars debate several aspects of the site and its transformation over time, it is generally believed that it originated as a part of an aristocratic estate, possessed a private deposit of martyr relics in a small shrine, and also included a house church.[105] What is so intriguing about this and other relic depositories within Rome is that they contravened strict legal restrictions against intramural burial sites within the city.[106] As Bowes notes, the initial intramural relics were of foreign extraction; local saints were readily present, a short walk outside the city walls.[107]

The Constantinian basilicas that were commissioned shortly after the emperor's accession in 312 and were dedicated to popular saints, including St. Lawrence and St. Marcellus, made public commemoration of the martyrs possible. Others followed in the decades to come, both in the city and outside it.[108] In suburban areas, most of these churches were, in effect, elaborate martyr shrines and cemetery basilicas that enabled a form of broad civic devotion that enhanced both their imperial patrons and the officiating bishop.[109] Within the city, most of the basilicas, like that of St. Clement, were associated with the memory of a particular martyr but not connected to a physical shrine.[110] Throughout the fourth and into the fifth century, funding for expansion, renovation, and decoration of these sites was provided by subsequent members of the royal family and, increasingly, by other members of the Roman aristocracy. It was only later that Roman bishops themselves had the resources to contribute to large-scale building and decorative projects like that of St. Maria Maggiore (commissioned by Sixtus III, Leo I's predecessor), which became a major site for Marian commemoration.[111]

Before the construction of the Constantinian basilicas, public commemoration of the martyrs took place outside of the city walls in the catacombs and at other locations that developed as martyr shrines.[112] Some of the most popular sites, in fact, were those of martyred Roman bishops, including Cornelius and Callixtus.[113] In many (but not all) cases, the suburban basilicas were built on previously established cultic sites. The construction of these large facilities both coincided with and enabled the Roman bishop to assert a measure of ecclesiastical authority and supervision over the cult that he likely did not fully enjoy in the pre-Constantinian period—the suburban basilica of St. Agnes, built in the 340s, offering a prime example.[114]

In a similar fashion, Roman bishops were able to exert their authority over the cult of martyrs through the promotion of a single festal calendar that assigned specific days of commemoration by the Roman Church that would be officiated by the bishop himself.[115] As we will see, Gregory I (likely drawing on an older tradition) ordered bishops of central and southern Italy, as well as those from Sicily, to attend the commemoration of the Feast of St. Peter in St. Peter's basilica on June 29. For now, it is worth noting that the oldest surviving evidence that the Feast of Sts. Peter and Paul was commemorated on June 29 is a calendar, known as the *Depositio Martyrium*, which dates to the year 354.[116] Interestingly, that calendar claims that Peter's relics reside *in catacumbas* (i.e., at a shrine on the Via Appia), not at St. Peter's basilica, which had been recently constructed on Vatican Hill.

To be sure, the consolidation of martyr festivals into a consistent and centralized form took time, and our surviving sources suggest that many cultic sites were held by rival factions well into the fourth century. For example, during the disputed papal election between Damasus and Ursinus in 366, the basilica of St. Agnes on the Via Nomentana and the basilica Liberii on the Esquiline Hill became rally sites for the party loyal to Ursinus.[117] Through violence and other tactics, Damasus gained the election but not without damage to his credibility. It may well be for this reason that Damasus spent so lavishly on the renovation of martyr shrines in the catacombs.[118] Indeed, Damasus' tenure serves as a case study of the way Roman bishops appropriated the enthusiasm for martyr cult for their own initiatives to root out rival factions through a reframing of Rome's Christian history.[119]

For our purposes, of course, the most intriguing aspect of Damasus' efforts to consolidate popular martyr cult under papal control relates to the fact that when he was elected in 366 there were two sites in the suburbs of Rome that had a claim to be the location of St. Peter's martyrdom—a cemetery on Vatican Hill that received a Constantinian basilica[120] (in effect granting imperial sanction to the site as the proper place for the commemoration of St. Peter) and another location in the catacombs on the Via Appia (underneath the present basilica of St. Sebastian), where commemoration of St. Peter went back, at least, to the middle of the third century.[121] Without burying ourselves within the scholarly quagmire that is focused on identifying the supposed original location of Peter's bones, we will simply take note that, even though both sites have archaeological and textual traditions that predate the fourth century, we have little understanding of what kinds of rituals actually took place at those sites.[122]

One of the more intriguing theories put forward to explain the existence of competing sites was that of M. K. Mohlberg, who submitted that control of the memorial for Peter and Paul on the Via Appia was in the hands of the Novatians.[123] That thesis has been appropriated and developed by Kate Cooper, who employs a literary analysis of the surviving texts to show how multiple groups used the amorphous figure of Lucina (an aristocratic patron of Christianity who, according to various texts, was responsible for burying Peter, Paul, and a host of pre-Nicene Roman bishops) to support their claim to authenticity.[124] The fact that there were competing sites for Peter's relics should not surprise us; such was the case with many famous saints in late antiquity.

Because Damasus did not have the financial resources to compete with the imperial and aristocratic patrons of St. Peter at the Vatican, he seems to have focused his patronage of Peter's cult on the alternate site at the Memoria Apostolorum on the Via Appia, where he commissioned a monumental crypt.[125] In one of Damasus' most famous epigrams,[126] the pontiff acknowledges that pilgrims might come to the Memoria Apostolorum to venerate the relics of St. Peter and St. Paul but that those relics are not there.[127] Damasus does not tell us where they are or when they were moved—in fact, he does not actually say that they were moved; he simply acknowledges that pilgrims will come to this site looking for the relics. Instead, Damasus informs the visitors that they should take note of the starlike quality of Peter and Paul and should be heartened that they too (i.e., the pilgrims) can be inscribed as stars by the patron of the shrine (i.e., Damasus). In effect, Damasus seems to continue the cult of Peter on the Via Appia, even though relics no longer existed there. Perhaps this was because the Memoria Apostolorum offers him an opportunity to link himself to Peter's cult in a way that he could not achieve at the Vatican, where patronage was still, primarily, in the hands of the imperial family and wealthy elite.

While Damasus may have been unable to maximize his authority at the Vatican, subsequent bishops would be more successful. Indeed, as we will see, Peter's tomb at the basilica of St. Peter became an important marker of papal authority and a prime site for papal performance. By Leo's tenure, the bishops of Rome were increasingly using the basilica to showcase the symbolic links between themselves and Peter. For example, Leo used St. Peter's basilica as a locus for assembling and speaking to subordinate bishops. When the Western emperor Valentinian visited Rome in 450, Leo made sure that he attended a vigil at St. Peter's; when Theoderic visited Rome in 500, Symmachus likewise arranged for the Gothic king to pay a visit to St. Peter's. By

590, Gregory the Great was requiring his agents to swear an oath at the tomb of St. Peter before beginning their commissions. Even in death, a Roman bishop could link himself to Peter's tomb and thus lay claim to a share of Peter's authority.[128]

The bishops of Rome linked themselves to the Petrine legacy through other physical forms beyond the basilica of St. Peter and the Memoria Apostolorum. It should not be surprising that the artistic pairing of Peter and Paul appears repeatedly in material objects from Rome in this period, including bronze and silver medallions, metal and terra-cotta lamps, engraved glassware, and gold-glass portraits.[129] Charles Pietri has argued that the increased artistic pairing of Peter and Paul that occurred in the mid-fourth century was, in some circumstances, funded by Roman bishops (especially Damasus) who wished to smooth over factional infighting through an ideological campaign Pietri deemed a *"concordia apostolorum."*[130] Pietri's thesis has been challenged for a few reasons. Among them is the observation that Roman bishops themselves often appear alongside the Peter and Paul pairing in these material productions. Obviously, the placement of the Roman bishop with the founding fathers of Roman Christianity offered a symbolic opportunity beyond the promotion of Christian harmony.[131] For example, Pope Damasus' image can be found alongside St. Peter's on a number of surviving gold-glass portraits.[132] While the patronage for these portraits is impossible to identify with certainty,[133] scholars have typically understood Damasus, who was involved in one of the most violent papal elections of the period, to have sought to authenticate his legitimacy through the visual and literary pairing of himself with specific martyr cults, including, of course, the cult of St. Peter.[134]

Just as the literary sources we have examined introduced important elements that connected the Apostle Peter to the city of Rome and the Roman bishop, so too the embellishment of Peter's shrines and ritualized cult should be understood to be important aspects of the multifaceted and ever expanding horizon of the Petrine discourse that was both available to the papal actors and, reflexively, made possible by them. Indeed, it was the intersection of speech, text, space, and ritual that allowed the bishops of Rome and their interlocutors to put flesh once again on Peter's bones.

The Petrine Discourse and the Emergence of the Roman Bishop

In this chapter, we have sought to identify those texts, traditions, and material sites that reflect the emergence of a Petrine discourse—a set of discursive possibilities that eventually enabled Roman bishops to connect themselves to Peter and to Peter's authority for the purpose of legitimizing and/or expanding their own. As we have seen, the literary and material elements of the Petrine discourse developed on multiple and uneven trajectories that lacked clearly defined boundaries or centralizing forces. While most of our surviving narratives emphasize Peter's miraculous deeds, his teaching authority, and his faith in Christ, there remain considerable differences among them. Some emphasize his martyrdom, others stress his missionary efforts, some place him in Rome, while others situate his activity in the Near East. Although Rome may not have been the only ecclesiastic center that could lay claim to a Petrine foundation, there is little denying that nearly all fourth-century Christians would have understood Peter to have held a unique position of authority in the early Church. As we will see, it was one of the great achievements of the fifth- and sixth-century papacy that it was able to recalibrate the collective Christian memory of Peter in such a way that all religious authorities came to acknowledge that Peter had founded the Roman episcopate and that his successors, the bishops of Rome, possessed a measure of his authority that other bishops did not.

As noted in the Introduction, the Roman Church in the second, third, and even the fourth century was a much broader constellation of religious networks, rituals, and beliefs than what we can realistically understand to have fallen under the Roman bishop's care. As elsewhere, the ascendancy of the Roman bishop to a position of moral, legal, and dogmatic authority within his city was a process that was often uneven and sometimes highly contested. By harnessing the various elements of the Petrine legend and by asserting themselves as the rightful leader of Petrine rituals, however, the Roman bishops of the fourth century began not only to consolidate their authority within the ancient capital but also to assert themselves in the affairs of other churches.[135]

It is perhaps surprising that we have so little evidence of the Roman bishops' attempts to employ the Petrine narrative for their own purposes before the middle of the fourth century. In some ways, the pontificate of Damasus marks a watershed in the way that Roman bishops began to think creatively about maximizing the popularity of the cult of Peter to their own advantage. As noted, Damasus' tenure is also important because it reminds us of the extent to which papal elections could be bitterly contested. As we progress through our study of the development of the Petrine discourse, we should not lose sight of the fact that Damasus' promotion of the cult of Peter can be viewed, in part, as an effort to legitimate his own authority. Indeed, as the subsequent chapters will show, the escalation of papal claims that were accompanied by hyperbolic Petrine language in the period 440–600 were, more often than not, precipitated by challenges or insults to the Roman bishop's authority (dogmatic, political, or moral).

CHAPTER 2

The Many Faces of Leo's Peter

As we might expect for a figure as significant as Leo "the Great," scholars have explored many different aspects of his career and thought, ranging from the ideological and theological to the political.[1] One historiographical trajectory in the scholarship of the twentieth century suggests an attempt to locate specific ways the pope appropriated or transformed imperial signs and symbols for his Christian purposes.[2] Walter Ullmann, for example, argued that Leo deliberately borrowed the phrase "unworthy heir" (*indignus heres*) from Roman legal terminology as he sought to strengthen the bond between his office and Peter's uncontested authority.[3] Bronwen Neil has sufficiently shown that there are problems with Ullmann's interpretation (Ullmann essentially missed the fact that Leo is, in a sense, inverting the phrase, because in Roman law an "unworthy heir" cannot legally inherit). Yet there is little doubt that Leo's styling of himself as the "heir" of Peter reflects a blending of Roman imperial traditions with what Conrad Leyser identifies in another context as a Christian rhetoric of "unworthiness."[4] This chapter will similarly focus on Leo's narrative decisions in his formulation of Roman authority. In some respects, therefore, I am indebted to Trevor Jalland's 1941 biography of Leo, which emphasizes Leo's "greatness" in terms of his ability to assert papal prominence on the basis of an imagined Petrine legacy that, in Jalland's eyes, had little hope of historical verification.[5] I am also appreciative of Susan Wessel's insightful comments regarding the importance of Peter for Leo's vision of Rome's universal reach and exercise of ecclesiastical justice.[6]

All historical studies of Leo, of course, must take note of the dramatic transformation of Roman society that occurred in the fifth century as a consequence of the Germanic invasions/migrations. At the same time that the authority of Western emperors increasingly gave way to Germanic warlords, the landholding aristocrats of Rome (men who held positions in the Senate as consuls or as the *illustri* of the state) managed to increase their wealth and influence in the city. As a result, these families continued to play an integral role in civic and religious dynamics, whether or not particular members of a family took on leadership roles in the Church.

At the time of Leo's election in 440, the Western empire was ruled by Valentinian III (425–455), first cousin to Theodosius II (416–450), his more powerful counterpart in the East. Typical of the political infighting of the period, Valentinian grew envious of his most effective general, Aetius, and murdered him in 454. Valentinian was himself murdered in March 455. Because Valentinian had no male heirs, the Western empire fell into a period of further instability that partly enabled the ascendancy of the Gothic kingdom of Italy a generation later.[7] One of the most remarkable features of Leo's large corpus is its almost complete silence about these political developments. Not only does Valentinian's murder go unmentioned, so do Attila the Hun's invasion of Italy in 452 and the Vandal siege of Rome in 455.[8]

We know little of Leo's life before his election as pope.[9] We do know that he served as an advisor and archdeacon to Pope Sixtus III (432–440) and was on a diplomatic mission in Gaul on his behalf when Sixtus died and Leo was elected his successor in 440.[10] While biographical details are scant, the surviving corpus is substantial. In fact, Leo is the first pope whose writings survive in relatively complete editions. Of the 173 letters in the extant corpus, approximately 140 are believed to be genuinely his (in addition to several spurious letters, approximately 20 letters are addressed to him or have been transmitted with his corpus).[11] His is the largest surviving papal correspondence before Gregory the Great. In addition to the letters, there are 96 surviving sermons, organized by topic rather than chronologically. As noted in the Introduction, Carolingian editors chose to begin the collection with those sermons that most forcefully advocate Roman authority and do so by connecting that authority to the Apostle Peter. For Leo's Carolingian editors, his legacy was tied directly to his promotion of Roman authority via Peter.

By paying close attention to where, how, and why Leo employed the Petrine topos in his sermons and letters, this chapter seeks to nuance previous assessments of the function of Peter in Leo's assertion of Roman authority. Among other things, the chapter maintains that we can learn a great deal about Leo's Peter, and ultimately about how the Petrine discourse functions in this period, by paying closer attention to the occasions where the pontiff avoids any reference to Peter. While it is certainly true that Leo was one of the earliest pontiffs to employ the figure of Peter as a key feature of his promotion of Roman primacy, his use of the topos was typically confined to a specific set of diplomatic circumstances. As we will see, some of the strongest assertions of Petrine privilege in Leo's corpus derive from the beginning of his tenure, when he was likely most concerned to establish his authority over the ecclesiastical leaders of the Western Church. As he grew more confident that he had earned their respect, and even when he was engaging Eastern correspondents for the first time, Leo was far less likely to invoke Peter and all his apostolic might. What this tells us, I believe, is that the strongest assertions of Petrine privilege in Leo's corpus should be interpreted as markers of diplomatic and theological anxiety.

The Peter of Leo's Sermons

While we do not know exactly how often Leo preached, we do have a large number of Leo's sermons, most of which correspond to particular Christian feasts (such as Holy Week, Christmas, Pentecost, and the Feast of Sts. Peter and Paul), various fasting periods (such as Lent and the September fast[12]), or the anniversary of Leo's elevation to the episcopate (September 29).[13] Apart from the anniversary sermons, Leo's homilies deal primarily with pastoral concerns, especially those related to fasting, penance, and almsgiving.[14] While those facets of Leo's thought are interesting in and of themselves, we will focus our attention in this section on the ways in which Peter functioned as a proxy for Leo's concerns, whether pastoral or otherwise, throughout the surviving sermons, beginning with those sermons that most deliberately link Leo's personal authority to the Apostle Peter.

The Anniversary Sermons and the Feast of Sts. Peter and Paul

Leo employed the Petrine topos most fully on occasions when other bishops were present—namely on the anniversary of his election and for the feast of Sts. Peter and Paul. That Leo was so much less likely to invoke the topos for audiences of laity and lesser clergy attests to the fact that it functioned primarily as a form of rhetorical performance and self-presentation in the presence of Leo's episcopal peers. As we will see, the routine gathering of Italian bishops at St. Peter's tomb at Vatican Hill (or elsewhere in Rome), provided

Leo an arena of display in which he could reinforce the symbolic connection between himself and Peter.[15] And early in his tenure as bishop, Leo made the most of those opportunities.

On the first anniversary of his election, September 441, Leo stood before the assembled bishops and threw down the gauntlet. After expressing his confidence that God's presence is made manifest in the gathered assembly of so many "saints," he articulated a link between Peter and himself that would become a permanent feature of subsequent papal self-promotion:

> Neither, I am certain, does the most blessed Apostle Peter withhold
> his pious honor and faithful love from this assembly. Nor has he
> forsaken your devotion, because it was out of devotion for him that
> you have gathered. He too is made happy by your affection and
> embraces this observance by those who have a part in this honor,
> [an observance] instituted by the Lord. He approves the most
> orderly love of the entire Church, which receives as Peter the one in
> Peter's see and whose love for so great a shepherd does not diminish,
> even in the person of an unworthy heir.[16]

While this was not the first assertion that St. Peter is present in his papal successor (as "heir")—Pope Siricius, for example, had suggested the same— Leo forcefully asserts that, as Peter's heir, he deserves the respect of the entire Church as though he were Peter himself.[17] Although the passage is couched in several rhetorical affirmations of humility—Leo refers to his "lowliness," protests that he has "no merits," and postures as an "unworthy heir"—there is little denying that this was a deliberate assertion of personal authority. Indeed, it was probably the single most important rhetorical development in the history of papal self-aggrandizement.

It is impossible to know how Leo's initial foray into Petrine self-promotion was received by the assembled bishops. There are no surviving accounts. Perhaps our only recourse is to examine the rhetorical features of the next surviving anniversary sermon, dated two years later to September 443, which offers a considerably longer treatment of the matter. Indeed, Leo's *Sermon* 3 defends his previous claims of Petrine authority through a series of interconnected moves. The first links the stability of the Christian faith to a hierarchical structure that begins with Christ, passes to Peter, and is then shared by those who recognize Peter's authority: "for the solidity of that faith, which was praised in the leader of the apostles endures because just as what Peter believed in Christ remains, there likewise remains what Christ instituted in Peter."[18] Leo's second move is to assert Peter's authority among the disciples through an analysis of the scriptures. Here, Leo rehearses the passage from Matthew 16 in which Peter affirms Christ's divinity and is then rewarded with the keys to the kingdom of heaven and the ability to bind and loose sin.[19] Leo's final move is to make explicit the link between Peter's authority and his own through a careful exegesis of the Matthew passage. It is, in fact, noteworthy that the assertion of Petrine privilege in the preceding anniversary sermon (*Sermon* 2) included no such exegetical, or even theoretical, justification for the claim to be Peter's heir—it simply asserted it at the close of the homily.

Among the many striking advances of Leo's exegesis of Matthew 16 in *Sermon* 3 is the assertion that St. Peter, in his activity as the head of the apostles, remains fully active in the Roman Church of the fifth century. Leo notes that Peter "now governs the things entrusted to him more completely and more effectively." The pontiff also instructs his episcopal peers that "anything we do correctly . . . is a consequence of his works and merits."[20] With this remarkable passage, Leo is, in a sense, usurping all agency for the good, whether of the bishops themselves or of some other spiritual agent (e.g., Christ, the angels, or the saints), and transferring that agency to St. Peter. As the passage unfolds, however, we see that Peter's agency is simply a proxy for the spiritual and theological authority encapsulated in the papal office. Indeed, the implicit becomes explicit as Leo moves to the ways Peter remains active in his successor: "in this see his power lives and his authority excels." And then, a few lines later, Leo delivers the payoff: "Understand him to be present in my humble person. Honor him. For in him continues the responsibility of all shepherds, along with the protection of all the sheep entrusted to them. And his dignity does not decrease even in an unworthy heir." In short, all pastoral care—the leadership of the entire Church—belongs to Peter and to Peter's "unworthy" heir.[21] Just to be sure that his episcopal colleagues could not claim that Leo was introducing anything novel, the pontiff adds, for good measure: "we preach to you nothing other than what [Peter] taught."[22]

In addition to the many creative advances in Peter's authority, the homily also includes a fascinating elaboration of how it is that someone can be Peter's heir. Leo distinguishes between the biological inheritance of priesthood according to the order of Aaron and the spiritual inheritance of the Holy Spirit according to the order of Melchizedek (cf. Heb 5.6). Thus, he implies that his own inheritance of Peter's authority is a form of spiritual election and that it is fundamentally unlike the normal laws of domestic inheritance.[23] One wonders, in fact, if this significant point of clarification by Leo was precipitated by some sort of negative reception to a previous iteration of Petrine inheritance.

Although no subsequent sermon in Leo's corpus was ever as thorough in its defense of Petrine authority as the sermon of 443, the anniversary sermon of 444, as well as the sermons for the feast of Sts. Peter and Paul (another occasion on which Italian bishops would have assembled in Rome to pay tribute to Leo), generally repeated many of the same features.[24] Throughout these sermons, Leo asserts Peter's historic authority among the apostles by virtue of his confession of faith (cf. Mt 16).[25] Interestingly, Leo does not avail himself of the apocryphal traditions that detailed the apostle's supposed activity in the city of Rome. Instead he bases his Christ-given apostolic primacy in scripture, and proclaims that he, as Peter's heir, continues in a position of authority and responsibility vis-à-vis other episcopal leaders.

Though similar in many respects, there are a few distinguishing characteristics of the two surviving sermons Leo delivered on the feast of Sts. Peter and Paul (June 29, 441 and 443). *Sermon* 82 offers what might be described as a sophisticated appropriation of key elements of an "imperial" discourse for the purposes of promoting Petrine authority. Leo models Peter and Paul as Christian "refounders" of Rome, showing how the two saints supersede, by their virtue and their faith in Christ, the fratricidal Romulus and Remus.[26] Although Leo very much believed that divine providence had made use of the *pax Romana* to spread Christianity to the known world, he was also perfectly willing to subvert imperial sovereignty for the sake of Petrine promotion. Ultimately, Rome is the center of the world, in Leo's imagination, not because of its imperial past but because it is the home of St. Peter. *Sermon* 83 makes this final point even more explicit. In a sermon that does not even mention St. Paul, Leo offers one of his most extended ecclesiological statements on the balance of authority between the See of Rome and other episcopal centers. Referring to the authority to bind and loose sin, Leo notes:

> Indeed, the right to use this power was transmitted to the other apostles, also. But not without reason was it handed over to one, even when it is implied for all. Indeed, in a singular way it was entrusted to Peter because the figure of Peter is placed before all the

leaders of the Church. Therefore, this privilege of Peter resides wherever a pastoral judgment has been made in accordance with his fairness. For there will not be undue [pastoral] severity or leniency so
long as nothing is bound or loosed outside of that which blessed
Peter has loosed or bound.[27]

Leo concedes to the assembled bishops that they too share in Peter's ability
to bind and loose. But, the pontiff reminds them, they share in this privilege
only to the extent that they affirm that Peter is Leo's predecessor and that
their own pastoral judgments are restricted by the confines of Peter's spiritual
judgments—in other words, their judgments can be overturned by Leo.

Again, it is impossible to know how these sermons were received. It is
noteworthy that there is no hint of a Petrine assertion in the sermon that Leo
delivered on the occasion of his election in 440 (*Sermon* 1). Leo's claim that
he was Peter's heir came a year later, on the first anniversary of that election.
The most complete articulation of that position was delivered on the third
anniversary, in 443. While we cannot know how the attending bishops
responded, we can be reasonably assured that Leo's aggressive proclamations
of Roman primacy by Petrine means were part of a deliberate strategy to
assert his authority over other Italian bishops in the early years of his pontificate—something akin to a rhetorical marking of his ecclesiastical territory. It
is noteworthy that the surviving sermons (on any theme) for subsequent years
provide no assertions of Petrine authority similar to those in 441–443. As we
will see in the next section, Leo continued to employ the Petrine discourse
in his correspondence with Italian and other Western ecclesiastical officials,
even after it disappeared from the homilies he delivered for "friendly" audiences.[28] Before we investigate Leo's correspondence, however, we will examine the ways in which he employed Peter in those sermons he delivered to
the lay audiences of Rome.

The Pastoral Function of Peter and Its Absence

For all the attention that Leo's Peter has garnered among papal historians,
one might get the false impression that the pontiff's sermons are filled with
references to Peter and his authority. The fact of the matter is that Peter
functions as a forceful tool for the promotion of Roman episcopal authority
in only four homilies, a tiny percentage of Leo's surviving sermons. As noted,

the distinguishing contextual feature of those sermons is the presence of other bishops in the audience. In other words, the rhetorical leveraging of Peter for papal self-aggrandizement in Leo's sermons was likely performed solely for the benefit of other bishops. As a consequence, the aggressive use of the Petrine topos was a not relevant feature of the normal rhythms of the pontiff's preaching. This is not to say that Peter goes unmentioned in the other sermons, but that he functions in very different ways.

As we will discuss in a subsequent section of this chapter, Leo's greatest theological contributions addressed the Christological controversies of his day, particularly as they related to his interpretation of the incarnation (God's becoming human in the person of Jesus Christ). One of the diplomatic arguments that Leo repeats in that controversy is that Peter's confession of faith (cf. Mt 16) enabled him to understand better than the other apostles the Christological implications of the incarnation—a fact that, in Leo's rhetorical rendering, gave the Christological teaching of the See of Rome an unparalleled orthodoxy. Given Leo's frequent framing of his Christological position as "Peter's teaching" elsewhere, it is rather perplexing that Leo's nine surviving homilies on the Nativity fast and ten surviving homilies on the Nativity itself (several of which were delivered in the midst of the doctrinal controversy) never connect Peter's confession of faith to the Christological interpretations that Leo offers for the Christmas event.[29] The Nativity sermons, perhaps more than any other set of sermons in his corpus, feature Leo's theological preaching at its most sophisticated, as they present a theological depth that he typically withholds from lay audiences.[30] That Leo chose against connecting Peter's confession of faith to the interpretation of the incarnation would seem to confirm one of the core arguments of this chapter—that, in most cases, Leo connects Peter to his own authority only when he is especially anxious about whether or not his authority is going to be respected by others or when his authority had been repudiated by others. Neither of those situations was likely to have occurred in the gatherings of laypersons for his Christmas sermons. Thus, the Petrine topos (as it was typically employed by Leo) was of no rhetorical value in the pastoral setting of the Nativity homilies.

Another interesting feature of Leo's Petrine preaching is to be found in his Paschal sermons, which constitute twenty-one of the surviving ninety-six sermons—the largest subset in the collection. For most years for which we have records, Leo preached three times between Palm Sunday and Easter. The topics of these sermons vary to some degree but never stray too far from the various Gospel narratives of Christ's passion. Included within those scriptural accounts are two incidents involving Peter that draw Leo's attention: Peter's striking of the high priest's servant and his denial of Christ. The first is treated in detail only once, in *Sermon* 52 (dated to Palm Sunday 441). Whereas many early Christian exegetes interpreted Peter's attack on the servant as an example of Peter's lack of understanding of the need for Christ's passion,[31] in Leo's hands, Peter's "error" is transformed into an act of unsurpassed loyalty.[32]

Even more developed, however, is Leo's consideration of Peter's denial of Christ. Two of the twenty-one sermons offer a detailed analysis of Peter's denial. The first, delivered on Palm Sunday 442, concedes little ground to those who might argue that the biblical Peter was flawed. Indeed, Leo never employs the language of denial, sin, or rejection in the sermon. Instead, he emphasizes Peter's "instability" and that the experience enabled Peter to be the first of the apostles to learn the depth of Christ's humility. In other words, rather than framing the episode as a failure of will or faith, Leo sets the scene as an occasion in which Peter, the victim "of a violent storm of cruel assault," received from Christ a sudden conversion and restoration, which enabled him to overcome his fear.[33] In some ways, this echoes the *Acts of Peter*, which engaged the story of Peter's denial to warn against the power of Satan. For Leo, however, the "assault" becomes an occasion for Peter's growth rather than a sign of his weakness.

Three years later, on Palm Sunday 445, Leo confronted Peter's denial more directly, but here too, the pontiff finds a way to turn the event into a progressive step in the development of apostolic primacy.

> When the Son of God prepared to assume the punishment for iniquity, the blessed Apostle Peter, whose faith burned with such devotion that he would be prepared both to suffer for the Lord and to die for him, frightened by the accusation of the priest's servant, incurred the infirmity of a denial. He was permitted to hesitate, it would appear, so that the remedy of penitence might be founded in the prince of the Church [*ut in Ecclesiae principe remedium paenitentiae conderetur*], and so that no one would dare to trust in their own strength when not even blessed Peter could escape the danger of fickleness.[34]

Remarkably, Leo is able to transform a passage about Peter's denial into an encomium on the apostle's devotion, one that includes a plug for Peter's primacy in the Church. Peter is "permitted to hesitate," Leo reckons, so that we might all learn the power of repentance. Indeed, a few lines later, Leo continues with an emotional account of the power of Peter's repentance, a theme that became increasingly important in subsequent paschal sermons.[35]

In an essay on penance in Leo's sermons, Kevin Uhalde aptly demonstrates, contrary to previous assessments, that Leo's promotion of justice and penance was directly tied to the power that Peter had achieved through the "weakness" of his denial.[36] For Leo, it was through the lesson of his denial that Peter both learned of Christ's power and further devoted himself to the Christian cause. Indeed, following the detailed assessment of Palm Sunday 445, Leo began to tie Peter's newfound understanding of the power of penance to his conversion of the Jews via penance (cf. Acts 2.41).[37] And while there is little doubt that Leo creatively drew on Peter as a source for both his theology of penance and his promotion of Roman authority, it is nevertheless remarkable that the vast majority of Leo's sermons that explore the importance of penance make little, if any, explicit use of the biblical Peter.[38] Given Leo's repeated use of Petrine themes and given his frequent exhortations to penance, it is surprising that the pontiff did not more frequently connect the two themes for pastoral purposes.

Perhaps the only homily intended for lay consumption that does convey some of the markings of a more robust Petrine discourse is the lone surviving homily (*Sermon* 51) for the Feast of the Transfiguration (cf. Mt 17.1–9). Delivered in 445, the homily begins with an extended reminder of Peter's confession of faith (Mt 16), which precedes Matthew's narrative of the Transfiguration. Leo, as elsewhere, stresses that Peter's primacy among the apostles was instituted as a kind of reward for his correct answer to Christ's question. Following that affirmation, however, Leo's homily takes an unprecedented turn in that it implies that Peter's faith was, at that point, still immature. In other words, Peter needed to experience the miracle of the Transfiguration to make his Christological understanding more complete.[39]

To make the point all the more clearly, Leo reminds his audience that Peter had made the mistake (just after his confession of faith) of attempting to prevent Christ from going to Jerusalem to be crucified (cf. Mt 16.21–28). Leo, of course, softens the extent of Christ's rebuke, irenically substituting the "get behind me Satan" exclamation of the biblical text with the summary that Peter received a "kindly reproach from Jesus that inspired him to want to share in his passion."[40] While most of the remainder of the homily focuses on the Christological dimensions of the Transfiguration, Leo does explore another of Peter's miscues from the biblical narrative—namely his suggestion that they build three altars, one for Moses, one for Elijah, and one for Christ (Mt 17.4).[41] To be sure, Leo does not dwell on Peter's mistakes for long. Like the paschal homilies that dealt with Peter's striking of the servant and his denial of Christ, Leo moves quickly to shift the topic away from Peter's lack of understanding to show how the experience benefited Peter in the long run. Nevertheless, this homily stands out as the most conspicuous example of Leo's willingness to acknowledge the limitations of the biblical Peter— something that he seems to have never done in the presence of other bishops.[42]

One final dimension of the use of Peter in Leo's homilies is the extent to which the saint functions as a patron and spiritual protector of the city of Rome. One of the tropes of Leo's sermons, in fact, was to conclude his homilies, especially those delivered during the various fasting periods, with the petition "let us keep vigil together with blessed Peter that through the intercession of his merits we might obtain that which we ask of the Lord."[43] The injunction to keep vigil with Peter might be a reference to Peter's keeping vigil with Christ in the garden of Gethsemane (Mt 26.36–45)—but the fact that the biblical Peter fell asleep, and thus did not keep vigil, would seem to be a problematic referent, even for the exegetically creative Leo. The petition might also, of course, refer to the fact that the relics of St. Peter were housed in the very church (St. Peter's basilica) where Leo was offering some of these sermons.[44] The physical placement of Peter's relics within the church (or in Rome more generally, if Leo was preaching from a church other than the basilica of St. Peter) would have been a powerful symbol for all of Leo's Petrine maneuvering, and there is no reason to doubt Leo's belief that the relics could serve as a conduit of miraculous power.[45]

Of course Leo's confidence in the power of Christian saints to protect the city of Rome from all trouble was not always matched by his congregation, as attested by his attempts to distinguish the power of the saints from the ancient pagan cults.[46] As noted, *Sermon* 82 identifies Peter as the saint par excellence who can provide spiritual protection for the city—a kind of protection neither Romulus nor Remus could provide. We should not lose sight of the fact that Leo's promotion of Christian cults at the expense of pagan rites and festivals would have been an indirect challenge to the traditional models of aristocratic patronage and therefore something of a challenge to the elite households in Rome. While there is little doubt that Christianity was increasingly replacing the ancient cults (and with them some of the avenues for aristocratic patronage and authority), Leo's *Sermon* 84 attests to the fact that Christian suppression of traditional forms of religion, entertainment, and patronage was far from complete.

As evidence, we should recall that by Leo's tenure the city of Rome held an annual commemoration of its "deliverance" from Alaric's famous sack of the city in 410. *Sermon* 84 informs us that Christian leaders, before Leo, had attempted to attribute the city's deliverance to spiritual protection provided by Christian saints, especially the intercession of Roman martyrs. By 442, however, enthusiasm for commemorating the event as a Christian holiday seems to have waned, prompting Leo to ask, rhetorically, whether Rome had been saved by demons and circuses or by the prayers of the saints (clearly, a great number of Rome's inhabitants preferred more traditional civic celebrations).[47] Not surprisingly, he concludes the sermon with an invocation of St. Peter who, more than any other saint, looks over the city's inhabitants.

While it is true that Leo's sermons provide evidence for the most potent Petrine claims in Leo's corpus—it is there that the very concept of the "unworthy Petrine heir" develops—the sermons are hardly consistent in their reflection of the Petrine topos as a discursive horizon for the advancement of papal hegemony. Indeed, the vast majority of Leo's sermons make no reference to Peter at all. Many of the sermons that do reference Peter do so without any attempt to link the biblical Peter or the cult of Peter to Roman ecclesiastical authority in any explicit way. Perhaps the most instructive aspect of our analysis of the sermons with respect to the Petrine discourse is the extent to which it was primarily employed in the presence of other bishops and, notably, only at the beginning of Leo's tenure, when he was likely to have been the most uncertain of the respect others would show to him and his position. What this tells us, I believe, is that the Petrine discourse enabled Leo to develop a rhetorical connection between the apostle and himself that assisted in the promotion of Roman ecclesiastical authority vis-à-vis other episcopal leaders. It was not, in any substantial way, a dominant theme of Leo's preaching or pastoral ministry.

Intervention and Recognition in the Western Church

As we will see in this section and the next, Leo's correspondence repeatedly employs the arguments of tradition and canonical precedent to promote

Roman jurisdictional authority. Like other ecclesiastical leaders of his era, Leo believed that ecclesiastical law (both conciliar canons and papal decretals) functioned according to a system of precedent that mirrored Roman secular law.[48] Perhaps the most important precedent of papal jurisdictional authority was that of the Council of Serdica (343), which had granted a condemned cleric from any jurisdiction the right to appeal his case to the bishop of Rome.[49] By the mid-fifth century, the canons of Serdica and the canons of Nicaea had been combined in Roman texts, such that Leo and all of his successors believed that this superjurisdictional appellate authority had been authorized by the hallowed gathering at Nicaea (rather than by a disputed regional council several years later).[50] Rome's appellate jurisdiction, like its understanding of canonical precedent, similarly followed imperial protocols—if the Roman appellate court (i.e., the pope) determined that a cleric had been wrongly convicted, a "universally binding" retrial could restore the person to his prior state.[51] Not everyone, of course, acknowledged the Serdican privilege (especially the Eastern churches that did not include the Serdican canons within their Nicaean collections), and one of the most important features of Leo's correspondence was the extent to which he tried to make good on what he perceived to be traditional Roman privilege as established at Nicaea. What distinguishes Leo from his papal predecessors and what is of particular interest to the present study is the extent to which he employed the Petrine theme as a rhetorical feature of his promotion of the Serdican precedent and Rome's appellate jurisdiction.

For simplicity, I have separated my investigation of the Petrine discourse in Leo's correspondence into two sections, dealing with the Western and Eastern churches respectively. Such a division is not without problems. For example, while it is true that many Western correspondents conceded a level of respect for Roman ecclesiastical privilege that was less consistently shown by Eastern leaders, it is certainly not the case that all Western correspondents did so. But some distinctions can be made between Leo's Eastern and Western correspondence. Most notably, in the West, Leo seems to have been more willing to employ the Petrine topos as part of his strategy at the outset of conflict or negotiations with potentially hostile recipients. In contrast, Leo's Eastern correspondence is more cautious with respect to its use of Peter. In the East, he employed the Petrine topos only reactively, when he felt that his personal authority (or the honor of his see) had already been insulted. We will also see below that Eastern and Western leaders (both secular and episcopal) were willing to consent to Leo's Petrine pretensions (and employ the language themselves) whenever they had a particular diplomatic need and believed that acknowledging the Petrine topos would be beneficial to their own objectives.

Italy, Illyricum, and Sicily

We begin with a summary of Leo's correspondence with those regions in which the Church of Rome had the longest-running contact and influence, namely Italy and Illyricum. In time, the Roman Church would develop vast papal estates in these regions (as well as in Sicily) from which it would derive a great deal of income, and it would impose its particular practices (especially those related to clerical celibacy and liturgical custom) on regional churches.[52] As a general rule, Leo does not employ the Petrine topos in any of his letters to the bishops in these regions. This is, no doubt, in large part the consequence of the historical relationship between the See of Rome and these regions, which would have diminished the likelihood that any of these bishops would have openly objected to Roman authority. The letters to Illyricum, in fact, deal exclusively with the appointment of the metropolitan of Thessalonica as papal vicar, and his activity in the region.[53] Nearly all the letters to Italian bishops deal with various pastoral matters, the criteria for the selection of candidates for the priesthood, or the suppression of heresy, especially Manichaeanism.[54] To be sure, Leo's efforts to assert his policies in each of these matters constitute a promotion of Roman ecclesiastical authority, just as the apparent acceptance of Leo's policies by his correspondents suggests regional acknowledgment of that authority.

The promotion and reception of Roman ecclesiastical claims in Sicily are especially interesting because the Christian community at this time was an amalgam of indigenous, Greek, and Roman ecclesiastical traditions. Sicily was predominantly Greek in language and culture, and its agricultural resources and strategic location were critical to imperial operations in the Western provinces.[55] Leo, in fact, provides the oldest surviving claim of jurisdictional authority by a Roman bishop. This claim is manifest in his *Epistle* 16, which was written to all the bishops of Sicily in October 447 and is the oldest surviving letter Leo sent to the island.

At issue is the Sicilian practice (almost certainly derivative of an Eastern Christian custom) of baptizing catechumens on Epiphany (January 6) rather than Pentecost, which was the practice of the Roman Church at that time.[56]

Leo begins the letter with a general assertion of his Petrine privilege and responsibility by noting that Christ had commanded Peter to shepherd the Christian flock (cf. Jn. 21.15–17), and, therefore, it is "out of reverence for the see [of Peter], over which we preside," that Leo is bound to instruct the Sicilian bishops about the error in their practice.[57] Whereas Pope Gregory I would be surprisingly amenable to liturgical variation in regional churches, Leo was, by comparison, openly hostile to it. He informs the Sicilian episcopate that their deviation is an "error," one that could have been easily avoided if they had simply "used as the foundation of [their] practice that same source from which [their] consecrated office is derived and if the See of Peter, the blessed apostle, which is the mother of [their] clerical dignity, were also the teacher of [their] liturgical practices."[58]

Following this critique, Leo launches into a lengthy theological justification for the Roman custom of performing baptisms on Pentecost.[59] His argument is capped with a turn, once again, to the Petrine theme, wherein he argues that the Roman practice is derivative of the historical Peter, who, according to Acts 2.41, baptized three thousand Jews on the original day of Pentecost. At the conclusion of the letter, Leo instructs the bishops that they should gather together at least twice a year and that they must send at least three of their number to the annual commemoration in Rome of his own election (September 29). These final injunctions are issued, he tells his readers, to prevent any scandal or heresies from erupting in their churches, because episcopal deliberations must always take place "in common and in the presence of the most blessed Apostle Peter, so that all [the Church's] decisions and canonical decrees may be kept without violation by all of the Lord's bishops."[60]

This letter serves as a prime example of the ways the Petrine discourse made possible the assertion of papal authority. Seeking to expand Roman influence in the region but uncertain of the degree of episcopal submission that he will receive, Leo repeatedly leans on the Petrine topos as his primary rhetorical strategy for achieving his goals. Leo informs his readers of the biblical justification of Roman authority (viewed through Christ's instruction to Peter to "feed his sheep") as well as the Petrine basis for Roman liturgical practice. What is more, Leo insists that the Sicilian Church participate in the annual celebration of his own authority, which is couched in the language of submission to St. Peter. That Leo insists in this letter (seven years into his pontificate) that the Sicilian bishops participate in the annual Roman synod suggests that they had not done so until this point. It also suggests that Leo

remained uncertain as to whether or not his instructions concerning baptisms
would be heeded. Rhetorically, Leo engages this uncertainty by presenting
his instructions through a Petrine register; practically, Leo orders the Sicilian
bishops to gather annually in Rome so that he can have more direct oversight
of their willingness to follow his instructions.[61] Both of Leo's advances on the
Sicilian Church (i.e., the rhetorical and the practical) constitute a significant
expansion of papal influence on the island.

Gaul

Whereas the bishops of Rome had asserted at least some measure of authority
in suburbican Italy and Illyricum for centuries, papal influence in Gaul, if it
existed at all, had been more theoretical than real before the fifth century.
Irenaeus of Lyons (d. ca. 202) may have recognized a type of Roman primacy
through the presence of Sts. Peter and Paul in the imperial capital, but there
is no reliable evidence to suggest that a Roman bishop attempted to exert
ecclesiastical influence in Gaul prior to the 380s or that the bishops of Gaul
ever sought Roman counsel.[62] It was not until Innocent I (401–417) that a
Roman bishop actively peddled papal influence in Gaul or was sought as an
appellate adjudicator, based on the Serdican privilege.[63] Indeed, as Ralph
Mathisen explains in his exhaustive study of the fifth-century Gallic Church,
it was the See of Milan, not Rome, that exercised Italian influence in Gaul
during the fourth century.[64]

During the fifth century, the Gallic Church experienced its own up-
swing. The monastic complex at Lérins, infused with John Cassian's ascetic
theology, proved a dominant force, not only in Gaul, but throughout the
Western Church.[65] But this expansion in Gallic ecclesiastical prominence was
accompanied by rancorous infighting between rival ecclesiastical factions that
sought to expand their influence as diocesan boundaries were redrawn
according to the ever-changing secular provincial borders.[66] It was in this
context that Leo's "apostolic" judgment was sought and asserted.

The occasion for Leo's most serious intervention in Gallic matters was a
dispute between Hilary, bishop of Arles (himself a graduate of the monastery
at Lérins), and neighboring bishops who believed that Hilary had unjustly
asserted his authority beyond precedent and fairness. The details of the case
have been amply explored by Mathisen and others and need not detain us,
apart from a few points related to Leo's interest in the case.[67] First, Leo

became involved in the controversy when Chelidonius of Besançon, one of Hilary's "victims," traveled to Rome to plead his case to Leo. Second, to Leo's great surprise, Hilary also came to Rome when he learned that Leo would grant Chelidonius an appellate hearing—interestingly, Hilary returned home before the end of the trial. Third, Leo's account of the affair (which differs dramatically from the *Vita Hilarii*) is summarized in his *Epistle* 10, written the following summer and addressed to multiple bishops of the Vienne region. Finally, it is within this letter, that we find Leo's most aggressive assertion of the Petrine privilege in his Gallic correspondence.

In the opening paragraph of *Epistle* 10, Leo begins by striking a balance between investing his episcopal correspondents with sufficient apostolic capital and at the same time preserving apostolic primacy for himself. That balance, however, is quickly discarded as Leo insists that all authority in the Church flows from Peter and from those associated with Peter. "[The Lord] desires that his gifts flow into the entire body from Peter himself, as from the head to the body. And any individual who dares to separate from the unity of Peter will come to know that he no longer shares in the divine mystery."[68] In other words, solidarity with Peter (i.e., the bishop of Rome) is framed as the lone criterion by which someone participates in the mysteries of God. Leo supports this audacious claim with what had by this time become his programmatic rendition of Petrine authority based on Matthew 16.[69] When he gets to his account of Hilary's actions, several paragraphs later, Leo presents the renegade bishop as a man who seeks the submission of others while not, himself, accepting the authority of the "blessed Apostle Peter." The "arrogance" of Hilary's statements, likewise, is described as an affront to "the most blessed Peter." And precisely because the pastoral care of the faithful was entrusted to Peter above all others, Hilary flaunts Peter's authority and the entire structure of the Church by asserting his own authority in the region of Vienne.

One of the most significant (and ingenious) features of Leo's use of the Petrine topos is his grammatical maneuver to allow St. Peter (as a noun in the nominative case) to serve as a proxy for Leo's own interests—a grammatical substitution that I refer to as the production of a "Petrine subject." Through this maneuver, Leo is able to present his own theological opinions as Peter's. Likewise, those who respect Leo's authority are said to respect Peter, and anyone who acts against Roman interests or snubs Roman authority insults Peter. This dynamic is in play frequently in Leo's use of the Petrine topos but perhaps nowhere more clearly than in *Epistle* 10. Indeed, Leo's entire narrative is framed not as a direct judgment of Hilary's overstepping of his canonical authority, but rather as a contest between those who acknowledge Peter's authority and those who ignore the scriptural basis for it and, therefore, usurp for themselves Peter's authority. As we will see in subsequent chapters, the Petrine subject became an important feature of the Petrine discourse, especially in those situations where subsequent popes had little actual leverage and relied instead on the rhetorical force of Peter's legacy.

Another interesting element of *Epistle* 10 from the vantage point of the Petrine discourse is that Leo seems to acknowledge that Petrine privilege is disregarded by those who are not predisposed to accept it. Leo, in fact, hints that Hilary (and possibly others) has already ignored Leo's claims to Petrine primacy.[70] To compensate for this, Leo both escalates his rhetorical assertions (anyone who disagrees with Leo's verdict disagrees with Peter) and defends the very connection between Peter and the papacy (not only stressing its biblical foundations but also inventing a Petrine tradition within the Gallic Church). Leo's admission that Hilary has been unmoved by the Petrine appeal reminds us, once again, that most papal claims to authority (like the use of the Petrine discourse) in this period evince papal desires, not ecclesiastical realities.

A final point that we must consider in our evaluation of this important letter, which has been missed by other scholarly investigations, is that the Petrine appeal is employed for the benefit of Leo's episcopal readers, not Hilary (who has already dismissed Leo's authority by abandoning Rome before the conclusion of Chelidonius' appellate hearing). Indeed, given the fact that some of the bishops addressed in the letter should have been the ready recipients of a condemnation of Hilary's actions (i.e., some of the bishops of Vienne would have seen their authority most at risk in the expansion of Arles' jurisdiction; others addressed had themselves been appointed by Hilary), it is somewhat surprising that the letter would contain such an unprecedented force with respect to Leo's Petrine rhetoric. In part, we can attribute the appeal to the Petrine topos to the simple fact that this is the first time that Leo had written to the bishops of Gaul, and, as we have seen, it was typical of Leo to assert his Petrine credentials (albeit in a variety of degrees) in most first encounters with non-Roman Western bishops.[71] But even so, the forcefulness of the Petrine agenda is unprecedented for what we would otherwise expect to have been a partially receptive audience. So what, we might ask, is Leo's endgame?

While we can never know Leo's full intentions, and there may, in fact, have been several motivating factors, it would seem to be the case that one of Leo's goals in *Epistle* 10 is to demonstrate that Roman intervention in Gaul is not unprecedented. Indeed, before he even engages the specifics of Hilary's poor behavior, Leo mounts a multifaceted argument for his involvement in what is essentially a distant regional dispute.[72] Assessed from this vantage point, we see that there would have been far more at stake in Leo's intervention in the Hilary affair than the simple checking of a rogue bishop's ambition. In some sense, the Hilary affair served as a trial balloon for the very cause of Roman primacy—not in terms of Chelidonius' appellate hearing per se, but in the court of episcopal opinion in Gaul. While Leo could count on the metropolitan of Vienne to support his censure of Hilary, he could not necessarily count on all of the bishops of the region to respect future Roman interventions in Gaul. But the occasion of Chelidonius' appeal provided Leo with an ideal opportunity to attempt to break the cycle of Gallic bishops paying attention to Roman decrees only when those decrees suited their purposes. To achieve this, Leo made the strategic decision to stress the figure of Peter as the basis for his censure of Hilary (a censure that some of bishops of Vienne would have welcomed). But by employing Peter in this way, Leo's censure of Hilary was accompanied by an expansion of Roman super-jurisdictional authority in Gaul that few bishops of Vienne would have wanted. And, thus, it is likely with an eye to the future (and not to the past deeds of Hilary) that the early paragraphs of *Epistle* 10 so forcefully link Peter to the justification for papal interference in Gallic matters.

What is perhaps most striking about the remainder of Leo's Gallic correspondence (both epistles sent to and received by Leo) is the extent to which the Petrine topos faded from Leo's own letters while the provincial bishops began to acknowledge it themselves when writing to Leo. Indeed, whereas Leo's subsequent correspondence includes several pointed instructions (mostly directed against the See of Arles), they never again leverage Peter to do so.[73] Even Leo's several letters to Gaul that describe his efforts in the Christological controversy of the East are devoid of references to Peter.

The same was not true of letters written to Rome. Among the many things that Leo had done in his attempt to check Hilary's abuse of power was to suspend his "metropolitan rights."[74] As metropolitan, Hilary would have had regional administrative authority for all of the dioceses within his metropolitan domain (an ecclesiastical border that mirrored the Roman provincial boundaries). What had angered Leo (and others) was that Hilary had exerted his metropolitan privilege over a larger jurisdiction than his metropolis, most notably among the sees within the administrative supervision of Vienne.[75] There is no evidence to suggest that Hilary stopped asserting his metropolitan rights after Chelidonius' vindication, despite the papal censure.[76] And when the charismatic bishop died in 449, his successor, Ravennius, continued Hilary's practices.[77] Despite his actions, Ravennius seemed to covet a form of legitimacy that only Roman recognition could provide. So, shortly into his own tenure as bishop of Arles, Ravennius organized the bishops of southern Gaul to write a letter to Leo that asked the pontiff to restore metropolitan rights to the See of Arles.[78] The petition employed a series of rhetorical strategies, including flattery and an appeal to Petrine authority. For example, it acknowledges that "the blessed Church of Rome has leadership over all the churches of the world through Peter, prince of the apostles."[79] It also links the origins of the Gallic church to Peter's sending of St. Trophimus to Arles. But as Mathisen has compellingly argued, this rhetorical recognition of Petrine authority was anything but a submission to Roman primacy in Gaul. It was rather a rhetorically sophisticated attempt to persuade Leo to acknowledge Ravennius' own primacy over southern Gaul.[80] Leo, not to be outdone by his own rhetorical inventions, resisted and, instead, subtly accused Ravennius of following in Hilary's footsteps.[81] Although other letters to Rome from Gaul do not go as far as *Epistle 65* in terms of the Petrine discourse, many employ flattery and affirm Rome's super-jurisdiction as their primary rhetorical strategies.[82]

As in the time of Pope Innocent, the requests for Roman adjudication in Gaul during Leo's tenure do not evince a singular respect for Roman authority and impartiality so much as they indicate an attempt to call on an external power structure to assist in the suppression of a rival ecclesiastical network. What the Gallic bishops learned from Leo's *Epistle* 10 was that the pontiff presented himself as the heir of Peter and that they would need to acknowledge this in future petitions to the Roman See if they hoped to achieve success. As if mirroring the patterns in Leo's own use of the Petrine topos, it would appear that the more exaggerated the rhetorical submission to Petrine authority (cf. *Epistle* 65), the less likely it was that Leo would submit to the request. What is more, it is important to remember that the Gallic willingness to employ the Petrine topos does not in any way evince whether the Gallic bishops actually believed Leo to be Peter's heir. We can never know what they thought of Leo's relationship to the apostle. All we know is that the Petrine discourse afforded the Gallic bishops a discursive register by which they could rhetorically submit to papal ambition for the purpose of satisfying their own interests.

Leo's correspondence with the ecclesiastical leaders of the Western Church mirrors, in important ways, the strategic deployment of the Petrine topos in his sermons. In those situations where Leo was encountering other bishops for the first time, especially if his purpose was to be critical of them (as in *Epistles* 10 and 16), Petrine authority was on full display. But in those situations where Leo was more certain of the loyalty of his correspondent, there was little need for the rhetorical performance and self-aggrandizement that the Petrine discourse enabled. Leo's correspondence with the imperial and ecclesiastical leaders of the East followed this same pattern but only to a certain degree. Prior to the Synod of Ephesus in 449, Leo was more tentative in his use of Peter's authority and rarely employed it in his initial contacts with Eastern leaders. As we will see, the so-called Robber Synod of 449 forever altered Leo's Eastern strategy, and, as a consequence, the rhetorical posturing of Eastern and Western Christian leaders has never been the same.

Leo, Peter, and Chalcedon

Leo, of course, is best known for his involvement in the Christological controversies, which dominated the theological debates of the Eastern Church during the fifth century. Other scholars have discussed at length both the content of those controversies and Leo's contributions to them.[83] We will continue to focus on the ways in which the Petrine discourse enabled Leo's rhetorical choices (and the extent to which Leo's rhetorical choices stretched the Petrine discourse in new ways) to achieve his theological and diplomatic goals throughout the controversies. And to understand more fully when and why Leo employed St. Peter as he did, we will begin with a brief summary of Roman involvement in the Christological controversy in the middle of the fifth century.

Eutyches, Leo's Tome, *and the Council of Chalcedon*

In 431, the archbishop of Constantinople, Nestorius, was condemned at the Council of Ephesus for having failed to properly explain the union of the human and divine natures in the person of Jesus Christ, particularly as it related to the divine presence within the womb of the Virgin Mary. Among Nestorius' most vehement critics was the Constantinopolitan priest-monk Eutyches. Eutyches was himself condemned by a Constantinopolitan synod in 448, in part because he audaciously claimed to find closet Nestorians behind every Constantinopolitan door. Following his condemnation, Eutyches appealed his case widely, even through an embassy to Rome, hoping to garner support anywhere he might find it.[84] Based upon his own belief that Rome possessed universal appellate jurisdiction, Leo initially agreed to consider the appeal and wrote to Flavian (the archbishop of Constantinople) in December 448, asking for a full account of Eutyches' condemnation.[85] When Leo was informed of Eutyches' teaching, the pontiff was aghast. Upon learning that the emperor, Theodosius, intended to convene an international synod in the East for the purpose of resolving the matter, Leo sent a flurry of letters to Eastern correspondents, including *Epistle* 28 to Flavian (commonly known as Leo's *Tome*), which provided an elaborate and sophisticated articulation of Leo's dual-nature Christology.[86] Given his theological investment in the impending council and his penchant for spreading Roman influence anywhere he could, Leo worked to guarantee that Roman interests would be represented at the synod, and widely announced his decision to send representatives.[87]

From Leo's perspective, the Synod of Ephesus in 449 was a complete disaster: Eutyches was restored to his prior position; the archbishop of Constantinople, Flavian, was condemned; the Roman representatives were barred from participating; and Leo's *Tome* was completely ignored. Not only had the council authenticated a Christological position that was fundamentally different from his own view, but Roman ecclesiastical authority had also been humiliated on an international scale. Leo's response was swift and multifaceted, employing every facet of the Petrine discourse he could muster to denounce the synod and nullify its authority.[88] To many of his correspondents, Leo proposed a new, universal council to be held in Italy. He lobbied the Western emperor, Valentinian, along with his mother and wife, to send their own requests to Theodosius for a new council to be held in the West and directed by Leo.[89]

In the meantime, both Flavian and Theodosius died. Flavian was succeeded by Anatolius, a protégé of Dioscorus, archbishop of Alexandria and an ally of Eutyches. In the end, Anatolius adopted Leo's Christological position, especially once it became clear that the new emperor, Marcian, also supported it. Marcian and Anatolius prepared for yet another council, with the emperor personally requesting Leo's participation.[90] Leo, having learned something of a lesson from the synod of 449, did two significant things following Marcian's invitation. First, he established the office of *apocrisiarius* in Constantinople—a permanent ambassador between the pope and the emperor.[91] Second, once he learned that the emperor supported the pope's theology but would not support a council in the West, Leo did everything he could to suppress or, at the very least, delay a new council.[92] As far as Leo was concerned, a new Eastern council posed greater risk than reward.

But, once again, Leo was not to get his way. The Council of Chalcedon, perhaps the most significant gathering of Christian leaders in history, met in the fall 451, despite Leo's efforts to postpone it. Theologically, the council was an enormous victory for Leo—his *Tome* was identified as one of the foundational articulations of Christological orthodoxy. But in terms of Roman ecclesiastical prestige, Leo and Rome were humiliated once again. At issue was Canon 28, which conferred on the See of Constantinople "equal dignity" with the See of Rome, "because it [was] New Rome."[93] Leo's initial response to the council was one of great ambivalence: he welcomed the condemnation of Eutyches and the exoneration of Flavian, but he would not, in any way, surrender his apostolic primacy to the See of Constantinople, whose claim to authority rested on imperial rather than apostolic credentials. And so Leo hesitated before confirming the verdict of Chalcedon.

As word circulated that the pontiff was withholding his support, those who objected to Chalcedon on theological grounds (Christians who would become known, derisively, as Monophysites) began to leverage Leo's hesitation to their advantage.[94] Utterly perplexed by the papal delay, Marcian and Valentian issued a joint request to Leo in late 452/early 453 warning him that if he did not publicly endorse the council all would be lost.[95] Leo relented and offered his begrudging support. In March 453, Leo wrote to the bishops who had convened at Chalcedon, ratifying their theological deliberations and insisting that nothing ever contravene Nicaea—he made no explicit comment about Canon 28.[96] In his private correspondence to Eastern leaders, however, Leo continued his assault on the canon.[97] The last surviving letter in which Leo complained about Canon 28 was dated to 454, but it was probably not until the rise of a new emperor in 455 that Leo made the strategic decision to drop the issue of Canon 28 from his imperial correspondence.[98]

Leo's Peter in the Midst of the Controversy

Within Leo's Eastern correspondence, the Petrine topos appears strongly (albeit in different forms and for a variety of rhetorical purposes) in eight letters related to the Christological controversy (*Epistles* 33, 44, 93, 105, 106, 119, 129, and 156). The first example is the letter that Leo sent to the bishops assembled for the council of 449. The letter opens with an audacious example of the pontiff's use of the "Petrine subject" to assert Roman primacy in all theological matters. He begins, in fact, by suggesting that the emperor himself has summoned the assistance of Rome and of Peter: "Our most clement emperor . . . has invoked the authority of the Apostolic See in order to effect a holy settlement. In this, he has shown reverence for divine institutions, desiring, as it were, that the most blessed Apostle Peter proclaim those words in his profession of faith which were praised [by Christ]."[99] Leo then quickly presents the Eutyches question not as a matter of Christological orthodoxy but as a question of submission to or rejection of Saint Peter. And while Petrine orthodoxy vis-à-vis Matthew 16 is implicit in Leo's framing of the options that he presented to the council, the pontiff explicitly attempts to turn the Christological question at hand into an acceptance or rejection of Petrine (i.e., his) authority.

Perhaps it should not surprise us that the assembled bishops rebuked Leo's interference as they did. While we can never know if Leo's self-promotion was a contributing factor to the assembly's disregard for Leo's *Tome*, and while Leo, in hindsight, must have understood the council to have been a complete failure, *Epistle* 33 marks an important escalation in the history of papal self-aggrandizement because it transformed the central theological debate into a question of submission to papal authority. For our purposes, what is so noteworthy about *Epistle* 33 is that the rhetorical strategy Leo employs to achieve this relied, almost exclusively, on the discursive possibilities available through the Petrine discourse. And, as we will see, the defeat at Ephesus only hardened Leo's Petrine resolve.

Shortly after Leo learned of the verdict at Ephesus, he sent a carefully constructed response to the emperor. Leo begins by hiding his defense of Petrine authority behind a mask of imperial flattery: "in your love for the Catholic faith, your Clemency sent a letter to the See of the blessed Apostle Peter." He goes on to transfer all blame for the outcome of the council to Dioscorus, archbishop of Alexandria, before pleading with the emperor to annul the synod's verdicts. Here too, Leo leans on the Petrine theme, beseeching the emperor to keep before his eyes "the glory of the blessed Peter . . . and [his] profession of the true divinity and true humanity of Christ."[100] In doing so, Leo repeats what was a familiar theme in his correspondence during the controversy, namely that Peter's confession of faith, guarded exclusively by the See of Rome (i.e., Peter's see), is the measuring stick of orthodoxy.

The Petrine topos also features prominently in Leo's letters to the East just before and just after the meeting at Chalcedon. Writing to the assembled bishops, the pontiff claims that the emperor has sought Leo's participation because he desires that the "rights and dignity of St. Peter be preserved."[101] Perhaps the strongest assertions of Roman (and Petrine) authority, appears, however, in a letter to the empress Pulcheria, shortly after Leo learned of Chalcedon's authorization of Canon 28. In many ways, the letter resembles one that he had sent to the emperor in the same dispatch of letters. But the letter to Pulcheria includes a more strongly worded rejection of Canon 28:

> But the bishops' consent [to Canon 28], which is contrary to the holy canons of Nicaea and not in conjunction with your faithful grace, we do not accept, and by the blessed Apostle Peter's authority we absolutely reject this [canon] in comprehensive terms. We do this in every ecclesiastical context obeying those laws that the Holy Spirit set forth by the 318 bishops [i.e., of Nicaea] for the peaceful observance of all priests in such a manner that even if a much greater number [of bishops] were to pass a different decree to [that of Nicaea], whatever was opposed to its constitution would have to be held in no respect.[102]

On this occasion, Leo invokes the Petrine cause, not so much to advance a particular point of view but simply to defend what he perceives to be an assault on his personal authority.

Indeed, Canon 28 prompted Leo to think in new ways about his own authority and about the potential for Petrine language to safeguard it. Writing to Anatolius, archbishop of Constantinople, Leo warns that Canon 28 is a rejection of Nicaea and an assertion of arrogance.[103] What it is more, it is an affront to the authority and antiquity of the Sees of Alexandria and Antioch, which, unlike Constantinople, have a direct link to Peter, the prince of the apostles. Leo chides Anatolius: "let the See of Alexandria not lose the dignity it earned through St. Mark the Evangelist, the student of blessed

Peter."[104] When Leo wrote to Maximus of Antioch the following year, he attempted to convince the archbishop that Canon 28 had undermined his own episcopal and Petrine dignity.[105]

A final, brief appearance of a Petrine appeal in Leo's Eastern correspondence survives in a letter to the new emperor, Leo, dated to December 457. By this time, Pope Leo had determined to abandon his campaign against Canon 28, resigned that East and West would simply agree to ignore their disagreement. But that resignation did not mean that the pontiff in any way abandoned the Petrine topos in his negotiations with the East. *Epistle* 156, in fact, required a delicate diplomatic presentation: on the one hand, Leo had to explain why the Council of Chalcedon had been necessary in the wake of disagreement over the Council of Ephesus in 449; on the other hand, he had to explain why a new council was not necessary in the wake of disagreement over the Council of Chalcedon. The pope's solution to this diplomatic conundrum was to argue that the Council of Chalcedon represents the faith of St. Peter in a way that the Council of Ephesus had not. To do so, Leo employs Peter's confession of faith in Matthew 16 as the proof-text of Petrine and Chalcedonian orthodoxy.

The Absence of Peter

What is perhaps most surprising about Leo's diplomatic efforts during the Christological controversy is that he does not employ any semblance of the Petrine discourse in those situations in which we might otherwise have expected him to do so. A careful observation of the contextual features of the various stages of the controversy reveals certain patterns in Leo's diplomatic strategy in this regard. For example, whenever Leo had a neutral or positive relationship with his correspondent and appeared to be at least partially (though not fully) successful in his efforts, the pontiff avoided using the figure of Peter. As noted, Leo tried repeatedly to either postpone or delay the synod that ultimately met at Chalcedon. Although he was not able to achieve that particular goal, he was reasonably assured of the court's commitment to his dual-nature theology, and he had been able to appoint several representatives to the coming council. Thus, Leo's *Epistles* 79 and 83 each attempt to obtain further concessions from Marcian and Pulcheria, but these letters reflect a calculated decision to pursue a gentler, less aggressive form of diplomacy that was devoid of the self-aggrandizement that characterized Leo's use of the Petrine topos.[106]

Whenever Leo wrote to an important Eastern official for the first time he was equally circumspect in his use of the Petrine appeal. So, for example, the pontiff's first letter to Anatolius, Flavian's successor as archbishop of Constantinople, refrains from employing the Petrine topos in a period that might be understood as the height of the crisis (the period between the Council of Ephesus in 449 and the Council of Chalcedon in 451). What is particularly significant about this letter is that Leo deliberately inserts himself in matters that would otherwise have been the exclusive domain of the archbishop of Constantinople (for example, how to deal with local bishops who had participated in the council of 449 but now wish to recant). But Leo inserts himself carefully, without any explicit mention of personal jurisdiction or privilege. This is a decidedly different posture than he had struck with his initial correspondence to the bishops of Sicily and Gaul. Two months later, Leo sent another letter to Anatolius, pushing papal authority a little more aggressively (he instructs the archbishop that all difficult cases should be referred to Rome), but here too there is no explicit recourse to his personal Petrine authority.[107]

Perhaps the most unexpected absence of an appeal to the Petrine discourse is in *Epistle* 114, the letter in which Leo formally affirms Chalcedon's condemnation of Eutyches and restoration of Flavian but does so in the context of his continued dismay over Canon 28. The letter, which had likely been prompted by Marcian and Valentinian's joint order to Leo, both affirms the theology of Chalcedon and rejects, vaguely, anything "contrary to the canons of Nicaea." By this oblique reference, Leo means to condemn Canon 28. But his censure of the council is muted by imperial expectations, and it is probably for this reason that Leo's bark lacks any Petrine bite.[108]

Taken as a whole, Leo's Eastern correspondence during the Christological controversy reveals both similarities to and differences from his activities in the West. To be sure, the Petrine discourse appears in its most aggressive form on those occasions when Leo believes that Roman authority is in the greatest jeopardy—this is seen most clearly in the wake of the snubbing of Roman authority at Ephesus in 449 and in the aftermath of Chalcedon's Canon 28. With one important exception and quite unlike his Western strategy, Leo did not avail himself of the Petrine topos when he began diplomatic efforts with his Eastern counterparts, nor did he employ it in situations in which he perceived negotiations to be difficult but possible. The one exception, of course, was the opening letter Leo sent to the delegates meeting at Ephesus in 449, in which he attempted to reframe the Christological debate as a matter of submission to Roman authority. The reception of that letter and the council that followed proved to be a total humiliation from the Roman perspective. But Leo seems to have learned a lesson from the experience, and it is worth noting that in the years that followed, the pontiff pursued lines of argument rooted in the Petrine discourse only in situations when he was the most vulnerable, the most unable to effect Eastern outcomes.

Recognition and/or Rejection of Leo and Peter

One final element of Leo's involvement in the Christological controversy that deserves some attention is the extent to which Eastern authorities either endorsed or rejected Roman claims of authority during Leo's tenure. Perhaps not surprisingly, the Eastern response to the papacy was mixed, almost always tied to individual circumstance and the fragmentation of ecclesiastical alliances. But what is particularly interesting is the ways some Eastern leaders spoke within the discursive matrix of the Petrine discourse as they sought to affect their own diplomatic goals.

POSITIVE ENDORSEMENTS

We begin our survey with those figures who, for a variety of reasons, evince the greatest respect for Roman ecclesiastical authority. Perhaps the most obvious reason that an Eastern cleric in this period would acknowledge Roman authority was if he had been condemned by an Eastern ecclesiastical court and sought Rome's appellate authority. While there is little tangible evidence that Eastern clerics appealed to Rome because of the so-called Serdican privilege, they did routinely seek support from Western bishops, especially the bishop of Rome, whenever they ran out of options in the East—the most famous case, of course, being that of John Chrysostom, who wrote to the bishops of Rome, Milan, and Aquileia seeking assistance at the time of his exile.[109] Thus, it should not surprise us that when Eutyches was first condemned in Constantinople in 448, he asked that Leo organize an appellate hearing for his case.[110] Perhaps even more intriguing, however, is the report that Eutyches had claimed at the time of his original trial in Constantinople that he had in his possession a written endorsement of his theological positions from Pope Leo.[111] There is absolutely no evidence that Eutyches ever possessed such a confirmation (although the two had exchanged letters), but the report serves as an important indication that the opinion of the Roman bishop was thought to carry some authority in Constantinopolitan proceedings, even if it was not enough to prevent Eutyches' excommunication.[112]

Theodoret of Cyrus, who had been condemned in absentia at Ephesus in 449, also sought recourse by appealing to Rome.[113] Unlike Eutyches, however, Theodoret fills his written appeal to Leo with rhetorical affirmations of Roman authority and, notably, the connection between Peter and Rome.[114] Drawing parallels to Paul's deference for Peter's instruction, Theodoret affirms Leo's primacy among the bishops of the world, stressing both the spiritual beauty and the imperial authority of the city of Rome.[115] The crowning reason for papal primacy, according to Theodoret, is that the see possesses the relics of Sts. Peter and Paul. The Syrian bishop adds, for good measure, that the glory of the two saints continues to enlighten the world through Leo himself. Theodoret's goal, of course, is to obtain vindication for his condemnation through an appellate hearing at Rome. His appeal contains multiple forms of flattery, a defense of his innocence, a condemnation of Dioscorus, and a willingness to travel to Rome. It is probably the most comprehensive affirmation of Roman prestige within Leo's Eastern correspondence.

In addition to the opportunity provided by an appellate hearing, Leo's Eastern correspondents occasionally endorsed Roman ecclesiastical privilege (and even Petrine authority) when they needed something specific from the pontiff in return or when they determined that it was in their best interest to maintain a positive relationship with the Roman Church. The two letters that most clearly reflect this latter scenario were sent by the imperial family. *Epistle* 73, issued jointly by Valentian III and Marcian, affirms Leo's *principatem* within the episcopate, and *Epistle* 77, written by Pulcheria, upholds Leo's *Tome* as the measuring stick of Christological orthodoxy.[116] Although neither letter takes the extra step of incorporating the Petrine topos, it is clear that their authors were, at that particular moment, keen to maintain a positive relationship with Leo, and that they were perfectly willing to endorse the rhetorical features of Leo's authority to do so.

The final scenario in which a correspondent in this period employed the key features of the papal discourse was if he or she determined that it was beneficial for a third-party relationship to appear to be in league with the bishop of Rome. Perhaps the best example of this type of situation is reflected in the series of letters (*Epistles* 55–58) written by members of the Western imperial family to their counterparts in the East in the months after the Council of Ephesus in 449. In December of that year, Valentinian, his wife,

Eudoxia, and his mother, Galla Placidia, all sent requests to Theodosius
beseeching him, to varying degrees, to annul the Council of 449 and sponsor
a new council in the West under the leadership of Leo. Not only do these
letters imply dissatisfaction with Theodosius' handling of the ecclesiastical
situation, but they also reveal key features of the Petrine discourse in their
narratives. For example, Valentinian describes the Council of 449 as an
"affront to St. Peter."[117] For her part, Galla Placidia, maintains that Flavian
should be granted the ability to appeal his condemnation to Rome, based on
Rome's Serdican privilege (which she, too, presents as a Nicaean privilege).
Perhaps more significantly, Galla Placidia combines that request with an
affirmation of Leo's primacy based on Peter's reception of the "keys of
heaven."[118] While it is beyond the scope of the present study to investigate
the complex and shifting relationship between Western and Eastern imperial
families, it is noteworthy that Leo was able to lobby Western leaders to his
cause and that he was able to do so to such an extent that they incorporated
the features of the Petrine topos in their diplomatic efforts. One almost wonders if he or his agents wrote the letters on their behalf.

REJECTIONS OF ROME

In addition to the various scenarios in which Eastern correspondents
endorsed the claims of Roman authority and Petrine privilege, we should, of
course, recall that there were several episodes during the span of the controversy in which some of very same ecclesiastical and secular rulers disregarded
or denied the Roman claims. No doubt the greatest affront to Roman pretension was the decision by Dioscorus and the other leaders of the council in
449 to refuse all Roman participation in the synod (many of the bishops who
participated in 449 were the same bishops who attended Chalcedon two years
later). We might also interpret Theodosius' indifference to Leo in the wake
of the council in 449 (he simply did not respond to Leo's Petrine-laden
critique of the council) as an indirect rejection of Roman primacy.[119] In fact,
when the Eastern emperor responded to the Western court's lobbying on
Leo's behalf (and did so by incorporating Petrine language), Theodosius simply claimed that the synod of 449 and Flavian's condemnation had been
just.[120]

We might also view Marcian's determination to hold a new council and
to hold it in the East as an implied rejection of Roman authority. As noted,
Leo initially attempted to convince the secular leaders of the East that a new
council should be held in Italy.[121] When Marcian expressed support for Leo's

dual-nature Christology, the pontiff attempted to postpone or delay a new Eastern council. Despite Leo's repeated efforts, Marcian was determined to hold a new council, and the very fact that he did so in the East can be seen as both an assertion of imperial authority and a dismissal of Leo's sense of his Serdican privilege (i.e., to hold an appellate hearing for Flavian in Rome).

ASSESSING ROMAN PRIVILEGE AT CHALCEDON

Thus far, our evaluation has surveyed those letters that demonstrate, at least on the surface, unqualified support for or resistance to claims of Roman and Petrine primacy. Of course, not all surviving sources are so clear. Perhaps the most intriguing sources, in fact, are those that offer ambivalent or ambiguous support for Roman claims. And there is probably no letter more ambiguous than that sent by the Chalcedonian assembly to Leo at the conclusion of the synod.[122]

The purpose of the letter was multifold: it applauded Leo's defense of Christological orthodoxy, it announced the condemnation of Eutyches and Dioscorus, and it attempted to persuade Leo of the legitimacy of Canon 28.[123] Following the rhetorical conventions of the era, the letter opens by flattering Leo, and does so with an explicit appropriation of the Petrine topos. Referring to Leo's Christological orthodoxy, the letter affirms: "you have steadfastly preserved this, being set before all as the mouthpiece of Peter and imparting the blessedness of his faith unto all."[124] Continuing, the letter rejoices in the theological glory of Leo's *Tome* and asserts that even though he was not present at the council, he led (*praesum*) it, "as the head does the body" through his representatives.[125]

The simultaneous affirmation and undermining of Roman authority that occur in the context of Canon 28, however, shows the epistle to be far more surreptitious than the opening sequence would otherwise suggest. The bishops introduce the subject of Canon 28 by noting rather blandly that they have ratified the canon of Constantinople 381, "which ordains that after your most holy and apostolic see, the See of Constantinople shall take second place."[126] In the hope of disarming Leo, the bishops continue by noting their confidence that the pontiff will, "out of his care for others, extend his apostolic prestige" to the Church of Constantinople because they know—wink, wink—how much he wants to share his good work with others.[127] Hoping further to mitigate Leo's reaction, the bishops even claim that the papal representatives objected to this canon, not because Constantinople should be denied this right, but only because the idea itself had not originated with

Leo. It is with this in mind, the bishops now claim, that they are writing to Leo so that he might "initiate" the proposal of Canon 28, even though both the emperor and the Senate have already ratified it.

In short, the entire passage is something of a rhetorical farce. The bishops of Chalcedon know that Leo is going to object to the canon. But in their presentation of the canon to him, they attempt to deflect his objections by appropriating for their own purposes the language of papal and Petrine authority. Thus, it would appear that the use of this language does not so much reflect an Eastern submission to Roman primacy as it suggests a resistance to that primacy through a co-opting of the very rhetoric designed to promote it.[128]

Contained within the acts of the Council of Chalcedon is a related affirmation of Petrine authority that has long been the source of Roman apologetic claims. When Leo's *Tome* was read during the second session of the synod (October 10, 451), the bishops of the council are reported to have proclaimed in unison: "Peter has spoken through Leo."[129] And while there is little doubt that the *Acta*, particularly during the second session, provide a consistent respect for both Leo and his *Tome*, there is likely more to this affirmation than a blind endorsement of Roman ecclesiastical authority.

Indeed, even though that acclamation represents an appropriation of Roman self-aggrandizement, we should not lose sight of the fact that the decision by non-Roman clerics to include this phrase in the *Acta* served other purposes, quite different than the promotion of Roman authority. First and foremost it was an attempt to lend apostolic credibility, through the figure of St. Peter, to the text that the council had selected to be the quintessential statement of Christological orthodoxy. This passage in the *Acta* reflects a unique possibility contained within the Petrine discourse that had little to do with the promotion of Rome and much to do with a specific articulation of orthodoxy that was perceived to be consistent with scripture, the Cappadocians, and especially Cyril of Alexandria.[130] In other words, although subsequent papal pundits would repeatedly employ Chalcedon's Petrine language as proof of Roman authority, the original function of the claim was very different in that it hoped to lend apostolic credibility to the council's Christological authority.

The Legacy of Leo's Peter(s)

There is little denying the significance of Leo's expansion of the claims of Roman ecclesiastical authority or the extent to which he both stretched the

Petrine discourse to achieve that expansion and relied on the discourse to defend his authority when it was brought into question by a rival power structure. Early in his career, Leo typically initiated diplomatic efforts with Western ecclesiastical officials by asserting his authority through the Petrine topos. I have argued that this was part of a deliberate strategy to assert his authority over nearby bishops and to expand it into neighboring regions where Rome historically had little direct influence—namely in Sicily and in Gaul. I have suggested that Leo's initial development of the Petrine topos (and its justification by Mt 16) between 441 and 443 may have been born of anxiety over the extent to which other episcopal leaders would accept his authority. While our sources are not as complete as we might like, we can be reasonably assured that bishops of Italy and Illyricum submitted to Leo's Peter sufficiently to escape the controversy of public censure. Leo's attempts to assert Roman authority in Sicily and Gaul (both of which drew on and expanded the Petrine discourse) met with mixed results, but he was successful enough that even the bishops of Gaul began to employ the Petrine topos themselves whenever they sought something from Rome in return.

It was Leo's experience with the Eastern Church, however, that would have the greatest influence on the way that subsequent popes styled their Petrine claims. Whereas Leo often incorporated the figure of Peter in his initial negotiations with Western bishops, the pontiff was generally far more self-conscious of appearing to be too self-aggrandizing when he opened negotiations with Eastern leaders. The one exception to this trend, of course, was when the pontiff sent a letter to the bishops meeting at Ephesus in 449 and attempted to recast the entire Christological debate as a matter of submission to Petrine (i.e., Roman) authority. In the years that followed, the Petrine topos appeared in Leo's Eastern correspondence only in those instances when his authority was most in question, when Rome was suffering its greatest international humiliations (namely in the repudiation of 449 and in Chalcedon's Canon 28). Leo never again employed the discourse when he was confident (or reasonably assured) that he was going to get his way. Indeed, understanding the Petrine topos to be a marker of papal insecurity rather than ecclesiastical strength is one of the hermeneutical lenses through which we will view the material in the following chapters.

It is, in fact, a testimony to Leo's great achievement on the international scene, through his *Tome* and his careful negotiations in the age of Chalcedon, that those bishops of Rome who came after him would view any slight of the *Tome* or of the Chalcedonian settlement as a direct insult to Roman prestige, to Leo, and, ultimately, to Peter himself. It is in this context, of course, that the Acacian schism (484–519) was so detrimental to papal aspirations of international significance.

By 482, the imperial court had grown weary of defending Chalcedon's dual-nature Christology against the unrelenting opposition of Christians in Egypt, Syria, and Palestine, who claimed that it was a subtle but significant rejection of Cyril's Christology and the original Council of Ephesus in 431. The emperor Zeno, together with the patriarch of Constantinople,[131] Acacius, signed a compromise (known as the *Henotikon*) with the de facto leader of the Egyptian Church, Peter Mongus, which attempted to bypass the explicit dual-nature Christology of Chalcedon and emphasize, instead, the orthodoxy of the first three ecumenical councils and the condemnations of Nestorius and Eutyches.[132] Although Roman legates were initially supportive of the *Henotikon*, Pope Felix III condemned the document in 484, along with Peter Mongus and Acacius of Constantinople, thus initiating the so-called Acacian schism.

As we conclude this chapter on Leo, the Christological particulars of the *Henotikon* and of the Acacian schism are less significant than the extent to which Felix and his successors viewed the controversy from the vantage point of Roman authority. Insofar as Leo's *Tome* was bypassed as the definition of orthodoxy, so too were Rome and the papacy being bypassed. The fact that the emperor, the patriarch of Constantinople, and the leader of the Monophysite party had reached this accord without papal consultation only fueled the growing sense in Rome of marginalization, isolation, and international irrelevance in the age of an empire now clearly centered in the East. The defense of Leo's honor and of Roman significance would be the primary international concern of Felix's pontificate. But it would be his archdeacon, the future pope Gelasius I, who would pack the greatest Petrine punch into that defense.

CHAPTER 3

Gelasius' Domestic Problems and International Posture

Pope Gelasius I, who sat in Peter's chair from 492 to 496, is familiar to all students of papal history because he simultaneously offered the most assertive of late ancient papal claims to ecclesiastical authority and was the first pope to propose a specific model for church/state interaction. For the ninth-century advocates of papal authority, Gelasius was of fundamental importance because his corpus offered several ancient precedents for papal sovereignty. Indeed, for the Carolingian editors of papal documents, Gelasius was significant because he had successfully instructed an emperor that secular authority was subordinate to priestly authority and that the source of priestly authority was the See of St. Peter. But as we noted in the Introduction, the ninth-century presentation of the late ancient papacy was based largely on the polemical interests of the day and therefore offered a particularly partisan account of papal history. A more thorough investigation of Gelasius' career reveals the extent to which his proclamations of authority represent a yearning for, rather than a recognition of, strength.

Gelasius' tenure, of course, came in the midst of the Acacian schism, a matter that simultaneously framed his diplomatic posture toward the East and provided him a platform of international significance at home. Gelasius' surviving corpus is substantial (approximately forty authentic letters, dozens of additional fragmentary letters, and several theological tractates), but despite the size of his corpus, his writings are shockingly understudied.[1] Between 1975 and 2010, for example, there were only two English-language peer-reviewed articles devoted to him. What is more, before the publication of this book, only a few paragraphs of his Latin had ever been printed in

English.[2] It would seem that there is a startling disconnect between Gelasius' importance for the development of the papal concept and the willingness of scholars to critique or just explore that supposed importance. This chapter, therefore, raises the possibility that Gelasius' assertions of papal authority, most famously prescribed in his *Epistle* 12 (also known as the *Ad Anastasium*) do not document ecclesiological or political realities as they were, but instead encapsulate a discourse of papal ambition born of frustration on the part of a bishop who, at the moment of writing, enjoyed little tangible authority either at home or abroad.

Following the adage that all politics are local (in this case, even ecclesiastical politics), this chapter begins with an assessment of Gelasius' ecclesiastical authority by scrutinizing his standing in Rome itself. As we will see, Gelasius neither enjoyed the respect of the Senate nor had the full support of the Roman clergy. His attempts to exert his authority throughout the Italian Peninsula were equally frustrated by communities and personalities who appear to have been unmoved by his repeated efforts. By viewing Gelasius' international claims and Petrine pretensions through the prism of local conflict, we obtain a very different picture of his pontificate and are led to rather different conclusions from those of previous scholars about the purpose and meaning of his Petrine claims. Indeed, it would seem that Gelasius asserted himself abroad not only because he thought that the heir of Peter deserved the submission of international bishops, but because he hoped that these assertions of prestige might help to alleviate an otherwise troubling situation at home.

The Reception of Gelasius' Authority in Rome

It is difficult to reconstruct what the citizens of Rome thought of their bishop. No direct accounts survive. Gelasius would have been well known in Rome prior to his election, having served as a deacon (likely the archdeacon) and close associate of his predecessor, Felix III, on whose behalf he may have authored several diplomatic letters.[3] We know nothing of the election itself; even the *Liber Pontificalis* is silent about it.[4] It is possible that Gelasius owed his promotion entirely to his close association with Felix.[5] Indeed, that might be the best way that we can explain the election of a man who had his share of political liabilities. Among them, of course, was the fact that Gelasius was not a Roman—he was from North Africa.[6] Nor was he a member of the aristocracy (either Roman or provincial)—he was, in fact, one of only a handful of popes in the period not to have been a member of the nobility.[7] This has led at least one scholar to propose that Gelasius' trouble with the city's aristocracy stemmed from his "outsider" status.[8] But, as we will also see, Gelasius' policies were not universally embraced by the local clergy either.

Trouble with the Roman Senate

As discussed in the previous chapter, the Roman nobility continued to enjoy hegemony in the city's political, cultural, and religious life long after the ascendancy of Christianity and the empire's recentering in Constantinople. The integration of the local aristocracy into the clerical ranks was part of the process by which a more powerful papacy would ultimately dominate those facets of Roman life, but this process was far from complete at the end of the fifth century. Indeed, despite the contemporary exaggerations of papal biographers and the bluster of papal rhetoric, members of the Roman Senate and other secular elites continued to dictate much of the cultural and religious life of Rome for centuries to come. Perhaps one of the best examples of the secular influence in this period is the continuation of the popular Lupercalia festival, which on at least one occasion set members of the local aristocracy in direct opposition to Gelasius.

Like most ancient Roman religious festivals, the origins and purpose of the Lupercalia remain somewhat uncertain, even though the festival is attested by a number of ancient authors (including Plutarch, Cicero, Quintilian, and Augustine) and seems to have continued, in a modified form, into the sixth century. In the time of Julius Caesar, the celebration included a ritual sacrifice performed by a brotherhood of priests, the initiation of new priests, a semi-nude race performed by members of the male aristocracy, and a good deal of drunken spectacle.[9] The current scholarly assessment of the festival, in fact, is that it was a ritual of the carnival type.[10] The suppression of pagan cults in Rome by the emperor Gratian in 382 C.E. and the subsequent disintegration of the pagan priesthood may have forced a retooling of the festival, but the rite certainly continued and, contrary to some assessments, did so without morphing into a Christian ceremony.[11] It is Gelasius, in fact, who provides the most comprehensive extant evidence that the festival remained popular among the inhabitants of Rome and funded by the local elite.

What we know of the altercation between Gelasius and the patrons of the festival derives entirely from a single Gelasian text, which Thiel lists as *Tractate* 6, but the *Collectio Avellana* transmits as an epistle entitled *Against Andromachus and the Other Romans Who Hold That the Lupercalia Should Be Celebrated According to the Ancient Custom.*[12] The difference in editorial designation is not surprising given the rather unusual and genre-defying characteristics of the text. The treatise sharply rebukes and threatens the excommunication of an unnamed Christian magistrate, whom the editors of the *Collectio Avellana* identified as the senator Andromachus.[13] It also delivers a series of loosely aimed critiques at other elite patrons along with a tongue-in-cheek criticism that they are failing to perform the ritual according to ancient custom.[14] But taken in its totality, the treatise might best be characterized as an extended charge of hypocrisy designed to undermine the credibility of lay Christians who have recently critiqued a member of the clergy.[15] How can they, Gelasius reasons, who are guilty of drunken buffoonery and demonic superstition be in a position to judge a minister of the Church?

A careful reading of the first paragraph, in fact, sets the entire treatise in context. A local priest has been found guilty of an adulterous relationship, bringing public scrutiny to the Church.[16] But more than being embarrassed by the scandal, Gelasius has come under personal criticism for not acting swiftly enough to punish the derelict priest.[17] Gelasius begins his treatise with an extended censure of those who, not knowing all of the information, have rushed to judgment in the matter.[18] The pontiff then, rather brashly, admonishes those hypocrites who condemn another for physical adultery when they are themselves guilty of the even greater sin of spiritual adultery. And it is here that Gelasius begins the connection to the Lupercalia, which he casts as a form of spiritual adultery because its celebrants have turned from love of God to the love of demons (a common late antique Christian accusation against pagan sacrifice).[19]

As reflected in the framing of the first paragraph of the text, there is clearly more at stake for Gelasius than a desire to disrupt a long-standing and popular event. But it is not until several paragraphs later that we are provided our surest clue. In paragraph 8, Gelasius notes that an added element in this particular year's festivities will be a theatrical mocking (through lewd songs) of the guilty priest.[20] Here, it would seem, is the primary motivation for Gelasius' extended rant. The pope is embarrassed that the clergy (including, by extension, himself) are going to be the target of drunken buffoonery. Andromachus, the leading patron of the event, has been unresponsive to

Gelasius' attempts to suppress this particular aspect of the ceremony (he has even posted a public announcement of the festival),[21] and so Gelasius responds with the maximum force that he can—a threat of excommunication.[22] But given that Andromachus is not actually named in the treatise and given that he may have had access to a private oratory, the threat of excommunication contained in the document may have amounted, in practical terms, to little more than bluster.

In the end, Gelasius can do nothing to stop the event, nor can he really do anything to diminish Andromachus' standing in the city. Gelasius' concluding declarations that the festival must come to an end should not be misconstrued as evidence of the cessation of the festival.[23] There is nothing in this text, in fact, to suggest that the Lupercalia came to an end. Instead, Gelasius' concluding exhortation must be read as a kind of political or religious slogan for reform—a hope or desire for moral change that was more idealistic than realistic and more likely intended to reinforce the ideology of those who already shared his viewpoint than designed to persuade those who did not. These realities set both the purpose and the audience of the treatise into greater relief. To what end does Gelasius attack Andromachus if he is not even willing to name him?[24] And why are the pope's criticisms of Andromachus' fellow patrons, which fill the majority of the text, so hollow?[25] Neil McLynn has provided one possible answer to these questions by suggesting that the tractate was written for the benefit of the local clergy; it was not, McLynn argues, an attempt to provoke the aristocracy into open battle over the celebration of a popular festival.[26] As we will see, Gelasius and his local clergy did not always see eye to eye, and even though Gelasius condemns the adulterous affair,[27] we might best view the treatise as a public show of clerical solidarity and an attempt to shield local clerics from the moral scrutiny of the secular elites.

But why was Gelasius, the bishop of Rome and heir of Peter, so powerless to shut down the Lupercalia and why would his declaration of excommunication have meant so little? The answers to both of these questions are to be found, in part, in recent scholarship on the private oratories of aristocratic Roman Christians from this period. Kristina Sessa and Kimberly Bowes have independently demonstrated that the continuation of the pre-Nicene domestication of Christian liturgical practice (such as daily prayer and domestic communion[28]) would have served as a formidable barrier to papal assertions of religious hegemony in the city.[29] One of the unique characteristics of the development of Christianity in the city of Rome was that the private households of the senatorial elite remained a space decidedly free of episcopal oversight (whether political, economic, or ethical). This was due, in large part, to the carefully guarded and ancient legal protections granted to all aspects (including the religious) of the private domain, the *domus*, through the principle of the *paterfamilias*. As Sessa notes, the Roman *domus* "was not a blank slate onto which the bishop simply etched his power to build his church."[30] Rather, the householder remained an active agent in the process by which Roman bishops did, eventually, gain access into the home. But that process was a long and uneven one, far from complete during Gelasius' tenure.[31] In short, the evidence Sessa, Bowes, and others have provided for household worship in Rome dramatically contradicts the traditional scholarly narratives that this period saw the "rise of the papacy," at the expense of the lay householders' religious and domestic autonomy.[32]

On this point, it is interesting to take notice the very first line of Gelasius' *Tractate* 6, which begins with the assertion that "Some people sit in their houses unaware of what they say or of what they approve of, judging others even though they do not judge themselves."[33] In short, Gelasius is suggesting that Andromachus and his fellow aristocrats are not adhering to the ethical parameters of the Christian life. Not only are they judging those to whom they should show mercy, but they are doing so from a vantage point that marks them as somehow *para-ecclesial*—outside the Church. Gelasius' implication is that the authentic Church is that of parish churches in the episcopal administrative system. The domestic worship spaces of the senatorial elite, despite their antiquity, fly in the face of that structure. They are both a threat to and competition for the episcopal network. It is not surprising, therefore, that we find in Gelasius' correspondence the most concerted attempt of any pontiff in the late ancient period to regulate the construction and consecration of new churches.[34] In one letter, he goes so far as to insist that the construction of any new church or oratory in all suburbican Italy must first gain papal approval.[35] As we will see, his unprecedented efforts to scrutinize clerical ordinations could also be interpreted as an attempt to prevent clergy from serving in these domestic churches.[36] For now, we can simply conclude that *Tractate* 6 reveals Gelasius' frustration with a fractured ecclesiological system for which he has no immediate recourse other than rhetorical performance.

For all the fascinating dynamics at work in Gelasius' condemnation of the Lupercalia (and what this tractate reveals of the limitations of papal influence vis-à-vis the senatorial elite) one aspect that scholars have over-looked is the fact that Gelasius never avails himself of the Petrine topos. Nowhere in *Tractate* 6 does Gelasius ever claim that he, as heir of St. Peter, has the right to shut down the festival or to oversee the city's religious celebra-tions. Nor does he ever make reference to the Apostolic See or Rome's apos-tolic inheritance. In fact, in the entire treatise Gelasius does not make a single claim to personal religious authority. Instead, his arguments emphasize the futility and superstitious character of the festival and offer what he believes to be empirical evidence that pagan rites do not achieve what their prac-titioners expect of them.[37] It is difficult to know why Gelasius pursues this strategy. Whatever his reasons, the altercation testifies to both the weakness of his position vis-à-vis the local aristocracy and a more limited application of the Petrine topos than we find elsewhere in his corpus.

Of course, the Lupercalia celebration was not the only occasion over which Gelasius would have competed with local aristocrats. It has become a commonplace in late ancient Christian studies to describe the various ways episcopal authorities appropriated the primary avenues for patronage (e.g., food doles and entertainment) from their pagan predecessors and aristocratic peers.[38] Indeed, we might view patronage in fifth-century Rome as something of a multidimensional competition for civic visibility and influence. Just as Andromachus and his fellow senators supported the Lupercalia because it provided an increasingly rare opportunity for local aristocrats to support a popular religious and cultural event free of episcopal oversight,[39] so did Gela-sius pursue opportunities for patronage that had traditionally been the domain of the aristocratic elite but now afforded the opportunity to raise his profile among the city's inhabitants.

In this regard, Gelasius' relatively brief biography in the *Liber Pontificalis* offers some evidence of the pontiff's efforts. In addition to a cursory discus-sion of the Misenus rehabilitation, the continuation of the Acacian schism, and his initiatives for clerical reform, the *Liber Pontificalis* describes only three other aspects of Gelasius' tenure: (1) his concern for the poor; (2) his construction of several churches; and (3) his discovery and persecution of a Manichaean community in Rome.[40] To be sure, episcopal support for the poor would have been both expected and commonplace by the mid-fifth century. The ever-expanding size of the Roman patrimony (farms owned by the See of Rome), combined with the individual wealth of many popes, enabled lavish benevolence.[41] And yet, interestingly, Gelasius is one of the very few pontiffs to be recognized by the *Liber Pontificalis* for his gifts to the poor. In fact, of the eighteen popes between Leo I and Benedict I (d. 579), only two are identified as having made distributions to the poor—Gelaisus and Symmachus. Whatever Gelasius' actual giving may have been, the surviving literary records place him among the most generous late ancient popes.[42]

The construction of new churches similarly would have provided Gelasius with an opportunity for civic patronage, as it had several popes before him.[43] Whereas old Rome was in decline—the population a fraction of its former size and the aristocracy unable to sustain any substantial public-works programs—the construction of new churches and refurbishing of old ones would have shown Gelasius to be an active civic patron and would have enabled him to target his patronage in a way that specifically reinforced papal prestige. The *Liber* credits Gelasius with the construction of a number of churches and basilicas in central Italy.[44] Among these projects is the (perhaps) surprising acknowledgment that he made possible the construction of a basilica, dedicated to the Virgin Mary, on the private estate of Crispinis. This may be the exception that proves the rule with respect to Gelasius' attempts to suppress churches that were controlled by aristocratic families.[45] Clearly, Crispinis and Gelasius had managed to come to some agreement about what would occur in this basilica.

Affirmation and Dissent Within the Roman Clergy

Evidence of clerical appraisals of Gelasius may be even less direct than those of the local aristocracy, but we are still able to glimpse a few important facets of the relationship between the pope and the city's clergy. Of note is the observation by Peter Llewellyn (building on the work of I. Kajanto) that Gelasius ordained nearly twice the percentage of non-Roman candidates to the priesthood (28 versus 14 percent) than his predecessor.[46] Llewellyn takes this as evidence that Gelasius, like Symmachus after him, made a conscious effort to tweak the social composition of the clergy who controlled the city's *tituli* parishes—an effort that could have slightly undercut aristocratic influence over clerical appointments and possibly even brought titular revenue more under episcopal influence.[47] Whether his ordination of non-Romans was deliberate or not, Gelasius would have been well aware that he did not have full support of the city clergy.

The most significant engagement between the pope and the city's priests recorded within the Gelasian corpus is a text that Thiel lists as *Epistle* 30. The document might best be described as a redacted and partisan transcript from a legal proceeding in which a local bishop, Misenus, is restored to his previous dignity after having endured a long period of excommunication.[48] Misenus, in fact, had been the bishop of Cumae during the tenure of Pope Felix III and, along with Bishop Vitalis, had served as a papal ambassador to Constantinople in 484 at the height of the altercation with Acacius.[49] Misenus and Vitalis had made the career-ending mistake of validating Acacius' orthodoxy by receiving the Eucharist from him.[50] Felix had been embarrassed, and his hard-line diplomatic stance toward the Eastern patriarch had been compromised by his envoys. Not surprisingly, Felix's response was swift. The bishops were recalled from Constantinople and then condemned by a Roman synod upon their return.[51]

As a likely consultant for Felix's Eastern strategy, Gelasius must have concurred with (if not orchestrated) the punitive action against Misenus and Vitalis.[52] Thus, the rehabilitation of Misenus in 495 (Vitalis had already died) is a rather surprising development. Although only a few scholars have taken notice of *Epistle* 30, it has led to radically divergent interpretations. J. N. D. Kelly, for example, sees Misenus' rehabilitation as evidence of an increasingly powerful clerical minority in the city that had grown tired of the schism with the East. Thus, Kelley argues, Misenus' rehabilitation should be viewed as a partial repudiation of the pope's Eastern policy.[53] In sharp contrast, Jeffrey Richards views Misenus' restoration as a sign of increasing papal strength.[54] Saying nothing of Gelasius' motives for seeking to restore Misenus, Richards emphasizes what he considers to be a surprisingly small minority of priests who boycotted the synod—eighteen of the seventy-six Roman priests did not attend, indicating a core group of Roman clerics who refused to abide by the exoneration.[55] But Richards' analysis leaves us with more questions than answers. Why, for example, should we view an 80 percent majority opinion as an example of strength when even Richards concedes that 100 percent agreement in such matters was typical at this time?[56] Moreover, how can we reconcile Gelasius' hard-line approach toward the East in all other matters if we are supposed to interpret the rehabilitation of Misenus as orchestrated by Gelasius—a change of course not only inconsistent with Gelasius' Eastern policy but rejected by a group of Roman priests supposed to be more rigid than Gelasius himself? But even if Richards is correct, and the decision to rehabilitate Misenus was the pope's (perhaps in exchange for Misenus' exaggerated public affirmations of Gelasius' authority during the trial of 495), the pontiff was clearly unable to gain full clerical support for the endeavor, which in itself evinces a concrete limit to papal efforts to control clerical opinion.

And it is precisely because of this weakness that the unprecedented affirmations of Gelasius' sovereignty contained within *Epistle* 30 are so arresting.[57] Following Misenus' confession of guilt and affirmation of faith (paragraphs 1–5), the document informs us that Gelasius asked the assembled bishops to offer their own opinions on the matter. Here, the text boasts: "All of the bishops raised themselves up, calling and saying: 'Christ hear us, give Gelasius a long life!' This was said twenty times. 'Since God gave you authority, rule!' This was affirmed twelve times. 'Do what [our] Lord Peter does!' This was said ten times. 'We ask you to be lenient!' This was said nine times."[58] This characterization of Gelasius in full control of a sycophantic synod, of course, echoes similar portraits of a Roman emperor whose authority was publicly proclaimed by both Senate and people. No doubt, this is not the first time that a discourse of papal authority had mirrored imperial models nor the first time that a Roman bishop had been cheered in imperial fashion, but the hyperbole is all the more noteworthy given the apparent divisions among the Roman clergy that this partisan account seems to have been designed to conceal.

The document concludes by transcribing a second episode of euphoric affirmation. Many of the previous assertions are repeated, but in this case there are two significant additions: "We acknowledge you as the vicar of Christ!" and "We see you to be the Apostle Peter!"[59] *Epistle* 30 is, in fact, the oldest extant text affirming the papal title "Vicar of Christ." The second addition, linking Gelasius directly to Peter, is perhaps less grandiose but no less rhetorically significant. Indeed, it is precisely because Gelasius is "Peter" that he is able to "loose" the sin of Misenus (cf. Mt 16: "what sins you bind are bound and whatever sins you loose are loosed").[60]

In addition to these rather dramatic recitations of Gelasius' authority, there are still other ways that *Epistle* 30 stretches the rhetorical possibilities of the Petrine discourse in new ways.[61] For example, during Misenus' confession, he is said to affirm his faith "in the sight of God and Blessed Peter and his vicar and the whole Church."[62] The assertion that the gathering occurs within the "sight" of the apostle is a powerful statement of the way that the authority of Peter is said to be present in a papal assembly and especially in his vicar—Gelasius.[63] An equally important rhetorical device is the linguistic insertion of the "Apostolic See" as the subject that acts on various objects. In other words, it is not Gelasius who acts, nor is it the synod. Instead it is the "Apostolic See" that "leads the entire Church," that rightfully "removed Misenus and Vitalis from communion," that now makes available a "place of mercy" for Misenus.[64] This further serves to cast Gelasius' actions as those of the apostle who founded his see. In paragraph 10, several of these components are brought together so that the "Apostolic See" is authorized to both exonerate Misenus and vilify Eastern heretics. The author goes so far as to anticipate that this verdict will not be approved by the Eastern Church—something of an odd assertion, given that Misenus had initially been condemned for his solidarity with the East. But any anticipated Eastern objection is preempted by the claim that the Apostolic See does not need the authorization of the East, because Eastern bishops have chosen to associate themselves with the heresiarch Acacius rather than with blessed Peter, which is here understood as the measuring stick of orthodoxy.[65]

While no objective interpreter would assume that *Epistle* 30 accurately reflects everything that took place during the synod, nor would anyone presume that the very public proclamations of Gelasius' popularity represent the universal view of the city's priests, the surviving evidence presents a real interpretive challenge for assessing Gelasius' functional authority among the Roman clergy. On the one hand, no Roman bishop has ever enjoyed universal support, and it may well be that Gelasius' efforts to defend and promote the Roman clergy made him more popular among that constituency than some other popes. On the other hand, it seems more likely that the letter's proclamations of Gelasius' authority, especially the introduction of new and more exalted titles such as "Vicar of Christ," were inserted into the only surviving record of the trial for the explicit purpose of masking what might otherwise have been understood to have been a humiliation for the pontiff. Indeed, it is significant that the entire document seems fixated on asserting Gelasius' authority vis-à-vis the rest of the Church (whether the assembled bishops who acknowledge his authority, the Eastern heretics who deny his sovereignty, or some silent third party who seems to have questioned the pope's right to overturn a previous synod).[66] The text does not seem to be at all concerned with the proposed matter at hand—the redemption and forgiveness of a penitent cleric. Whatever the historical circumstances of the trial, *Epistle* 30 presents a powerful and well-respected pope.

The Broader West

Although he was not as internationally active as Leo had been, Gelasius was likely the most involved pontiff in the ecclesiastical and political affairs of Italy, Sicily, and the Latin-speaking Balkans of any pope between Leo and Gregory the Great. Both his correspondence and his theological tractates testify to his attempts to raise clerical standards and prosecute heresy throughout Italy. His corpus also offers a few glimpses of the initial papal posture toward Theoderic, the Ostrogothic king, who would play a more definitive role in the lives of Gelasius' successors.

Clerical Discipline as Papal Prerogative

There are more letters in the Gelasian corpus dedicated to the restriction of clerical abuse and/or the standards for clerical ordination than any other matter. The episcopal recipients of these letters generally resided within those regions that had historically been part of Rome's super-diocesan jurisdiction, including the immediate dioceses around Rome, suburbican Italy, Sicily, and the southwestern coast of the Balkans. The presence of papal patrimonies in those regions (especially in Sicily and the Balkans), of course, made possible a more direct papal intervention in the affairs of local churches. And Gelasius seems to have taken every opportunity to dictate precisely what he expected of subordinate clergy.

The most extensive of his instructions regarding the clergy are contained in *Epistle* 14, which presents dozens of regulations concerning clerical candidacy, clerical discipline, and the boundaries between the various clerical ranks. Concerning the latter, Gelasius explicitly prohibits priests from assuming episcopal roles, especially those related to the celebration of baptisms, ordinations, and the Eucharist.[67] At this point in the development of the priestly offices, these sacramental rites were performed primarily by bishops, but they could also be conducted by priests who had the explicit permission of their bishops to perform them on the bishop's behalf. Gelasius' proscription against priests who act without episcopal sanction, of course, indicates that priests were serving these sacramental roles without sufficient episcopal oversight. Given the dynamics of Italian domestic worship, it is conceivable that Gelasius has in mind the sacramental rites that were being conducted in the private churches and oratories of the aristocratic elite—liturgical spaces that were too far removed from episcopal oversight for Gelasius' liking. Indeed, twice in *Epistle* 14 Gelasius condemns the consecration of any new church or oratory that does not have the consent of the Apostolic See.[68] One interesting element of Gelasius' proscriptions against priests who usurp episcopal roles is the related critique of bishops who are not sufficiently supervising those churches within their jurisdiction.[69] Gelasius, in fact, proffers that such bishops will be held accountable for the sins of their priests.

The letter contains several other regulations, including the assigning of specific days for ordination or the veiling of virgins, a proscription against the female deaconate,[70] a proscription against slaves or soldiers becoming monks,[71] and an insistence that clerical advancement be governed by seniority. What most concerns us in the present study, however, are the rhetorical strategies by which Gelasius asserts these measures. Throughout *Epistle* 14, Gelasius appeals to two distinct but overlapping arguments to justify his intervention. First, he claims that his instructions are rooted in the ancient canons and practices of the Church.[72] Second, Gelasius asserts that his authority to issue these regulations is directly linked to his relationship to St. Peter, in whom "the Lord of the whole Church has placed primacy."[73] Indeed, he begins paragraph 9 by noting:

> Since we desire that nothing against our reverence for the salutary rules be allowed by chance, and since the Apostolic See, with the Lord protecting, desires to hold those things which have been established in a pious and devout way by our ancestors' canons, it is an indignity if anyone, either a bishop or a member of the lower orders should refuse to observe what the seat of St. Peter follows and teaches. And it should be fitting enough that the whole body of the Church is in accordance with this observance, which anyone can see to be thriving where the Lord of the whole Church has placed primacy.[74]

Thus, the justification for Gelasius' intervention in the affairs of southern Italy is made explicit by the connection of a series of binding faith-based principles: (1) Christ invested Peter with primacy; (2) Peter instituted rules for the regulation of the Church in Rome; (3) the See of Rome has maintained those rules down to the present day; therefore (4) Gelasius, as Peter's successor, has the authority to reinstitute the ancient customs that have fallen out of use because of the disruptions of war and famine.[75] In short, Gelasius frames his intervention in the suburbican churches as a return to ancient practice, rooted in the authority of St. Peter.

A great number of letters in the Gelasian corpus repeat one or more of the clerical regulations (sometimes word for word) that are contained in *Epistle* 14. Among these, two letters deserve some comment. The first, *Epistle* 20, is addressed to two bishops in Rome's immediate vicinity.[76] What is noteworthy about this letter is that it exists at all. In other words, presuming that bishops Martyrius and Justus reside adjacent to Gelasius' immediate circle, why is it necessary for the pope to repeat the regulations concerning who can and who cannot be ordained to the priesthood, especially if the regulations of *Epistle* 14 stem from a Roman synod in which both these bishops should have been present?[77] Either Gelasius has exaggerated the compliance of other bishops with the pope's edicts at the Roman synod or *Epistle* 20 should be viewed as evidence that Martyrius and Justus have resisted (or have simply been unable to adhere to) Gelasius' regulations. Either way, it is clear that not all bishops have complied with Gelasius' instructions concerning the ordination of the lower clergy.

Epistle 25, which is addressed to bishop Zeja (of an unknown provincial diocese), begins with the rather provocative assertion that Zeja, being a provincial bishop, needs to adhere to the synodal decisions that are based on ancient canons that originate from "our see." At issue is the consecration of churches that do not have papal approval. The letter echoes an assertion of *Epistle* 14, which defines the traditional practices of the Apostolic See as the measure by which all churches are to be held accountable.[78] It also appears to mimic the approach of imperial legislation in this period, which often asserted that the laws promulgated in the capital were automatically binding throughout the provinces.

Of course Gelasius' assertion of papal authority via Peter in the Western Church was not limited to issues of clerical discipline and church construction. For example, *Epistle* 17, which is a very brief letter to the bishops of Sicily, begins with an explicit assertion of Roman authority in Sicily. There is also the brief letter to Aeonius of Arles, which is saturated with multiple references to the Apostolic See and St. Peter's authority, including the provocatively direct assertion that Christ the Lord had instituted St. Peter as the primary caretaker (*gubernatio principis)* of all the sheep throughout the world.[79] Brotherly fidelity to ancient tradition, Aoenius is reminded, requires that he acknowledge this. It is worth noting, however, that this is the only surviving letter to Gaul within Gelasius' large corpus. Not only does this suggest that the Gallic bishops were no longer appealing to Rome to resolve internal matters, but it also implies that Gelasius seems to have been unable to find an occasion for interfering in the routine operations of the Gallic Church.[80]

Engaging the Ostrogoths

While the impact of the Ostrogothic presence in Italy will be a focus of the next chapter, there are a few points that are worth introducing in the context of Gelasius' involvement in Italian affairs. We should begin, in fact, with the observation that the transition from the last Roman emperor of the West into a period of Ostrogothic rule (famously occurring with the accession of Odoacer in 476) was something of a nonevent for the daily operations of the Catholic Church in Italy. Indeed, the bishops of Rome and the Ostrogothic rulers of Italy seem to have achieved more than a peaceful coexistence with one another. John Moorhead, in fact, has argued that Gelasius' predecessor, Felix III, owed his election to the intervention of Odoacer, whose senatorial ally, Basilius, proved instrumental in the decision.[81] Few documents survive that speak directly to Gelasius' interaction with the Ostrogoths, but there is little reason to believe that there was any open hostility between them.[82]

Given the Arian confession of the Gothic rulers, this peaceful coexistence has surprised not a few scholars.[83] We might think that it is particularly unexpected for Gelasius, given the pontiff's proclivity to find and persecute all other forms of heresy on the Italian peninsula.[84] But among the undisputed letters, there is no evidence that Gelasius actively engaged Odoacer or Theoderic on the matter, nor does he seem to have complained to anyone about their Arianism, apart from one brief snicker after Odoacer's death.[85] And that remark was designed to show that even a "barbarian heretic" had greater respect for Catholic bishops of Italy than the Eastern emperor. There are, of course, a handful of additional brief letters that are reputed to have been written by Gelasius to Theoderic.[86] But even if these letters are authentic, they show Gelasius to have done little more than pepper Theoderic with requests that he not impose any civil restrictions on the Catholic clergy. The same collection includes a pair of letters to Theoderic's mother, supposedly a Catholic, whom Gelasius hoped might be able to effect her son's eventual conversion to orthodoxy.[87]

To be sure, Theoderic's irenic religious policy would have played a large part in the dogmatic détente between Ravenna and Rome, but the fact that the normally fiery Gelasius seems to have completely ignored the situation perhaps tells us a great deal about the pope's ability to measure his dogmatic pugnaciousness with political pragmatism.[88] If anything, the radically different posture that Gelasius struck for the Arian king versus the pseudo-Monophysite emperor might underscore the extent to which Theoderic was, and Anastasius was not, a foreboding presence in Italian affairs in the mid-490s.[89]

On this score, it is also important to note that there remained an uncomfortable and ever-shifting four-way coalition between the emperor, king, Senate, and Church (neither of the latter two, of course, existed as a monolithic front).[90] On three occasions (in 489, 493/4, and 497), Theoderic sent leading senators on diplomatic missions to the East in search of imperial recognition of his rule in Italy (finally achieved in 497).[91] On at least two of those occasions, the same ambassadors took part in negotiations that were intended to resolve the Acacian schism. Though little ever came of those efforts, we must not lose sight of the fact that each of these four parties was engaging with the others on multiple levels and with competing allegiances. In 497, for example, the *caput senatus*, Festus, promised the emperor Anastasius that he could guarantee Pope Anastasius' acceptance of the *Henotikon*, should the emperor offer an official recognition of Theoderic's rule.[92]

The surviving evidence is so limited that there is little we can say about a Petrine appeal in Gelasius' interaction with the Goths. The one undisputed fragment sent to Theoderic does, interestingly, include a reference to Peter—perhaps not insignificant given the fact that the entire text is little more than a sentence.[93] One of the two disputed letters allegedly sent to Theoderic's mother also refers to St. Peter.[94] There is also another authentic fragmentary letter from Gelasius to two bishops that refers to Theoderic as his "son"—a type of rhetorical subordination of authority that we will discuss in detail in the next section.[95]

Perhaps the most relevant historical consequence of the Gothic presence in Italy during Gelasius' tenure was the destructive force of the civil war between Odoacer and Theoderic. In several of his letters to Italian clergy, Gelasius complains of the disruption and destruction caused by the barbarian wars.[96] In fact, he uses the political crisis as the occasion for distributing his clerical reforms to the Italian dioceses. While it is possible that Gelasius actually believed that barbarian unrest had been the cause for clerical laxity, it may be more likely that the pontiff simply used the Gothic civil war as a pretext for issuing his clerical regulations—regulations that provided an occasion for the assertion of a new mode of Petrine authority, but which he framed as a return to ancient practice.

Peter's International Stage

We turn now to Gelasius' use of the Petrine topos in his correspondence with the emperor and Eastern clerics and to the possibilities that the Petrine discourse enabled in those diplomatic efforts. It was in this theater that Gelasius issued his most assertive claims—claims that have been the bedrock of traditional interpretations of Gelasius' career and have all too often been misinterpreted by polemicists and scholars alike as evidence for both the growth of and actual adherence to papal claims to authority.[97] As we will see, however, a more careful analysis of the relevant documents reveals that the escalations of Petrine rhetoric contained in them were actually born from diplomatic frustration and weakness rather than strength. As a consequence, the same documents attest to the relative insignificance of papal influence in the East at the close of the fifth century.

The Ad Anastasium

Gelasius is, of course, best known for a letter (*Epistle* 12) he sent to the Roman emperor Anastasius in 494 that included a provocative distinction between priestly and imperial authority and suggested how the two spheres of influence, both authorized by God, should cooperate with one another. Paragraph 2 begins:

> As you know, Emperor, there are two primary means by which this
> world is ruled: the hallowed authority of the pontiff and royal
> power. Now, if we were to compare the two of them, the sacerdotal
> burden is as much heavier as the responsibility [of priests] is more
> serious for they will render an account even for the kings of men at
> the divine judgment . . . [And] if all the priests are essentially han-
> dling divine affairs correctly and it is deemed appropriate that the

faithful submit their hearts to them, how much more should everyone follow the opinion of him who presides in the chair, he whom
the most high God desired to preside over all the other priests,
whom the whole pious church has celebrated without ceasing?[98]

It is easy to understand why this passage has drawn so much attention: Gelasius articulates a form of diarchy and at the same time proposes that priestly
authority is ultimately more important than imperial authority because even
emperors need the sacraments for salvation.[99] Equally significant is that Gelasius establishes himself as the *pontifex* of priestly authority—a sort of mirror
image of the emperor's leadership of the imperial government. Rhetorically,
Gelasius presents both positions as first principles that the emperor will naturally accept. Thus, the argument placed before the emperor in this particular
passage is predicated on related principles and functions, like a legal syllo-
gism: (1) priests and secular authorities are placed by God in their respective
realms of responsibility; (2) the clergy adhere to the civil laws of the empire;
therefore (3) the imperial authority must yield to the priesthood in theological matters.[100] In other words, because the Acacian schism is a theological
matter, it can be resolved only through deference to priestly authority, and
the locus of priestly authority is the See of Rome.[101]

What little attention scholars have paid to Gelasius in the past century
has been focused primarily on this lone passage and, regrettably, almost
exclusively on the semantic distinction between the *auctoritas* of priestly
authority and the *potestas* of imperial authority.[102] With that singular focus,
scholars have failed to acknowledge many of the other significant moves that
Gelasius makes in the letter. What is more, that preoccupation has likely
also contributed to the failure of scholars to differentiate between Gelasius'
embellished presentation of papal authority and the reality of ecclesiological
politics in the period.

Among Gelasius' impressive rhetorical demonstrations is his transformation of the argument for the divine derivation of imperial authority into an
argument for the subordination of the emperor to the priesthood. Of course,
the idea that the emperor held his position by divine fiat had both Greco-
Roman and Christian origins.[103] Gelasius pounces on an important corollary
of that maxim, namely that a person in authority was accountable to God for
his subordinates. More than merely a commonplace of Christian pastoral
literature, this principle also had important classical precedents, going back
to both Homer and Aristotle.[104] Perhaps even more significant in the current

context, however, the principle was consistent with elements of the Roman imperial tradition as reflected in Augustus' *Res Gestae* and the Roman legal tradition of the *paterfamilias*.

In paragraph 4 of *Epistle* 12, Gelasius both affirms and undermines the divine sanction of Anastasius' rule and responsibility. Noting that imperial governance is a *beneficium* from God for which the emperor will be accountable, Gelasius quickly notes that he too will personally be required to render an account before God for whether or not Anastasius properly administers the imperial *beneficium*. In other words, Gelasius boldly inserts himself into the ruling/responsibility paradigm to imply that his own responsibility (and, therefore, his own authority) was superior to that of the emperor. The emperor, of course, retains a certain responsibility for the Roman population, but above that hierarchical paradigm exists another, more exalted layer, placing the pope between the emperor and God. It is for this reason that Gelasius must speak truthfully to the emperor about his error (i.e., his support for the memory of Acacius).

The subordination of the emperor to the pope is further achieved by Gelasius' frequent reference to Anastasius as his "son."[105] Although it was a commonplace of late ancient and medieval episcopal correspondence to address a secular correspondent from a paternal vantage point, Gelasius was one of the first popes to employ the father/son paradigm in his imperial correspondence.[106] By framing the emperor as "son," Gelasius is able to present himself as a nurturing spiritual father who is concerned for the religious well-being of his disciple. But, at the same time, he clearly subordinates the emperor in the process—there would have been no mistaking the subservience of "sons" to "fathers" in the Roman world.

One might argue, in fact, that Gelasius repeatedly challenges the emperor's authority. By Gelasius' tenure, it had become customary for a newly elected pope to send a letter to the emperor announcing his election.[107] Gelasius, however, had failed to send such a letter. Whether this oversight stemmed from personal intransigence or from the fact that Rome and Constantinople were in schism at the time of Gelasius' election is impossible to know.[108] Either way, Gelasius begins the *Ad Anastasium* by noting his surprise that the emperor is disappointed that Gelasius had not written to him. He is surprised, Gelasius tells us, because only a few months earlier there had been a rumor circulating through Rome that Anastasius had forbidden his representatives to meet with the pope. So Gelasius, being dutiful to that rumor, had taken the further step of not sending any letters to the emperor.[109] In other words, Gelasius spins his failure to announce his election to Anastasius as an act of obedience, rather than disobedience. He concludes this explanation by noting: "you can see that this situation did not arise from a desire to conceal my election from you, but rather from my precaution: I did not want to annoy one who rejects me."[110] The very acknowledgment that the emperor might interpret his previous silence as an act of deception should, in fact, be an indicator that Gelasius knew full well that he was breaking protocol—and thereby insulting the emperor—by not writing to him.

The letter then immediately transitions from a justification for past silence into a proclamation of the pope's patriotism and loyalty. Gelasius declares: "O glorious son, I, as one Roman-born, love, cherish, and highly esteem you both as a Roman Prince and as a Christian."[111] Gelasius' claim of Roman birth is a fascinating assertion. As indicated earlier, Gelasius was not technically born a Roman. He was born in North Africa.[112] We should, therefore, interpret the passage as having a double meaning. Ostensibly, Gelasius' statement of Roman-ness is an affirmation of his patriotism and is followed by his pledge of loyalty to the emperor.[113] But the same claim serves as a rhetorical mask for one of Gelasius' most significant political liabilities at home (that he is not Roman born). Is it also possible that Gelasius' subsequent claim of loyalty is likewise a subtle attempt to deflect an accusation of insubordination? That Gelasius had refused to send the announcement of his election and failed to follow imperial directives with respect to the memory of Acacius could both have been interpreted in imperial circles as acts of political rebellion.

The various means by which Gelasius undermines and subordinates the emperor's authority, of course, serve the explicit purpose of the letter as a whole—to convince Anastasius that he needs to take the Acacian error more seriously. As *pontifex* of priestly authority, Gelasius is the most qualified citizen to assess and manage theological challenges. Left to his own devices, Anastasius has mistakenly supported the memory of Acacius—an error that could only have been made by someone ill-prepared to understand theological subtlety. Eminently better informed, and authorized by God to adjudicate theological matters, Gelasius presents himself as the lone citizen able to discern that the emperor has not only put his personal salvation in jeopardy, but has also endangered the very survival of the empire.[114]

Anticipating the emperor's objection that there are theological advisors in the East as well, Gelasius asserts the fundamental preeminence of the

Roman See, which alone guarantees orthodox teaching. He begins paragraph 9, in fact, by acknowledging that the bishops of the East have been "grumbling" because the Apostolic See has not written "these things" to them. What, exactly, the Apostolic See has not written is not entirely clear. What is clear is that Eastern bishops will not yield to the papal condemnation of Acacius. While that fact is both obvious and well known, it must be acknowledged that the Roman See simply did not possess the international respect in doctrinal matters that Gelasius so forcefully claims throughout the letter.[115] As a consequence, we must read every one of Gelasius' claims to ecclesiastical authority as an indication of what the pontiff wants, not what he enjoys.

Paragraph 9 is equally important because it provides Gelasius with the opportunity to assert his version of the Petrine topos in its fullest form. Addressing the obstinacy of the Eastern Church directly, Gelasius argues that it is absurd to think that the authorities of the Eastern Church, men who harbor and conspire with heretics, could possibly interpret the teaching of St. Peter more effectively than the Apostolic See. Thus, "true teaching" is "Peter's teaching," and vice versa. Gelasius, in fact, smirks that it is inconceivable that bishops who harbor heretics could possibly help the "Apostolic See" to interpret properly the teaching of Peter, just as it is unlikely that they could even have received the Petrine teaching uncorrupted.[116] Here again, Gelasius' logic is presented in syllogistic fashion: (1) orthodoxy is enshrined in the teaching of Saint Peter; (2) the Apostolic See, more than any other see, remains faithful to that teaching; therefore (3) the Apostolic See is the guardian of orthodoxy.

Just as we saw in *Epistle* 30 (which concerned Misenus' restoration), the *Ad Anastasium* routinely situates the "Apostolic See," rather than the author, as the grammatical subject. One of the important ways that the *Ad Anastasium* marks a further escalation of Gelasius' use of the Petrine discourse is the progression of subjectivity from the "Apostolic See" to St. Peter himself. The Apostolic See, through its *pontifex* (Gelasius), acts on behalf of St. Peter, in solidarity with St. Peter, because it is St. Peter.

In addition to this stretching of Petrine discourse in *Epistle* 12, there are two equally significant things to note about Gelasius' engagement with the Eastern bishops (men Gelasius presents as not understanding the significance of Peter). First, it is possible that the Eastern bishops had been expecting Gelasius to send them a confession of faith—the "unsent" letter. In the subsequent century, it would become customary for the leader of each of the five major Christian sees to send a personal confession of faith to the others at the time of his election.[117] Assuming that this pattern was in place by Gelasius' tenure, there would be a certain consistency between Gelasius' failure to announce his election to the emperor and the pope's unwillingness to submit his confession of orthodoxy to the scrutiny of others—especially bishops Gelasius believed to be themselves guilty of heresy. While the specifics remain a matter of speculation, there is no denying that Gelasius was aware that the Eastern bishops had been critical of him to the emperor—this is why he tries to address the matter on his own terms. It is, in fact, an astonishing admission by the pope that the Eastern bishops believe that it is within their purview to evaluate the orthodoxy of the bishop of Rome. And that acknowledgment is a rather dramatic internal contradiction of the claims of papal sovereignty asserted throughout the letter.

Second, it is worth noting that Gelasius always restricts the designation "Apostolic See" to the See of Rome. As we saw in the previous chapter, Leo had cautiously extended the "Apostolic" title to the See of Alexandria and the See of Antioch as part of his diplomatic strategy to recruit those Eastern sees against the growing pretensions of the See of Constantinople. Pope Gregory I would do the same thing during the crisis over the "Ecumenical" title in the 590s. But in the 490s, the political landscape was such that both the See of Antioch and the See of Alexandria were in league with Constantinople and offered little hope of diplomatic leverage in the dispute over the memory of Acacius. Whether it was an ideological shift or a diplomatic strategy is impossible to know; either way it is clear that Gelasius chose to confine the "Apostolic" designation to the See of Rome alone. That rhetorical move, of course, further stressed the singularity and preeminence of Rome over all others—two factors that have certainly contributed to the Gelasian legacy.

Perhaps this is all the more reason to be careful not to succumb to Gelasian hyperbole. The escalation in Petrine claims is not, in and of itself, evidence of international deference to papal authority.[118] On the contrary, it would appear that the Gelasian pronouncements of universal prestige and international recognition were akin to a fifth-century version of an echo chamber (in that only Gelasius and his inner circle initiated the claim of international supremacy; once the same proclamation was repeated, others who did not understand the dubiousness of the initial claim began to adopt it as well). It is clear that neither the emperor nor the Eastern bishops were going to defer to Gelasius on the issues related to the Acacian schism. With this in mind, we might interpret Gelasius' words in paragraph 9 as an attempt to mask his own recognition that the Eastern bishops do not accept the claims of a Roman monopoly on orthodoxy. Here, he reminds the emperor of the antiquity of Roman prestige and the extent to which all bishops, for all time, have respected that authority:

> Indeed, the authority of the Apostolic See, because it has been given in all Christian ages to the universal Church, is strengthened both by the series of canons of the fathers and a multifaceted tradition. But indeed if anyone, contrary to the constitutions of the Nicene Synod, should dare to take some authority for himself, this should be made plain to the assembly of one communion rather than opened to the minds of the outside world.[119]

Given the patterns established elsewhere in the text, Gelasius' insistence on the antiquity and orthodoxy of Roman preeminence serves as yet another sign that neither the bishops of the East nor the emperor himself respected the antiquity or the universality of Roman privilege.

Beyond the Ad Anastasium

Gelasius' Eastern diplomacy, of course, was pursued through concurrent efforts—his imperial correspondence being only one of them. The richest store of surviving evidence of the pope's Eastern initiatives exists in the correspondence with the Catholic leaders of Dardania. Situated in the southwestern corner of the Balkans, this region was critical to Gelasius' strategy because of its proximity to the Eastern Empire and its centuries-old loyalty to the See of Rome. Five surviving letters attest to Gelasius' efforts to prevent support for Acacius in the Balkans.[120] These letters, of course, have common themes, including a pro-papal account of the sequence of events linking Eutyches to Peter of Alexandria to Acacius, and the perceived danger of failing to denounce the Acacian error.

Two of the letters, *Epistle* 8 (to the abbot Natalis) and *Epistle* 18 (to the bishops of Dardania and Illyricum), provide ample evidence that Gelasius was fully aware that previous papal attempts to suppress the Acacian party had failed. *Epistle* 18, in fact, devotes considerable attention to the fact that the Metropolitanate of Thessalonica, a see that had been elevated to a papal vicarage for the Balkans earlier in the century, had abandoned Rome and followed Constantinople in supporting Zeno's *Henotikon* and the memory of Acacius.[121] Gelasius' only recourse in this stunning defeat is to warn the Latin bishops in Illyricum that the metropolitan has been severed from communion with the Apostolic See and removed from "society with the blessed Peter the Apostle."[122]

However, what is perhaps most interesting about these five letters is that they reveal, more clearly than any of our other surviving sources, the rhetorical strategies that Eastern clerics were employing against Gelasius and the See of Rome—namely the claims that Acacius' condemnation had been conducted contrary to the canons and that Rome's refusal to reinstate the memory of Acacius stemmed not from a meaningful theological disagreement but from the international humiliation that Rome suffered when Acacius refused to submit to Rome's primatial claims.[123] Through these letters, Gelasius provides his Balkan correspondents with a specific rejoinder to each of these pro-Acacian arguments. *Epistle* 26 is especially pertinent because it not only functions as the most thorough engagement with the Eastern accusations but also offers the most detailed articulation of Roman authority vis-à-vis other episcopal centers of any of Gelasius' letters written to "friendly" clerics.

While much of Gelasius' defense can be reduced to an extended affirmation of the antiquity of Roman privilege (he never really provides evidence for the claim—he just asserts it), there is an interesting element here not emphasized elsewhere in the correspondence. Rather than lambast Acacius' theological errors or even his association with the heretic Peter of Alexandria, Gelasius' primary critique of Acacius is that he had failed to adhere to canonical procedure when the disputed election between John and Peter of Alexandria first emerged—the event that precipitated the schism. According to Gelasius, a contested election in the See of Alexandria, the "second See" according to international ranking, could be adjudicated only in Rome.[124] Gelasius' predecessor, Felix, had determined that John was the rightful bishop of Alexandria. According to canonical statute, Gelasius opines, Acacius was bound to adhere to the Roman decision. But Acacius, without deference to the See of Rome, without recourse to a council of bishops, and without recognition that John of Alexandria outranked him, chose to fracture the unity of the Christian world by supporting the pretensions of the heretic Peter of Alexandria.[125] In short, Acacius' primary error was not theological; it was that he failed to adhere to a hierarchical system that placed the See of Alexandria and the See of Rome ahead of the See of Constantinople.

Epistle 10, written to the Roman senator Faustus, also preserves otherwise unrecorded evidence of the pro-Acacian Eastern party's diplomatic posture during the mid-490s.[126] It was Faustus who had been sent to Constantinople in 493/4 on the second of Theoderic's three embassies to the East. While he was in the Eastern capital, Faustus made some efforts (it is impossible to know how vigorously) to find a diplomatic solution to the Acacian schism.[127] It would appear that the immediate context of *Epistle* 10 is that Faustus has sent word to Gelasius of the continuation of the impasse and this letter provides Gelasius an opportunity to reply to Faustus' report.[128]

Among other things, *Epistle* 10 responds to two Eastern challenges not found elsewhere in Gelasius' corpus. The first is the pontiff's argument against the exoneration of Acacius on the basis that a sinner can be restored to communion only through a willful act of contrition (something that the now dead Acacius cannot possibly perform).[129] Gelasius adds, of course, that the ability to loose sin is the unique privilege of St. Peter (and his heirs), and therefore the Eastern bishops on their own could not exonerate Acacius, even if he were still alive.[130] The second argument is equally intriguing in that it reveals a potent Eastern retort to the Roman narrative of the schism. In short, Gelasius responds to the accusation that Acacius had been condemned by a single person (Pope Felix), rather than by a synod, which on the Eastern reckoning rendered the papal excommunication meaningless.[131] Gelasius attempts to deflect this charge by insisting that Council of Chalcedon had, for all intents and purposes, condemned Acacius in 451 (twenty years before he became patriarch) because he had communed with Peter of Alexandria, who was guilty of the heresy condemned by Chalcedon. Here, as elsewhere, Gelasius is at pains to make clear the link from Eutyches to Peter of Alexandria to Acacius. But it is only in this letter, *Epistle* 10, that we learn why such a connection is designed to do more than simply paint Acacius with the brush of Eutychian heresy—it is an attempt to deflect the charge that the See of Rome is operating beyond the bounds of its canonical jurisdiction.

On this point, it is equally important to note that *Epistle* 10 (in a form very similar to that of *Epistle* 26) further attests to the pro-Acacian party's belief that Acacius had not done anything contrary to the canons. Instead, they argued, it had been Pope Felix, followed by Gelasius, who had been operating beyond legitimate canonical authority. Whereas *Epistle* 26 fits well within the normal Gelasian rhetorical standards, *Epistle* 10 contains a fiery response to Faustus that incorporates the most assertive statement of Roman

canonical authority vis-à-vis other ecclesiastical centers of Gelasius' entire
corpus. In fact, *Epistle* 10 offers the most assertive claim to Roman privilege
in all of late antiquity! In paragraph 5, Gelasius responds directly to the
charge that Rome is acting beyond its canonical authority. He begins by
insisting that it is they, the pro-Acacian party, who are ignoring the canons,
because they have "refused to obey the first See, which is urging healthy and
right things."[132] That initial claim serves as the platform for a series of subsequent statements about Roman privilege, including

- "the whole Church has been entrusted to the examination of [the
  Roman] See."
- "[the Rome See] ought to judge the whole Church."
- "[the Rome See] cannot be judged by anyone."
- "a [Roman] verdict cannot be scrutinized by another [See]."
- "a [Roman] verdict can never be overturned by another [See]."[133]

Gelasius is at pains to make these points to Faustus because Faustus' experience in Constantinople would have almost certainly indicated that none of
these claims was actually true. In other words, it is precisely because the
Church in Constantinople and the emperor reject Roman privilege that
the schism continues. However much Gelasius might posture and protest,
the Roman Church has virtually no authority in the Eastern capital at the
very moment when Gelasius is making the most exaggerated claims to date
about that authority.

 While the escalation in Roman privilege is fascinating in and of itself,
perhaps the most intriguing element of these claims is that they occur in this
form only once in Gelasius' substantial correspondence and that the recipient
of these assertions is not the heretical emperor, an Eastern cleric, or any cleric
for that matter, but a member of the Roman Senate. Why, we might ask,
does Gelasius push this far only once? And why does he do so in a letter to a
senator who is serving the Ostrogothic king on an embassy to the East?
Who, exactly, is Gelasius hoping to persuade with these claims? Is it Faustus,
Patriarch Euphemius, or Emperor Anastasius? Or is it, perhaps, Faustus' senatorial colleagues, who would also have seen the papal letter?[134]

 Before, in conclusion, we assess the "audience" for whom this incarnation of the Petrine discourse was intended, it is worth noting that within
Gelasius' substantial corpus there are only three surviving letters to Eastern
clerics.[135] Gelasius sent *Epistle* 3 to Euphemius, patriarch of Constantinople,

Epistle 27 to the "bishops of the East" and *Epistle* 43 to the bishops of Syria. Each of these letters contains one or more characteristics of the papal discourse found elsewhere. The letter to Euphemius, for example, repeatedly refers to Rome as the "Apostolic See," the "first See" and the special relationship between Rome and St. Peter. The final paragraph, in fact, equates the orthodox confession of faith with the faith of Peter himself—a not-so-subtle attempt by Gelasius to assert dogmatic authority over his junior colleague in the East.[136]

Epistle 27 is the longest of the letters to Eastern bishops and includes a protracted narrative of the entire affair from a particularly Roman point of view. As in *Epistle* 10 and *Epistle* 26, Gelasius stresses the links between Acacius, Peter of Alexandria, and Eutyches. He insists that Acacius acted contrary to the canons when he vindicated Peter of Alexandria, because only the Apostolic See has the authority to absolve another bishop.[137] Gelasius then adds that Acacius was fully aware that Peter had been condemned by a Roman court when he chose to commune with him. So why, Gelasius asks, would Acacius have communed with Peter unless the patriarch of Constantinople had deliberately sought to sever communion with Rome, the Apostolic See?[138]

As elsewhere, Gelasius presents the error of the pro-Acacian party of the East (like the error of Acacius himself) as a failure to adhere to canonical and institutional structures—the error is never really framed as a dogmatic or heretical fault. Though he insists that he has no personal interest in international honors or privileges, Gelasius is unable to ignore that the decision to support Peter of Alexandria had been made (and was maintained) in full knowledge that the Roman Church had already condemned him.[139] The breach is thus a breach of communion with the primatial see of Christendom. In short, despite a rather weak protestation to the contrary, the sin of the Eastern Church is that it does not respect Roman privilege.[140]

Audience, Petrine Rhetoric, and Its Reception

The goal of this chapter has been to scrutinize the circumstances and methods by which Gelasius employed the Petrine topos to achieve his goals and, simultaneously, was enabled by the Petrine discourse to make the rhetorical choices he did. It has also been the objective of this chapter to assess, as best as possible, the extent to which Gelasius' domestic and international correspondents endorsed his ever-expanding view of Roman ecclesiastical privilege. Whereas previous scholarship has emphasized his international pretensions, focusing almost exclusively on the *Ad Anastasium*, this chapter began, quite deliberately, with an assessment of the limits of Gelasius' domestic authority. Our examination of the Lupercalia episode reveals the extent to which the pope was virtually helpless to disrupt a popular pagan ceremony—an especially embarrassing defeat because a priest was going to be a primary target of mockery in that particular year. But even more important, the affair underscores the extent to which the domestic oratories and *tituli* churches of the city's elite continued to provide a locus of Christian life and practice that remained, at least partially, beyond the bishop's control. Gelasius' repeated attempts to scrutinize the construction of new churches and to enforce more rigorous standards for ordination, in a sense, only confirm the limits of papal authority over Christian patronage and pastoral direction in suburbican Italy at the close of the fifth century.

The rehabilitation of former bishop Misenus provided an equally important glimpse into the limits of papal influence over the city's clergy. Through a careful analysis of the rhetorical structures of *Epistle* 30, we found that the effusive affirmations of Gelasius' authority function as a mask for the rather embarrassing absence of nearly 20 percent of the city's priests. Whatever Gelasius' motivation for rehabilitating Misenus and whatever the reasons for the clerical dissent at the council, *Epistle* 30 served as a post-event partisan account of the synod, designed to showcase a powerful and universally respected bishop who was simultaneously Vicar of Christ and Vicar of Peter.

Given Gelasius' domestic troubles and the rhetorical steps he and his staff took to conceal them, the pontiff's international posturing is all the more arresting. While it is in this context that Gelasius offers his boldest and most rhetorically sophisticated assertions of both Roman privilege and specifically the Petrine privilege, we should not lose sight of the fact that the emperor and the Eastern bishops posed no tangible threat to Gelasius' authority in Rome. The Roman Senate and clergy, however, provided daily reminders of the empirical disconnect between the assertions of international prestige that were sent abroad and the tangible limits of Gelasius' authority to effect change in the city of Rome itself. Or did they?

In other words, perhaps Gelasius' bold international claims were doubly intended (or even primarily intended) to provide a platform for displaying international relevance as a means to inspire local respect. Given Gelasius' overbearing rhetorical posture in the letter to Anastasius, it is difficult to believe that Gelasius ever expected this letter to heal the Acacian schism or to effect imperial subordination to the papacy. Instead, it is conceivable that Gelasius' Petrine posturing in the *Ad Anastasium* allowed the pontiff to assert for his domestic audience that foreign bishops and the emperor himself (Gelasius' "son") took their theological cues from the heir of St. Peter. Whatever role the *Ad Anastasium* may have played in Gelasius' Eastern diplomacy, it allowed the pontiff to conjure an illusion of international respect that no other domestic authority (lay or ecclesiastic) could equal.

This was possible in part because Gelasius' domestic audience could not possibly have understood how little attention foreign leaders (both lay and ecclesiastic) paid to Gelasius' Petrine bluster, at least until Faustus, one of Rome's leading senators, got a firsthand account of just how insignificant Gelasius was in the minds of the pro-Acacian Eastern clerics who governed the Church of Constantinople. Perhaps it is not so surprising after all that the most pronounced statements of international prestige—claims that no contemporary bishop outside of the Roman superjurisdiction would have accepted—were delivered not to a foreign ecclesiastic but to the very Roman senator who was about to return to the city and inform his peers of Gelasius' shocking lack of international standing. It is fascinating, indeed, that centuries later, it would be these very claims to singular authority that would come to dominate papal self-importance and self-identity.

CHAPTER 4

The Petrine Discourse in Theoderic's Italy and Justinian's Empire

Whatever Gelasius may have claimed with respect to the superiority of priestly authority to imperial authority, the sixth-century papacy rarely, if ever, enjoyed a position of privilege over the secular rulers of Italy or the empire. To that end, this chapter examines the continued interplay between the discursive possibilities available to papal actors through the Petrine discourse and the ways those actors employed the Petrine topos to their advantage. The chapter also seeks to understand the reception of Petrine claims from the vantage point of the discursive intersection of secular and ecclesial authority in sixth-century Italy. Here, as elsewhere, we find that the rhetorical use and expansion of the Petrine theme often tells us more about local crises (and secular investments in them[1]) than it does about the dynamics of international prestige or the influence of the papacy.

Whereas other chapters in this study examine the Petrine discourse largely from the perspective of a single author (considering, of course, the social, theological, and political conditions that helped to frame that author's concerns), this chapter will approach our topic from an altogether different vantage point. Here, we will examine the ways in which a variety of authors—authors with varying degrees of affiliation to the See of Rome—employed elements of the Petrine and papal narratives in the early decades of the sixth century. Very few of the texts under consideration in this chapter were, in fact, written by Roman bishops. But that did nothing to limit the range of rhetorical options linking Peter to Rome made possible by the Petrine discourse.

The chapter begins with an assessment of the so-called Laurentian schism, which began with the contested papal election between Symmachus and Laurentius in 498 and lasted until 506 or 507. While some attention is paid to the ways the contenders for Peter's chair sought or rejected Ostrogothic interference in the Roman Church, the section examines the significant expansion of the ways imagined narratives of a papal past were created to assert contemporary claims and mask contemporary humiliations. Through the creation of new literary forms and a targeted building program, the pro-Symmachian party was able to conjure a tale of papal sovereignty and innocence that helped to insulate it from its ecclesial competition and the threat of secular oversight.

The second half of the chapter examines the ways the emperor Justinian manipulated the See of Rome for his own purposes and surreptitiously employed the most ambitious rhetorical affirmations of Roman prestige for the purpose of gaining papal concessions. Whereas historians of many stripes have chronicled Justinian's engagement with the papacy, particularly in the context of the Fifth Ecumenical Council (Constantinople, 553), few have examined this relationship from the perspective of Justinian's use (or lack thereof) of Petrine language. To address this scholarly lacuna, we will look specifically at the ways in which imperial legislation from this period employs the rhetorical markers of papal self-promotion. What we will discover in this investigation is that the imperial government adopted papal and Petrine language for the very purpose of undermining papal sovereignty and asserting its own influence in Italy. In the end, both sections of the chapter suggest that the papacy in the sixth century, despite its many assertions to the contrary, rarely enjoyed in practice the authority it claimed to possess.

Peter, Theoderic, and Narrative Weapons in the "Laurentian" Schism

In the days after the death of Pope Anastasius II in 498, two men were elected pope by competing factions in the Roman clergy: the deacon Symmachus and the priest Laurentius. With partisan supporters resorting to mob violence, and neither candidate willing to yield to the other, both claimants agreed to have the matter resolved by the de facto secular authority of Italy, Theoderic, king of the Ostrogoths. Both Symmachus and Laurentius traveled to Ravenna in 499 and made their case to Theoderic.[2] The king determined that Symmachus should be recognized as the legitimate pontiff, arguing that he had been elected first and that he had greater support. The Laurentian

faction complained that Theoderic's verdict had been purchased—a claim
that has some scholarly support—but that accusation did not prevent a "confirmation" synod, held later in 499 in the basilica of St. Peter, which ratified Theoderic's verdict and offered Laurentius the See of Nuceria as a
consolation.[3]

When Theoderic visited Rome in the year 500, Symmachus joined the
Senate in greeting the Gothic ruler at the city's gates and escorted him on a
tour of the area, which included a stop at St. Peter's basilica.[4] Whatever
concord there may have been during the state visit, however, was dashed the
following year when a resurgent Laurentian faction complained to Theoderic
that Symmachus had celebrated Easter on the wrong date, that he had squan-
dered church property, and that he had improper relationships with women.[5]
Theoderic begrudgingly agreed to intervene and ordered both Symmachus
and Laurentius to Ravenna once more. En route to the Ostrogothic court,
Symmachus appears to have had second thoughts and, fearing that the
impending meeting was a trap, decided to ignore the summons and returned
to Rome. Upon his return, Symmachus took up residence inside the basilica
of St. Peter, which lay outside of the city itself on Vatican Hill, which was
on the western side of the Tiber River.[6] Symmachus may have been reduced
to living outside of the city's walls, but his control of St. Peter's basilica
would prove to be an important symbol in the propaganda war that ensued
between the pro-Symmachian and pro-Laurentian factions.

In the wake of Symmachus' retreat, Laurentius' supporters, most notably
among the senatorial class, lobbied the Ostrogothic court to take control of
the situation. Theoderic, in turn, determined to appoint Peter of Altinum as
a visitor to the Roman See, which some interpreters take to mean that the
king had effectively suspended Symmachus from office.[7] Peter arrived in
Rome in the spring 502 and, in his capacity as visitor, presided over the
baptism of Rome's catechumens for that Easter—an important sacramental
role for any city's bishop. The Symmachian and Laurentian documents, of
course, offer contradictory accounts of how and why Peter of Altinum came
to Rome, but whatever the circumstances of the visitation, the event stands
out as a glaring lacuna in the ever-growing narrative of papal sovereignty.[8]

Later in 502, two different synods sought to resolve the impasse—the
first was an intermittent gathering, beginning in the spring and lasting until
possibly October; the second was much quicker, likely occurring in November. The details of the two synods are difficult to decipher with any certainty,
but they are ancillary to our primary concern and need not detain us. For

our purposes, we can simply note that Symmachus is thought to have been injured attempting to traverse the city to attend the first meeting and, having returned to the shelter of St. Peter's, refused to try again.[9] Not knowing what to do, a large number of the Italian bishops who had assembled for the synod abandoned the cause and returned to their sees. Those that remained ultimately determined that they could not (or would not) judge a sitting bishop without his testimony, and decided that the case against Symmachus would be judged by God. In effect, this was an exoneration of Symmachus and a symbolic blow to the Laurentian cause. Under Symmachus' direction, a second synod was held in St. Peter's in November. Not surprisingly, this later synod absolved Symmachus of all charges and condemned Peter of Altinum's interference. It is noteworthy, however, that neither of these synods did anything to change the actual situation in Rome—Symmachus remained barricaded in St. Peter's across the Tiber, and Laurentius retained control of the Lateran and many of the city's churches, including a large portion of the *tituli* churches, which numbered twenty-nine at this time.[10] It was not until Theoderic ordered the Senate to return all of the city's churches to Symmachus in 506 or 507 that Laurentius lost his control of the city and its clergy.[11] What prompted Theoderic's change of heart is difficult to ascertain and remains a source for a great deal of scholarly speculation.

Interpreting the Schism and Theoderic's Role

The surviving evidence for the schism is fragmentary and contradictory. It is also polemical in nature. It is, therefore, not surprising that historians have offered such divergent interpretations of the causes for the schism. Some scholars, for example, believe that it was the consequence of and represents a debate within Rome about what policy should be pursued with respect to the Eastern Empire. The Roman Church had been isolated from the East since the tenure of Felix III, and it is generally believed that Pope Anastasius II had been willing to pursue a much more conciliatory policy than had either Felix or Gelasius. Thus, for scholars such as John Moorhead and Charles Pietri, the pro-Symmachian and pro-Laurentian factions (both of which comprised senatorial and clerical elements) reflect a division between the pro- and anti-Eastern constituencies in the city.[12]

An alternative thesis has been offered by Peter Llewellyn, who believes that the papal factions were primarily fueled by a clerical rivalry between the diaconal and priestly orders.[13] Apart from the fact that Symmachus had been a deacon and Laurentius a priest, Llewellyn argues that the priests would have been more sympathetic to Laurentius because they were the ones who inhabited the *tituli* churches and would have had the most to lose by the efforts to consolidate the Roman Church under the centralizing authority of a bishop in the Gelasian mold, as was Symmachus.[14] While Llewellyn may overstate the distance between the Roman bishop and the titular clergy, he does remind us that the *tituli* churches were not a geographic division of parishes by a centralized system but independent and self-contained units with their own traditions and practices.[15] It was for this reason, he believes, that the senatorial families to whom these *tituli* churches were often linked supported Laurentius and the priests rather than Symmachus.[16] The fact that Symmachus was a Sardinian, and not a Roman of Rome, only fueled senatorial antipathy toward the diaconal candidate.[17]

Perhaps the most inspired interpretation of the entire affair has been offered by Kristina Sessa. Rejecting all previous interpretations that sought to cast the schism as a division based on theological or imperial politics, Sessa argues instead that the controversy was a contestation over stewardship, succession, and clerical sexual discipline. "In short, the causes of the Laurentian schism were *domestic* and revolved primarily around debates over the ideal relationship between *oikonomia* and episcopal authority."[18] While that characterization does not account for all aspects of the dispute (e.g., the debate over the proper dating of Easter), it is a stunning and compelling reconsideration of the entire episode.

Scholars have, of course, offered additional explanations for the division.[19] Some, such as Thomas Noble, have sought to understand Theoderic's involvement in the matter. Given the stature of Theoderic in Italy and the increasing significance of the bishop of Rome in both Italian and international affairs, one would expect that there would have been a great deal of interaction between the Gothic ruler and the papacy. Instead, our surviving sources reveal a shocking lack of contact between them.[20] What is more, with respect to the Laurentian schism, Noble argues that there is very little evidence that Theoderic wished to be directly involved in the controversy.[21] Against those who have argued that Theoderic endorsed Symmachus in 499 because he wished to suppress pro-Eastern sentiment in Rome, Noble compellingly explains that the Ostrogothic ruler stood to gain little from a continuation of the Acacian schism in the period in question. If Theoderic had really sought to leverage the ecclesiastical dispute to his advantage, Noble maintains, he would have backed Laurentius, because that would have allied him with the majority of the city's senators.[22]

Whatever Theoderic's motivations, and despite the lack of surviving evidence to explain them, there is little denying that the Ostrogothic king was involved in the controversy at key points. This was a cause of much consternation for later papal biographers (such as the editors of the *Liber Pontificalis*). As we will see, the literary productions of the pro-Symmachian faction not only harnessed the Petrine topos more effectively than did the Laurentians, but they also did all they could to rebuke and/or erase the traces of secular interference from the narrative of papal sovereignty.

Papal Biography as a Narrative Weapon

At this juncture, it is perhaps necessary to recall the sage advice provided by Kate Cooper and Julia Hillner in their introduction to *Religion, Dynasty, and Patronage in Early Christian Rome*[23]—namely, that we should not view our surviving sources from this period as a pure excavation of the past, but rather as the evidence of past victors who won, in part, because they were able to develop new narrative "technologies" to promote the Roman episcopal institution as an autonomous entity free of imperial and Ostrogothic influence. Indeed, the vast majority of the surviving documents produced in the midst of the Laurentian schism reflect the factional interests of the partisans who created them.[24] The protracted schism witnessed an unprecedented pamphlet war between rival parties that offered competing narratives of the experience of Christians in Rome that stretched back decades, sometimes longer, in the hope of benefiting their cause in the present. It is in this context, in fact, that papal biography emerged and did so for the explicit purpose of producing "foundation" narratives that offered an unambiguous polemic—one that spoke primarily to contemporary concerns rather than the past lives and events that they purport to reflect.[25] These texts were designed, first and foremost, to mark difference—the difference between those on the side of the saintly popes of the past, especially St. Peter, and those not. While there was likely more to Symmachus' ultimate victory than the mere success of his marketing efforts, there is a striking difference in the degree to which his partisans, as opposed to Laurentius', sought to harness the Petrine topos in the pamphlet war that continued even after Symmachus' death. What is more, it was the pro-Symmachian texts, rather than the pro-Laurentian ones, that sought to backdate the authority of the Roman bishop vis-à-vis other Roman clerics and to shield him from any form of lay scrutiny (whether imperial, senatorial, or Ostrogothic).

The Liber Pontificalis

We have, of course, encountered the *Liber Pontificalis* in the previous chapters. And while we have engaged its narratives, we have not yet had reason to examine its origins. The prevailing scholarly opinion, in large part derivative of Louis Duchesne's nineteenth-century investigation, is that the *Liber Pontificalis* was produced in multiple stages, the oldest of which no longer survives but likely stems from the period around 530.[26] According to Duchesne, this first edition emerged as a part of the continuing literary battle to narrate the true causes, victims, and victors of the Laurentian schism. Specifically, Duchesne believed that the *Liber Pontificalis* sought to respond to the so-called *Laurentian Fragment*, a *vita* of Laurentius authored shortly after the death of Symmachus in 514, which was designed to portray Laurentius as the legitimate pontiff and victim of Symmachian scheming.[27] Not only does the *Liber Pontificalis* refute that position through its biography of Symmachus, but many of the other biographies of the late fifth- and early sixth-century popes in the text can also be viewed through the prism of the Laurentian/Symmachian conflict.[28] Despite its pro-Symmachian bias, however, this early edition of the *Liber Pontificalis* evinces an attempt by papal biographers in the years after the schism (as well as successive editions) to smooth over the bitterness of a previously divided Roman clergy and to do so by emphasizing the historic link between St. Peter and his successors.[29] We are so accustomed in the modern world to the narrative of Roman bishops standing in an ancient lineage back to St. Peter that we often neglect to appreciate how significant it is that the original author and editors of the *Liber* sought to make that very idea prominent in the consciousness of their Christian readers. Indeed, the *Liber* represents the first attempt by papal partisans to offer a cohesive narrative of papal history and importance through a string of biographies that began with Peter and continued to the then present.[30]

To emphasize that the *Liber*'s biographies, especially those of the Symmachian period, were designed to present a specific and purposeful narrative of the pro-Symmachian party, we might note that the text is extremely hostile to Symmachus' predecessor, Pope Anastasius II. It is generally assumed that

Anastasius had sought to reverse Gelasius' hard-nosed diplomacy toward the Eastern Church and that he was willing to compromise with the Acacians to bring the schism to an end.[31] The editors of the initial recensions of the *Liber Pontificalis* clearly did not share Anastasius' position and were so antagonistic in their biography of him that they declared that God had "struck him dead" for his secret diplomacy.[32] In contrast to the negative portrayal of the *Liber Pontificalis*, however, the authors of the *Laurentian Fragment* supported Anastasius' efforts. For example, the surviving text of the *Laurentian Fragment* actually begins halfway through a sympathetic biography of Anastasius, which differs significantly from the *Liber Pontificalis* presentation. The same section of the *Fragment* notes that the Acacian schism had "foolishly" divided the Church.[33]

Given the contentious context of its production, it is not surprising that the original author and subsequent editors of the *Liber Pontificalis* would include only those details of Anastasius' and Symmachus' life that supported their polemical needs, and that they would deliberately exclude additional details or contextual information that might compromise that position.[34] Thus, it is all the more interesting to see the ways the text attempts to make the most out of otherwise humiliating circumstances. For example, one way of reading the extraordinary number of ordinations attributed to Symmachus by the text is to understand that the contemporary Roman clergy were so in league with Laurentius that Symmachus needed to replace them. An alternative interpretation could suggest that the author/editor of the *Liber Pontificalis* wanted to advance the idea that it was necessary for Symmachus to perform so many ordinations because many clerics had been killed by the pro-Laurentian mobs instigated by evil senators.[35]

As in its presentation of Gelasius, the *Liber Pontificalis* emphasizes Symmachus' generosity to the poor and his patronage of church building projects.[36] Joseph Alchermes has noted that nearly half of Symmachus' entry in the *Liber Pontificalis* is devoted to his building projects.[37] Both Alchermes and John Moorhead keenly note that most of the building projects mentioned in the *Liber* have little to do with actual churches, and those that do are in the suburbs of Rome, rather than in the city itself. This distinction is typically explained by the fact that the Laurentians continued to control most of the churches within the city walls.[38] As noted, the one basilica Symmachus did have access to was St. Peter's, and he spent a great deal of effort to refurbish it. Symmachus added an episcopal residence, a sub-basilica, and eight oratories, as well as many expensive decorations throughout the structure.

Alchermes has noted that the Symmachian building program at St. Peter's did more than replicate the episcopal structures at the Lateran—it outdid them in both size and symbol.[39] The refurbishing of the oratories is particularly significant because it allowed Symmachus to perform large-scale baptisms at Easter, which in turn enabled him to fulfill a key ritualistic role as bishop, even if he was cut off from the basilica of St. Constantine, at that time the customary site for performing baptisms in Rome.

Although the *Liber* identifies several pontiffs of the fifth century who made expensive gifts to St. Peter's, only Leo and Symmachus are credited with improving and/or expanding the structure itself. As the basilica was his home base during the contested years of 501–507, it is quite logical that Symmachus would have taken an interest in it. But the pontiff's building program at St. Peter's certainly entailed more than a mere remodeling; it offered a dramatic symbol of the connection between the apostle and Symmachus' personal claim to Peter's throne. Not only did Symmachus reside at the site of Peter's relics, but he, and not Laurentius, was also responsible for providing a suitable shrine for those relics. The significance of that connection was not lost on the author/editors of the *Liber Pontificalis*, who stressed Symmachus' refurbishing of St. Peter's and thereby purposefully identified the otherwise controversial pontiff as one of the apostle's greatest patrons.

One final thing to note about the *Liber*'s presentation of Symmachus is its treatment of Theoderic. As noted, one of the key features of the *Liber Pontificalis* is its projection of papal sovereignty against all potential threats, especially secular ones. This is certainly true of the life of Symmachus, for whom the interference of Theoderic and his episcopal lackey, Peter of Altinum, had been great embarrassments. Whereas we know from other sources that Theoderic typically did not interfere in papal matters and at times was a strategic partner for the many popes who served during his tenure, the earliest recensions of the Symmachian biography in the *Liber* are quite strong in their condemnation of Theoderic, referring to him as a heretic and portraying his actions as uncanonical and unjust.[40] The same criticisms are shared in some (but not all) of the other papal biographies in the *Liber* from the era of Theoderic, especially the biographies of those popes who suffered the most from Theoderic's interference.[41] In this way, too, we see that the *Liber*'s author/editors produced and sustained a partisan memory of papal/Ostrogothic interaction—a revisionist narrative that stressed papal sovereignty against the realities of a more challenging experience.

The Symmachian Apocrypha

In addition to the *Liber Pontificalis*, which in later editions had institutional purposes beyond the immediate scope of the Laurentian-Symmachian stand-off, the pro-Symmachian party produced during the height of the controversy a number of imagined papal biographies that either related directly to the charges against Symmachus or hoped to insulate him further by offering legendary accounts that emphasized the authority and autonomy of Peter's successors. Although the stories are very different in content, they contain a series of interrelated theses concerning the inability of anyone (whether lay or ecclesiastic) to judge the bishop of Rome. They also offer specific justifications for many of the accusations recently lodged against Symmachus. Thus, the heroes of these papal biographies all serve as proxies for Symmachian interests and demonstrate a new form of papal rhetoric born in the traditions of the hegemonic claims of the Petrine topos. In recent years, the Symmachian forgeries have garnered increased scholarly attention, including a critical edition.[42] For our purposes, it will suffice to summarize some of the more pertinent texts and examine, in particular, their use of the Petrine theme.

The *Gesta Liberii*, for example, tells an apocryphal story of how Pope Liberius (352–366) was exiled from Rome by the heretical emperor Constantius.[43] When Easter approached and it was time for the pontiff to perform his annual baptism of catechumens, the citizens of Rome came to him on the outskirts of the city so he could perform the ritual in an Ostian cemetery. Not only does this text provide a "papal precedent" for performing baptisms outside of the city (as Symmachus was doing at St. Peter's), and claim that the orthodox catechumens of Rome would seek to be baptized by the authentic pope, it also emphasizes that Liberius had performed these baptisms on the very same site that St. Peter had performed baptisms, when he was the bishop of Rome. In other words, the *Gesta Liberii* carefully makes a narrative link between the baptisms of the historic Peter, a previously exiled but holy pope, and Symmachus who was at that time performing baptisms in the church that housed the relics of St. Peter. What is more, it would also be plausible to interpret the anti-Arian slurs against Constantius, the emperor who had exiled Liberius, as a condemnation of the "Arian" Theoderic, who was, in part, responsible, for Symmachus' exile across the Tiber.

In another of the Symmachian apocrypha, the *Synodi sinuessanae gesta*, we find a fictional tale of how Pope Marcellinus (296–304) had been brought to trial by a local synod for having offered incense to pagan idols during the

Diocletian persecution.[44] At the moment when the synod was about to pass judgment against the pope, a miraculous voice was heard by all to proclaim: *prima sedes non iudicabitur a quoquam*—"the first See will not be judged by anyone."[45] Here again, papal biography serves as a narrative weapon to insulate Symmachus from his enemies—namely the first synod of 502, which had been ordered by Theoderic to evaluate the charges against Symmachus. The biography invents the account of a divine voice proclaiming papal sovereignty because the reality of the present circumstances demonstrates just how limited Symmachus' authority really was.

In the *Constitutio Silvestri*, yet another narrative proxy for Symmachian concerns, we find a similar injunction, *nemo enim dijudicet primam sedam*—"no one, indeed, can judge the first See," which is designed to insulate the papacy from both secular and rival ecclesiastical interference.[46] In this case, the decree is put in canonical form, authorized by hundreds of bishops, Pope Sylvester, and the emperor Constantine. The text maintains that a cleric can be accused only by a peer (meaning a bishop can be accused only by another bishop, not by a priest or deacon) and that the pope can be accused by no one. The text also stresses the importance of celebrating Easter in unity and emphasizes the pope's role in determining the date of Easter. As with the other texts, these matters relate directly to Symmachian concerns and offer a counter-narrative to Laurentian accusations and Symmachian humiliations.[47]

In some cases, the narratives of the Symmachian apocrypha are so similar to the accusations against Symmachus that one wonders if they ever fooled anyone. The *Gesta de Xysti purgatione*, for example, notes that Pope Sixtus III (432–440) had been accused by wealthy Roman landowners of poorly managing church property and of having an adulterous affair with a nun.[48] In addition to the obvious connections to Symmachus' troubles, Kristina Sessa has made the important observation that this text in particular seeks to assert episcopal authority over the Roman *domus*. During the trial that exonerates Sixtus (a trial in which the emperor Valentinian III presides, accompanied by the entire Senate and clergy of Rome), the body of the council, once again, refuses to pass judgment on the *pontifex*. But more important, the bishop of Rome is made to be the emperor's proxy, to literally sit on his chair, and to serve as the city's leading moral and legally constituted authority in his absence.[49] All this, it would seem, at the expense of the Roman householders and their domestic churches.

Although several of the Symmachian apocrypha do not explicitly operate within the matrix of the Petrine discourse, we might say that they take its constitutive thesis as their starting point. In other words, the primary association embedded within the Petrine topos at this time was that the bishops of Rome, by virtue of being the heirs of Peter, were the uncontested ecclesiastical authorities—both in terms of orthodox teaching and Christian behavior. As ecclesiastical sovereigns, it is they who preserve the right to pass judgment on others; they cannot themselves be judged. The Symmachian apocrypha, even if they do not explicitly appeal to Peter, ultimately serve a similar purpose in asserting papal sovereignty. What makes these texts partisan within that pro-papal context is that they narrate the trials and tribulations of past papal sovereigns through thinly veiled comparisons to Symmachus' own troubles. But they always do so in a way that both reinforces papal autonomy and exonerates Symmachus.

Laurentian Martyrdoms and the Roman Households

The Symmachian faction, of course, was not the only one that resorted to the production of one-sided "foundation" narratives or biographies in the hopes of manipulating popular opinion. While far fewer of the pro-Laurentian texts survive, we do have enough material to make a few tentative observations with respect to their own application (or lack thereof) of the Petrine topos. What is perhaps the most significant aspect of this pro-Laurentian material, in fact, is that there is no direct appeal to or comparison with St. Peter.

The *Laurentian Fragment* stands out as the most directly affiliated text of Laurentian sympathy. As already noted, the text begins in medias res with a brief account of Anastasius' tenure before going on to chronicle the Symmachian/Laurentian split. The text is really more of a one-sided account of the schism than it is a biography of Laurentius and, in that regard, should not be considered a direct alternative to the *Liber Pontificalis*. While it is true that the text has a bias toward ending the Acacian schism (and thus might be considered pro-Eastern), that does not, in turn, make it hostile to Theoderic. In fact, it is far less hostile to the Ostrogothic king than the surviving pro-Symmachian texts (especially the *Liber*). What is perhaps the most intriguing aspect of the treatise for our purposes is that there is nothing within the text that could be remotely construed as an appeal to Petrine, or even a papal, authority. While there is hardly enough here (or among the other surviving pro-Laurentian sources) to draw any firm conclusions,[50] one wonders if the Laurentians simply did not avail themselves of the Petrine topos, even though they would likely have witnessed the Symmachians doing so. And if that is the case, one has to wonder why this is so.

In addition to the *Laurentian Fragment*, the pro-Laurentian faction produced additional biographical and foundational narratives to assist their cause. As noted in Chapter 1, Albert Dufourcq argued more than a century ago that many of the *Gesta martyrum*, in fact, were not penned as eyewitness accounts of the acts of the Roman martyrs (as they purport to be) but rather date to the Ostrogothic period and reflect the partisan concerns of that time.[51] Although the *Gesta martyrum* is notoriously difficult to navigate, Peter Llewellyn has drawn from the Dufourcq thesis to argue that several of the *Gesta* reflect an anti-episcopal, domestic orientation that would suggest that their authors were in league with the landowning secular elite and would, therefore, have favored Laurentius in the time of the schism.[52] Llewellyn's primary examples are the *Vita Pudentianae* and the *Vita Praxedis*, which he takes to be foundation narratives for domestic churches, in the guise of martyrdom accounts, whose purpose is to authenticate the churches' legal standing as independent of episcopal authority.[53] Not only do these texts offer a protracted defense of ecclesiastical sovereignty within the household (in a sense, a rejoinder to the diminution of household autonomy found in the *Gesta de Xysti purgatione*), but Llewellyn has shown that they may also offer a further critique of Symmachus' legitimacy by emphasizing the importance of celebrating Easter on the proper day (recall that one of the charges against Symmachus at the initial synod of 502 was that he had celebrated Easter on the wrong day).[54]

While it may be the exception rather than the rule that we can directly link the *Gesta martyrum* to the pro-Laurentian faction, it is certainly true that many of these texts emphasize the importance of a cult of legendary Roman martyrs, other than St. Peter, and that many of the titular churches and domestic chapels in the city owed their establishment to those cults. In some ways, then, we might see the papal promotion of the cult of Peter as an attempt to elevate the specific martyr cult that was most closely tied to its own ambitions. This did not necessarily mean the erasure of the other martyrs, but rather the subordination of their cults to the cult of St. Peter. And this is precisely what the *Liber Pontificalis* sought to achieve by fabricating a papal role in the creation and organization of the *tituli* churches.[55]

Laurentian Schism: Concluding Observations

In the church of St. Paul's in Rome, there is a gallery of papal portraits from the period of the Symmachian/Laurentian schism. It is worth noting that it is Laurentius, rather than Symmachus, who stands between Pope Anastasius II and Pope Hormisdas.[56] It is perhaps surprising that the portrait of Laurentius was never replaced. But whatever the reasons it survived the pro-Symmachian purge of Laurentian pretensions, the portrait provides a vivid testimony that the bishops of Rome in the early years of the sixth century never enjoyed the ecclesiastical or urban hegemony that they emphasized with their rhetoric and their supporters promoted through partisan biographies.

Symmachus may have spent nearly half his tenure barricaded across the Tiber in the basilica of St. Peter, but it was from there, the locus of Peter's cult, that he and his supporters developed new ways to support his claim of a link to the historic Peter. It was in this context that papal biography and the *Liber Pontificalis* gained momentum. Although later editors and propagandists might try to have it otherwise, this was not part of an ambitious program to extend papal influence abroad, to remedy the Acacian schism, or to subordinate an Arian Theoderic to an orthodox pope. It was done because Symmachus' very survival, perhaps literally, certainly symbolically, depended on a demonstration of legitimacy only the cult of St. Peter could provide.

In the decades that followed, Symmachus' successors would suffer an endless series of humiliations at the hands of the secular rulers of the Roman world. In one famous episode, Theoderic forced Pope John I (bishop of Rome 523–526) to lead an embassy to Constantinople in the hopes of ending the persecution of Arians in the East.[57] Although the Roman emperor Justinian was in large part responsible for allowing the Acacian schism to end on papal terms (including an official condemnation of Acacius and the emperor Zeno),[58] during the course of his long reign Justinian interfered even more directly than Theoderic had in papal affairs. He imprisoned uncooperative pontiffs, replaced them with hand-selected candidates, and forced the Roman Church to accept unpopular theological positions, such as the *Theopaschite Formula* and the condemnation of the *Three Chapters*. Even a cursory examination of the entries of popes John, Agapetus, Vigilius, and Pelagius in the *Liber Pontificalis* reveals that the patterns of narrative embellishment and pro-papal editorial bias established during the Laurentian crisis continued as a

means of counteracting and rewriting a history of humiliation and subordination to the secular authorities. If there was anything that the papal propagandists learned during the Symmachian/Laurentian schism, it was how the
production of papal biographies, especially those that could be carefully
linked to St. Peter, were an effective means of maintaining a narrative of
papal hegemony in the face of empirical evidence to the contrary.

Justinian's Peter and His Regard for the Papacy

Now we will examine the Petrine discourse from yet another perspective—
namely by investigating the ways the Petrine discourse made possible the
imperial court's use of the Petrine topos for its own benefit. We will also
examine the ways in which Roman ecclesiastical authority was acknowledged
but manipulated by the court. As we will see, the Roman emperor Justinian
(527–565), perhaps the most significant Roman emperor after Constantine,
endorsed the rhetorical claims of the See of Rome but, like many secular
authorities before him, did so to advance his own causes.[59] Whereas previous
studies have chronicled the long and sordid history of Justinian's exploitation
of the mid-sixth-century popes, we will focus our attention solely on the
ways Justinian's imperial legislation incorporated or ignored Roman claims
to jurisdictional authority. This examination shows that Justinian's legislation
affirms the papacy's most ambitious claims and simultaneously undermines
those claims—an ambivalence that raises fundamental questions about the
way Christians outside Rome understood Roman ecclesiastical authority at
the close of late antiquity and the extent to which others were able to leverage
the legacy of Petrine privilege to their own ends.

The Absence and Presence of Peter in the Justinianic Codex

The *Corpus juris civilis* is the modern name we apply to the massive collection
and codification of previous Roman laws commissioned by the emperor Justinian in 529 and likely completed around 534. For generations of scholars,
the *Corpus juris civilis* has served as one of the most important collections of
source material for the study of the late Roman/early Byzantine interaction
between an ascendant Christian Church and the Roman state.[60] The *Novellae*, or "new laws," issued mostly by Justinian himself, are especially illustra-
tive of the emperor's conception of diarchy, a system in which church and

state constitute two distinct but overlapping spheres of authority.[61] This same material provides critical evidence for both the ambiguity and flexibility of imperial attitudes toward papal jurisdictional claims vis-à-vis other episcopal powers.[62] In fact, the Justinianic legislation provides unparalleled access to the way the sixth-century relationship between the Roman Church and other leading ecclesiastical centers (especially the See of Constantinople) was understood by the imperial officials who authorized ecclesiastical legislation, and who, not incidentally, knew that in certain situations they might need to incorporate in their legislation either the claims of the Roman Church or those of its regional competitors to ensure that specific laws would be accepted and disseminated according to imperial designs. As such, the *Corpus* offers a prime source for scholars who wish to understand how late ancient Christians living beyond the immediate reach of the Roman bishop understood papal jurisdictional claims.

A cursory reading of the *Corpus juris civilis* suggests a convoluted and ambiguous view of the institutional organization of the Christian world: in some often-cited instances, the Roman Church is afforded the privileges that its most vocal advocates claimed—Rome is described as the "head of the Church" and it is the only see to be characterized as "Apostolic."[63] Elsewhere, Rome is presented as little more than one of several regional centers united under the umbrella of the imperial *oikoumenē*.[64] Perhaps most surprising, however, is the fact that the See of Rome is typically ignored by the Justinianic legislation altogether. Of the twenty-one *Novellae* that touch on ecclesiastical matters, the See of Rome is mentioned explicitly in only four.[65] It is with this final point—the absence of Rome in the *Novellae*—that we begin before going on to consider how and why the *Corpus* employs Petrine language to affirm Roman jurisdictional claims. I believe that this ambivalence provides an important contextual framework to help us understand the See of Constantinople's designation as the "Ecumenical Patriarchate," in the same legislation.

THE ABSENCE OF ROME AND PETER

The *Novellae* are distinguished from the rest of Justinian's legislation in that they represent new laws, often reforms or clarifications of previous laws, issued by the emperor in the years following the compilation of the *Institutes, Digest,* and *Codex*. The *Novellae* were never published as a uniform body of legislation, and with only a few exceptions they were issued in Greek, whereas the rest of the *Corpus* was promulgated in Latin.[66] Twenty-one of the 134

Novellae that date to Justinian's reign touch on ecclesiastical matters. Of these, the great majority seem to have been prompted by concerns or abuses evident in Constantinople, which by this time had served as the center of the Roman Empire for more than two hundred years. Indeed, nine of the ecclesiastical *Novellae* are addressed to the patriarch of Constantinople himself, whereas only one is addressed to the bishop of Rome; most of the remainder are addressed to civil magistrates.[67] Despite their local origins, however, most of the ecclesiastical *Novellae* claim empire-wide jurisdiction,[68] and, on a few occasions, individual laws instruct regional metropolitans, archbishops, and patriarchs to disseminate the new legislation throughout the churches in their jurisdictions.[69] While it is not surprising that the majority of the ecclesiastical *Novellae* were prompted by concerns in the East, what is surprising is that the See of Rome is typically omitted from the dispatch lists contained in the epilogues of these new laws.

For example, *Novella* 6, which regulates the election of bishops and the ordination of priests and monks, is addressed to Epiphanius, patriarch of Constantinople. The first epilogue states that "the patriarch of every diocese" is to safeguard the regulations of the *Novella*; none of the individual patriarchs or their sees are named.[70] A second epilogue chronicles the international figures who were to receive a copy of the law. This list includes the archbishops of Alexandria, Antioch, and Jerusalem (in that order)[71] and two civil magistrates: John, a praetorian prefect (whose province is not defined), exconsul, and patrician, and Dominicus, the praetorian prefect of Illyricum. According to Schoell and Kroll, the law dates to April 535, when Pope John II, a supporter of Justinian's *Theopaschite Formula*, would still have been alive. *Novella* 6 is often identified as one of the most important of the ecclesiastical reforms because it includes Justinian's famous distinction between "divine things" and "human things," as well as the emperor's examination of the two heavenly gifts: priesthood and empire (i.e., this law, as much as any, promotes the Justinianic model of diarchy).[72] It is, in fact, intriguing to consider the possibility that this *Novella* was designed to counter Gelasius' *Ad Anastasium* (now more than forty years old), which had sought to subordinate imperial authority to priestly. One possible explanation for why Rome is not included in the distribution list, in fact, would be that *Novella* 6 provides the legal basis for an imperial role in the affairs of the Church, and could have been interpreted as a challenge to the then well-established papal narrative, most famously articulated in Gelasius' letter.[73] But whatever the reason, the absence of Rome from the distribution list of such an important *Novella* is quite remarkable.

We must consider, of course, whether or not the infrequency of *Novellae* addressed to the See of Rome, and the absence of the See of Rome from the distribution lists of other *Novellae*, represent an ecclesiastical snub or simply reflect the current political disjuncture.[74] At the start of Justinian's sole rule in 527, the Italian Peninsula was still governed by the Ostrogoths from Ravenna. That situation changed, of course, with Justinian's invasion of Italy in 535 (the same year as *Novella* 6). Although Justinian's troops were in Rome by December 536, the suppression of the Goths was quite slow, and much of Italy remained a battlefield for the remainder of the emperor's reign.[75] Is it possible that the Roman Church was excluded from the surviving distribution lists of the ecclesiastical *Novellae* because the city of Rome was not consistently under imperial control?

To answer this question, we might begin with a consideration of the four *Novellae* that were sent to Rome. The earliest were *Novella* 9, which affirms the property rights of the Roman Church, and *Novella* 42, which deposes Anthimus of Constantinople by quoting Agapetus' condemnation of him. Both of these *Novellae* date to the short period between the imperial invasion of Sicily in 535 and the successful capture of Rome in December 536.[76] One might conclude that these two *Novellae*, both of which promote Roman ecclesiastical privilege, reflect a direct attempt by Justinian to secure papal support for his military designs in Italy. Claire Sotinel, for example, has argued that many Italian aristocrats were lukewarm about Justinian's impending invasion, preferring Ostrogothic rule.[77] If she is correct, then *Novella* 9 and 42 could suggest that Justinian was deliberately promoting Roman ecclesiastical claims as a quid pro quo to lobby for Agapetus' support.[78] Such concrete political concerns could certainly explain why these two *Novellae*, unlike so many others, were sent directly to Rome and why the privileges of the Roman See feature so prominently in them. Following the same logic, one might explain the omission of Rome from the distribution list for the ever-important *Novella* 6 as a deliberate attempt by Justinian to avoid conflict with the pope at roughly the same time. In other words, to the extent that *Novella* 6 might seem to curtail papal power in favor of balancing it with imperial authority,[79] one might argue that Justinian circulated his mandate on diarchy only among those churches closer to home.

Novella 123 and 131 (the only other *Novellae* that we know with certainty to have been sent to Rome), however, do not provide the same type of corroboration. Both of these later *Novellae* date to the mid-540s. Although that period was also a time of great military uncertainty in Rome (the city changed hands between the Gothic and imperial armies several times), there is no way to link the dissemination of either *Novella* to Justinian's political interests in Italy. More to the point, *Novella* 123 and *Novella* 131, likely Justinian's most famous ecclesiastical laws, served as direct challenges to specific papal claims. As we will see, *Novella* 123 provides the legal mandate for the ecclesiological concept of Pentarchy, which divided the administration of the Church into five autonomous jurisdictions, directly undermining Roman claims to universal appellate authority. And even though *Novella* 131 did incorporate some Roman rhetorical claims to preeminence, it simultaneously described the See of Constantinople as equal to Rome in ecclesiastical rank—hardly an effective way to court papal favor.

In the end, it would seem that there are at least four reasons the political isolation of Rome cannot, on its own, explain the neglect of Roman ecclesiastical concerns in the *Novellae*. First, whatever the realities of the troubled Gothic-imperial alliance in the early sixth century, Justinian never let the political snares of Italy stand in the way of his inclusion of the Roman See in ecclesiastical controversies when he felt that it would be beneficial to his interests. For evidence of this, we need look no further than his efforts to employ the authority of Pope John II in 533–534 to endorse the *Theopaschite Formula* or his leveraging of Pope Agapetus to dismiss the intractable Anthimus in 536.[80] Second, at no time did Justinian allow the situation in Italy to scuttle his attempts to bring the leading sees of Christendom into communion with one another. It was with Justinian's assistance, for example, that his uncle, Justin I, ended the thirty-five-year Acacian schism in 519. That Justin and Justinian forced the Eastern Church to accept Roman conditions for rapprochement can be taken as evidence that Justinian was committed to ecclesiastical union, even with sees beyond the realistic borders of the empire.[81]

Third, even after Rome tentatively returned to the imperial fold in 536, there was not a single *Novella* addressed to Rome, nor was there a significant increase in the number of *Novellae* that are identifiable as having been distributed to Rome. Indeed, of Justinian's twelve ecclesiastical *Novellae* issued after December 536, only *Novellae* 123 and 131 include Rome on their distribution lists. As noted, these are likely the two most significant of all the ecclesiastical *Novellae*, and we can reasonably assume that they would have been distributed to Rome, whether imperial or Gothic armies controlled the city.

Finally, it is worth noting that Justinian's famous Pragmatic Sanction, which was brought to Italy by Pope Vigilius in 554 and was intended to (re)assert Roman law over the Italian Peninsula following a major victory over the Goths, claimed that Italian authorities had received both the *Codex* and the *Constitutions* at the same time as every other region of the empire and that those laws had been in effect ever since.[82] That Justinian needed to issue the sanction suggests that most of Italy had likely been operating independently of the imperial government and therefore needed to be reminded of certain things. Nevertheless, the Pragmatic Sanction provides further evidence that Justinian believed the Church of Rome to be a part of the broader institutional Church and that it was subject to all laws of the empire.

In short, the absence of imperial *Novellae* addressed to the Church of Rome and the absence of Rome from the explicit distribution list of other empire-wide ecclesiastical reforms is startling. We might simply conclude that Rome, despite its own claims of self-importance (and Justinian's occasional exploitation of those claims), was too far removed from imperial concerns to receive the same measure of attention as the Church of Constantinople. It would also seem that it was only when Justinian needed the assistance of the bishop of Rome directly or when he was distributing the most important of his ecclesiastical reforms that he made certain to inform the Roman See of new laws governing the Church.

The Subordination of Rome

In addition to being directly ignored by the *Novellae*, the interests of the Roman See are sidelined in the *Corpus* in other ways as well—namely in those cases where the promotion of the rights of other individuals or their sees would have been seen as an infringement on the narrative of Roman and Petrine privilege. For example, some scholars have interpreted *Novella* 11's promotion of Justinian's hometown in Dacia, renamed Justiniana Prima, from a local diocese to an autonomous archdiocese, as a direct affront to Roman claims.[83] Prior to the promulgation of *Novella* 11 in 535, Justiniana Prima was a minor diocese in the Metropolitanate of Thessalonica, which was at that time a papal vicarage.[84] As noted in previous chapters, Rome had for many years owned property and asserted its authority throughout Illyria and Dacia.[85] Its influence in Thessalonica, no doubt, proved valuable in its interaction with the churches of the region. *Novella* 11 acknowledges that the advancement of the See of Justiniana Prima would come at the expense of the Metropolitanate of Thessalonica, but there is no reference in the legislation to the See of Rome, or to the fact that Thessalonica was a papal vicarage.[86]

Novella 123, the most explicit statement of the Pentarchy in the Justinianic *Corpus*, could also be viewed as an affront to traditional Roman claims. As noted in previous chapters, beginning in early fifth century, the bishops of Rome consistently claimed appellate authority to review the case of any cleric condemned anywhere in the Christian world. The basis for this claim was rooted in the canons of the Council of Serdica, which Roman scribes had combined with the canons of the Council of Nicaea since the early fifth century. Justinian's *Novella* 123, however, offers an implicit rejection of the so-called Serdican privilege. According to chapter 22 of *Novella* 123, the ecclesiastical world is divided among five autonomous jurisdictions, each headed by its own patriarch (i.e., Rome, Constantinople, Alexandria, Antioch, and Jerusalem).[87] Each patriarch provides a court of appeal for clerics condemned by lower episcopal bodies within their mega-jurisdiction. Chapters 23 and 24 affirm similar decrees in slightly revised forms. *Novella* 123 does not provide for an appellate system between the patriarchates, and there is not a single specific mention of Rome in chapters 22–24.[88] In short, *Novella* 123 rejects Rome's super-jurisdictional judicial oversight, which had emerged from and grown steadily since the tenure of Pope Innocent I.[89]

It is *Novella* 131 (dating to April 545), however, that makes the most explicit statement about the relationship between the ecclesiastical centers of Rome and Constantinople. Chapter 2 reads:

> Hence, in accordance with the provisions of these [ecumenical] councils, we order that the most holy Pope of ancient Rome shall hold the first rank of all priests, but the most blessed Archbishop of Constantinople, or new Rome, shall occupy the second place after the Holy Apostolic See of ancient Rome, which shall take precedence over all other sees.[90]

To be sure, *Novella* 131 grants legal standing to the most foundational of papal claims—that the See of Rome holds first rank. It also acknowledges that this primatial status had been upheld by the ecumenical councils. Nevertheless, the same text includes two elements that the bishops of Rome in this period fundamentally rejected.

The first objectionable point is the insinuation, implied in the language of "ancient" and "new," that both the See of Rome and the See of Constantinople derive their ecclesiastical primacy from the imperial structure (the See of Rome has primacy because Rome was the ancient capital; the See of Constantinople has second-place status because it is New Rome, the new capital). Since the early fourth century, the bishops of Rome had grown increasingly concerned about the movement of the capital to the East and had, since that time, contrasted the apostolic credentials of the See of Rome with the far less significant imperial credentials of the See of Constantinople.[91]

The second objectionable point in this passage from *Novella* 131 is the second-place status afforded to Constantinople. As noted in Chapter 2, Leo refused to acknowledge Canon 28 of the Council of Chalcedon, which had afforded second-place status to Constantinople and effectively demoted the "Petrine" Sees of Alexandria and Antioch.[92] Even before Leo, Pope Damasus had refused to acknowledge Canon 3 of the Council of Constantinople (381), which, like Chalcedon, had attempted to grant second-place status to the new imperial capital. Thus, *Novella* 131 directly affirms previous conciliar decisions despite persistent objections from Rome.

In short, whereas *Novella* 131 might at first sight appear to be a direct affirmation of Roman claims, it was, equally, a humiliation. Despite the repeated Roman claim that it was apostolicity and not imperial affiliation that determined the pecking order of regional churches, *Novella* 131 effectively added the weight of imperial law to the See of Constantinople's claim to second rank after Rome.

THE PROMOTION OF ROME AND PETER

How then are we to understand the affirmation of Rome's first-rank status in *Novella* 131 and other examples of Roman privilege in the Justinianic *Corpus* when they do occur? The most explicit affirmation of Roman authority exists in Book I of the *Codex* and relates directly to the Theopaschite controversy, which came to a head in 534. The *Codex* preserves four sequential texts (I.1.5–8) that affirm Justinian's *Theopaschite Formula*: "one of the Trinity suffered on the Cross." The first, second, and third articles all relate to the emperor's promotion of the formula in the East and need not concern us.[93] The final article, however, presents itself as a legally binding correspondence between Pope John II and Justinian (the text in question is a letter from John to Justinian but includes lengthy quotations from a previous missive from Justinian to John). The reason that the letter is included in the *Codex* is because it grants papal sanction to Justinian's formula.

John's acceptance of the Justinianic doctrine is itself significant, because it was a reversal of previous papal policy and has, for that reason, been read by a number of historians as a capitulation to imperial desires.[94] Perhaps it was in anticipation of the charge of capitulation that Pope John so forcefully asserts papal sovereignty throughout the letter. As we have seen in so many instances before this, the bishops of Rome and their allies consistently hid anything that might be construed as papal weakness behind a mask of rhetorical strength. In this particular case, Pope John had to have known that he was changing papal policy on the *Theopaschite Formula* (Pope Hormisdas openly opposed it) in accordance with the emperor's wishes.[95] But his letter states counterfactually that the formula had always been taught in Rome.[96]

If this interpretation of Pope John's posturing is correct, it was not the only example of rhetorical performance contained within this brief correspondence. As David Olster has argued, what distinguishes the Justinianic elements of the correspondence from the previous three edicts (articles 5–7) is a clear rhetoric of deferential submission to John's authority in ecclesiastical matters.[97] Not only does Justinian repeatedly affirm that Rome is "the head of all the holy churches,"[98] but the emperor also states that his court has worked to "unite all of the priests of the East and subject them to the authority of the [pope]."[99] Later the emperor affirms that the unity that binds the Holy Apostolic Church originates in Rome, through the office of the pope.[100]

Despite the *Codex*'s explicit assertions that Christian unity originates from the bishop of Rome, Milton Anastos has emphasized that the fragments from Justinian's letter that remain embedded in the law also contain implicit threats to the continuation of papal authority.[101] According to Anastos, Justinian slyly affirms that the "unity of all the churches will be preserved undamaged *as soon as* the most blessed bishops learn from [the pope]" his opinion in this matter.[102] In effect, Justinian suggests that the only acceptable papal opinion is the one that has been presented to him. Sotinel, who leans more toward Anastos' interpretation than Oster's, also notes that the letter from Justinian, although employing a certain rhetoric of papal prestige, does not abandon the emperor's position over the Church because it effectively asks the pope to consent to a formula that has already been produced rather than to state one out of whole cloth.[103]

Whether John understood Justinian's letter to be a threat or not, two things are certain: (1) Pope John affirmed the *Theopaschite Formula* against papal precedent, and (2) he used the correspondence as an opportunity to assert precisely what he saw as his authority within the Church. Specifically, John claims that Rome's authority over the other sees is an ancient right, repeatedly affirmed by the fathers of the Church and by previous imperial edicts.[104] Even if Anastos and Sotinel are correct that *Codex* I.1.8 contains a veiled affirmation of imperial sovereignty in ecclesiastical matters, it is important to note that the inclusion of the correspondence between pope and emperor in the *Codex* explicitly gave the imperial stamp of approval to a self-aggrandizing rhetoric of Roman authority vis-à-vis other ecclesiastical centers and did so because Justinian clearly wanted papal recognition for his policy. The inclusion of Pope John's letter in the *Codex*, therefore, must be read as something of a papal victory. And, as a consequence, we ought to reconsider the reasons Justinian was complicit in that papal victory.

On this score, I would submit that Justinian's appropriation of the rhetoric of Roman privilege should not necessarily be understood as his endorsement of a specific ecclesiological view but, instead, might reflect the emperor's willingness to do whatever was necessary to build a theological consensus for the *Theopaschite Formula*. From the emperor's perspective, catering to the rhetorical claims of Roman ecclesiastical authority in order to gain support for the formula was simple enough—especially when he already had the leaders of the Eastern Church solidly committed to it.

Moreover, Justinian's willingness to endorse Roman rhetorical claims was likely reinforced by the correspondence's direct coincidence with the invasion of North Africa, which was a critical preliminary step for an invasion of Italy. If it is true that Italian aristocrats were divided as to whether or not they would support that endeavor, it would have been vital for the emperor to secure the support of the Roman pontiff before an invasion. Thus, it is plausible that Justinian would be willing to adopt the rhetoric of Roman ecclesiastical prestige in order to secure papal support for his expansionist plans.[105]

There is one final observation to make regarding *Codex* I.1.8. Despite the unreserved endorsement of papal claims contained within it, neither component of the article (i.e., Justinian's abridged letter to John, John's letter to Justinian) actually uses Petrine language to assert these claims, apart from the rather vague identification of the See of Rome as the "apostolic" See. It is difficult to reckon why this is so. Certainly John was able to convey many of the boldest of Roman claims without rhetorical reference to the Petrine topos—including the assertion that his see is the head of all the churches and that it was he who authorized theological teaching. But it is nonetheless surprising that his letter (if, in fact, we have the entire letter) did so in an era in which Petrine language was increasingly employed to assert Roman claims.

There are very few explicit appropriations of Petrine language in the Justinianic legislation. But at least one of those examples occurs in a very prominent place—in the first sentence of the *Codex*. Indeed, Book I of the

Codex affirms that the Roman Empire is a Christian empire, rooted in the belief of the Trinity (anyone who does not believe in the Trinity as defined by law is marked as "demented" and "insane").[106] The first law included in the *Codex*, in fact, is a rescript from the Eastern and Western emperors Theodosius (379–395) and Gratian (375–383) that famously outlawed all religious practices other than orthodox (i.e., Trinitarian) Christianity. The law declares: "we desire that all of the subjects of our rule should practice that religion that the divine Peter the apostle gave to the Romans, as the religion which he introduced makes clear to this day. It is evident that this is the religion that is practiced by the pontiff Damasus and by Peter, bishop of Alexandria, a man of apostolic discipline."[107]

The sentence is a dramatic example of the extent to which the constitutive elements of the Petrine discourse had permeated the Christian consciousness as early as the late fourth century, when the law was originally promulgated.[108] Not only is Peter responsible for introducing Christianity to the Roman Empire, but he is also said to have "introduced the faith" altogether. In this way, we see the "totalizing" dimension that the Petrine discourse makes possible. What is more, Pope Damasus is singled out, alongside Peter of Alexandria, as offering a testimonial that the faith of the Apostle Peter is still the faith that is believed more than three hundred years later.[109]

To understand the logic behind the claims of the original law, it is important that we not read it anachronistically. Indeed, the rhetorical punch behind the Petrine claim does not lie with the promotion of the Roman See but with the contention that the faith of the co-emperors (as represented in their legislation) is consistent with the faith of St. Peter. As was the case in 451, when the chorus of delegates at Chalcedon is reputed to have proclaimed that "Peter has spoken through Leo," here too the appropriation of Petrine language was designed to grant apostolic credibility to a specific and contentious theological position. In other words, its purpose was to authenticate the orthodoxy of the emperors and their policies; it did not explicitly advance the See of Rome.

However the law might have been understood in the late fourth century, by the mid-sixth century the use of Petrine language in the context of Trinitarian orthodoxy and the proximity of the Petrine claim to a papal figure like Damasus could have elicited different readings. To be sure, it may be that Justinian privileged the law and retained its original language because he, like Theodosius before him, simply wanted to authenticate his own orthodoxy via Peter. It may also be the case, however, that Justinian perceived that the

ever-developing discursive association between Peter and the papacy could
also offer an additional degree of authenticity for his own cause. While we
might not wish to make too much of this text (unlike *Codex* I.1.8, it was not
a Justinianic creation but simply included in the *Codex* by Justinian's legal
experts), it is nonetheless significant that the very first line of a lengthy document that seeks to define the precise vision of Justinian's Trinitarian orthodoxy does so on the basis of a Petrine claim.

Finally, it is worth noting that the most thorough appropriations of
Roman ecclesiastical rhetoric, whether Petrine or otherwise, in the *Corpus* are
contained in the *Codex* and date to a period early in Justinian's reign and
before the invasion of 535. For example, none of the ecclesiastical *Novellae*
describe papal privilege as robustly, although *Novella* 9 does make a quick
reference to the "venerable See of Peter," and *Novellae* 42 and 131 certainly
attest to a form of Roman primacy. In fact, the *Novellae* appear to undermine
the contemporary claims of papal super-jurisdictional authority. And, as we
will see, the same *Novellae* actively promote the ecumenical title, which by
the end of the century would be viewed as a direct affront to Petrine privilege.

Constantinopolitan Humiliation and the Ecumenical Title

The earliest surviving evidence of the title "Ecumenical Patriarch" being
applied to the patriarch of Constantinople is a letter from the clergy in Antioch to John II of Constantinople dating to 518.[110] In the same year, two
regional synods in the East also referred to John as "Ecumenical Patriarch."[111]
By the end of the century, the patriarchs of Constantinople began to include
the title in the signature of their official correspondence. What little scholarly
attention has been given to the emergence of this title has focused almost
exclusively on the debate between Pope Gregory I and Patriarch John IV,
which occurred at the end of the sixth century and will be examined in the
next chapter.[112] What scholars have essentially ignored is that the title
emerged in the East at nearly the precise moment that the See of Constantinople was suffering its greatest international humiliation of the late ancient
period—the public acknowledgment that it and its leaders had been in error
throughout the thirty-five-year Acacian schism.[113] Indeed, the Church of
Constantinople had to remove the name of Patriarch Acacius from its dip-
tychs (i.e., its official records). While there is no direct evidence that the

ecumenical title surfaced as a deliberate strategy to rehabilitate the international prestige of the Constantinopolitan Church, the timing is noteworthy.
Just as the Roman bishops cultivated the Petrine discourse to mask humiliation and advance hegemonic claims, so too the Church of Constantinople
would learn to develop its own rhetorical traditions and apostolic narratives—in the form of the cult of St. Andrew—to protect its interests. Indeed,
any plausible explanation for why individual patriarchs would promote the
title at this time must relate in some way to their ever-increasing competition
with the See of Rome.[114] But why, we might ask, was Justinian willing to
endorse the ecumenical title through imperial legislation, and what might
that say about his view of papal authority?

Each of the nine *Novellae* addressed to the patriarch of Constantinople
describes him as the "Ecumenical Patriarch,"[115] as do the specific regulations
of two additional *Novellae*, addressed to civil magistrates.[116] The title is also
incorporated a few times in Book I of the *Codex*, including the very first
mention of the patriarch of Constantinople found in Book I (I.1.7).[117] In
short, the Justinianic legislation defines the patriarch of Constantinople by
means of the title "Ecumenical Patriarch" at nearly every opportunity.

The primary reason that the title became a source of contention in the
latter part of the sixth century (and has remained a matter of dispute down
to the present day) is because the actual meaning of the title and the privileges
that it conveys are notably slippery. Technically, the noun *oikoumenē* means
"the inhabited earth." Byzantine political propaganda, drawing from Roman
models, understood the borders of the empire to constitute the "inhabited
earth." Given this context, it might be possible to understand the adjectival
form, *oikoumenikos*, as a synonym for "imperial," because the "inhabited
earth" was the empire. Knowing that Justinian's ecclesiastic policies, diverse
as they may have been, were based on a vision of a single imperial church,
the temptation is to read *oikoumenikos* as "imperial." Such an interpretation
would conform to a long-standing Western historiographic tradition that
views Justinian as a Caesaro-papist who subordinated the church to the
state.[118] Thus, one might easily conclude that Justinian endorsed the ecumenical title because he wanted a single "imperial" patriarch at the head of
the Church—ideally one located in Constantinople, rather than Rome,
who could be hand-selected and easily "persuaded" to support imperial
concerns.[119]

This interpretation, however, is not without problems. Perhaps the most
important reason to resist eliding *oikoumenikos* with "imperial" stems from

an observation of the way that the sixth-century Latin scribes handled the Greek term. The *Codex*, officially promulgated in Latin, employs a transliteration of the Greek word: *oecumenicus*. More significant, however, is that the Latin translations of the Greek *Novellae* (as noted above, unlike the rest of the *Corpus*, most *Novellae* were issued in Greek) typically rendered the Greek *oikoumenikos* as *universalis* in Latin. Thus, neither the *Codex* nor the Latin *Novellae* employ the most obvious Latin equivalent for "imperial": *imperialis*. Which is to say that neither the authors of the *Codex* nor the translators of the *Novellae* sought to exchange "imperial" for "ecumenical."

There are other reasons as well for resisting the idea that Justinian endorsed the ecumenical title because he wanted to elevate a single "imperial" bishop. For starters, the emperor's active promotion of the Pentarchy would seem to defy the idea that he desired a single ecclesiastical figure to lead the Church. Of course, given the extent to which Justinian attempted to control the dogmatic decisions of the Church, his ultimate support for the Pentarchy is somewhat ambiguous. A possible solution to this inconsistency is that Justinian theoretically believed that the Church should be administered like the empire (i.e., as independent and regional administrative units that were ultimately submissive to the centralized authority). But, if so, it leaves unanswered what that centralized authority would have been. Was it the bishop of Rome, the bishop of Constantinople, or the emperor himself? The laws themselves never make this clear. For his part, John Meyendorff argues that Justinian's actions did as much to undermine the Pentarchy as his legislation did to promote it.[120] As noted, *Novella* 123 grants legal autonomy to each of the five patriarchs and makes no arrangement for inter-patriarchal legal suits.

Another reason that we should resist the notion that Justinian promoted the title to enable a single "imperial" patriarch is that if we ignore the title itself, there is nothing in the *Corpus* to confirm the notion that the See of Constantinople is the leading see. *Codex* I.1.7 (ch. 2) does define the Church of Constantinople as the head of the Church *in his partibus* ("in these parts"), presumably meaning the East, but only Rome is acknowledged as the head or unifying center of the universal Church.

This ambiguity, of course, should not lead to the conclusion that the title is irrelevant or that Justinian did not have specific reasons for promoting it. While it would be an exaggeration to suggest that Justinian used the title to promote Constantinople over Rome, it is certain that he consistently raised the profile of the See of Constantinople in the wider Church, and the inclusion of the title in the *Corpus* offers a rhetorical confirmation of the see's

increasing prestige.[121] Justinian's use of the title might also indicate a willingness on the part of the emperor to endorse a rhetoric of Constantinopolitan
authority in exchange for patriarchal support of imperial efforts[122]—a move
similar to the emperor's endorsement of a rhetorical embellishment of papal
prerogatives represented by *Codex* I.1.8. In fact, when we compare the frequent support for the rhetorical claims of patriarchal privilege as represented
by the ecumenical title to the relative paucity of support for Roman claims
in the *Novellae*, it becomes evident that Justinian, on balance, invested his
legislative capital in the See of Constantinople rather than the See of Rome.

Justinian's Legislation: Some Concluding Observations

Despite the seeming ambiguity between the affirmation of Roman privilege
in the *Codex* and the relative insignificance of Rome in the *Novellae*, there
is an underlying consistency in the Justinianic legislation: the majority of
ecclesiastical legislation from this period was prompted by concerns arising
in the East and, as a consequence, often emphasized the bishop of Constantinople as the authority who, with imperial support, would oversee the solution
to those problems. With the exception of the correspondence between Justinian and Pope John II (recorded in Book I of the *Codex*) and a single *Novella*,
which affirmed the property rights of the Roman Church, the See of Rome
is typically characterized in the Justinianic legislation as little more than the
administrative center of a provincial church, albeit one that needed occasional, if empty, affirmations of a grander prestige.

    If we were to rely exclusively on the Justinianic legislation for our knowl-
edge of how the Roman Church was perceived by Christians in the East, we
might come to the conclusion that it was, for all intents and purposes, irrelevant. The breakdown in ecclesiastical order that prompted the *Novellae* was
witnessed in Constantinople and reflects the situation in Constantinople, but
the laws were theoretically extended to the entire Church with no apparent
concern to have them affirmed by the bishop of Rome.[123] One gets the sense
from reading the *Novellae* that the patriarchs of Constantinople have enough
of the ear of Justinian that they are able to guarantee that most new legislative
acts reflect patriarchal concerns.[124] It was only when Justinian needed papal
support for other endeavors that he could be bothered to incorporate the
rhetorical claims of Roman ecclesiastical prestige into Roman law. As a consequence, this legislation not only reflects the shifting alliances in ecclesiastical

and imperial politics in the sixth century but helped to reinforce Eastern ambivalence regarding Roman jurisdictional claims for subsequent
generations.

Theoderic, Justinian, and the Petrine Discourse

Unlike other chapters in this study, which seek to provide a more comprehensive assessment of the ways in which a particular pope's rhetorical choices
fit within the discursive possibilities afforded by the Petrine discourse, this
chapter has pursued an altogether different approach to our topic by examining the ways in which a variety of texts—texts that served very different
purposes and did so with distinct voices—employed elements of the Petrine
and papal narratives in the early decades of the sixth century. Thus, the
purpose of this chapter has not been to offer a cohesive account of papal
history from this period, but rather to try to understand some of the contextual features that prompted an expansion of the Petrine discourse and to
ascertain the extent to which that discourse can be seen to have permeated
the various iterations of episcopal authority as far away as the legal courts of
Constantinople. While it is obvious that the two sections of this chapter offer
a great deal of variation in terms of content and analysis, they also provide at
least three important points of connection.

First, this chapter has shown that the secular rulers of Italy and the
empire were not nearly so concerned with the "rise of the papacy"—whether
the political, economic, or legal components of that rise—as we often presume. Scholars of the early and medieval papacy are in part to blame for this
miscalculation because all too often they have examined the church/state
relationship in the sixth century from the vantage point of what that relationship would become later in the Middle Ages, and, thus, seek in their sixth-
century investigation traces or constitutive principles for what would later
develop—namely the contest and one-upmanship between pope and (German) emperor. And while it is true that Justinian did seem to care a great
deal about the cooperation between the imperial and ecclesial spheres, little
evidence from his massive legal corpus suggests that his formula for cooperation privileged the bishop of Rome as a monolithic representative of ecclesial
interests. What is more, there is essentially no evidence in our surviving
sources to suggest that either Theoderic or Justinian viewed the bishop of

Rome as the single leader of the Christian people, or even as the undisputed leader of the Christian episcopate.

Second, although it might be unwise to propose any direct connection between the Petrine discourse and the emergence of the ecumenical title, there appear to be significant similarities between the respective escalations of rhetorical claims in the Roman and Constantinopolitan Churches—insofar as in both cases those escalations emerge in moments when the Churches are the most vulnerable and most in need of an infusion of rhetorical strength, even if that rhetorical claim to strength seems to defy all other empirical evidence. It is likely more than a coincidence that the title "Ecumenical Patriarch" was attributed to the See of Constantinople at the same time that the see was suffering its greatest international humiliation. Indeed, the Constantinopolitan development of rhetorical claims follows a remarkably similar, albeit delayed, pattern to those of the See of Rome. In the seventh century, in fact, the similarity between Roman and Constantinopolitan efforts would track even more closely, as the Eastern See began its own narrative of apostolic origins through the cult of St. Andrew, the "elder brother" of St. Peter who supposedly "founded" the ecumenical see in the mid-first century.[125]

Finally, this chapter has demonstrated that despite the international ambition and Petrine creativity of popes Leo and Gelasius in the mid- and late fifth century, the pontiffs of the early to mid-sixth century were rarely significant figures in their own right. When they were not preoccupied with contentious struggles to retain their authority against rival factions within the Roman clergy, the popes of this period were frequently subjected to the interests of the secular rulers of their age. Both Theoderic and Justinian made and unmade Roman bishops, and the clergy of Rome could do little to oppose them. In Justinian's case, the emperor went so far as to dictate Christological orthodoxy to the Roman Church in the form of the condemnation of the *Three Chapters* at the Council of Constantinople in 553. The impossible task of enforcing such an unpopular policy in the West would fall to the bishops of Rome, with little assistance from Constantinople. The failure of Roman bishops to implement this charge fully led to a situation in which the major sees of northern Italy (Aquileia and Milan) were in schism with the Roman Church for much of the latter half of the sixth century.

And, yet, despite the infighting and the frequent humiliations handed to them by Theoderic and Justinian, the bishops of Rome continued in this period to advance the narrative of papal sovereignty through the creation of new literary forms and through the careful erasure of alternative histories. At times, the bishops of Rome were even able to provide enough political and theological leverage that they could persuade the same secular rulers to acknowledge the Petrine claim (whether it was Theoderic's visit to St. Peter's or Justinian's affirmation of Peter's authority in the *Codex*), even if such an acknowledgment brought little actual relief from their subordination to the state.

CHAPTER 5

Restraint and Desperation in Gregory the Great's Petrine Appeal

Gregory the Great was born in 540 in the midst of the Justinianic war against the Goths. The devastation of central Italy (and Rome in particular) was acute and was exacerbated by floods, famine, and plagues.[1] In 568, just a few years before Gregory would begin his public career as *praefectus urbi* (prefect of the city of Rome), another Germanic tribe, the Lombards, crossed the Alps into Italy—a development that only furthered the desperation and increased the complexity of the political situation. The Italian Church also had serious problems. When Gregory assumed Peter's chair in September 590, the metropolitan of Aquileia and several of the suffragan bishops of Milan remained steadfastly opposed to the Fifth Ecumenical Council's condemnation of the *Three Chapters*—a condemnation that, in their opinion, was a capitulation to the Monophysite heresy.[2] Politically insulated from both the Byzantine exarchate in Ravenna and its military authority in central Italy, these northern Italian bishops were free to opine that the bishops of Rome had, for the greater part of the past fifty years, been little more than the puppets of heretical Eastern emperors.

Gregory was a man of exceptional skill and ascetic character. As Carole Straw eloquently narrated, Gregory's thought was balanced in sophisticated ways—an outlook she identified as finding "perfection in imperfection."[3] To be sure, both Gregory's writing and activity strike a balance between monastic idealism and practical responsibility—he desires ascetic retreat but undertakes a remaking of the papal curia; he aspires to abandon the world but organizes lumber shipments and facilitates the rebuilding of Rome's military defenses. As we will see, Gregory's development and assertion of the Petrine topos was similarly balanced and nuanced. Although he would, on occasion, emphasize some of the same discursive points as his predecessors, both Gregory's theological examination of the biblical Peter and his use of the Petrine topos in his international diplomacy suggest a far less aggressive and more nuanced application than either Leo or Gelasius had pursued.

The premise of this chapter is that Gregory, like many of his predecessors, typically employed the more assertive elements of an inherited Petrine discourse in moments of international weakness, and only after other diplomatic efforts had failed. What is so intriguing about Gregory's career is the extent to which he both restrained and expanded Petrine claims. As we will see, his theological treatises (and even certain aspects of his correspondence) show little interest in exploiting Peter's authority vis-à-vis other bishops, which had become pro forma during the tenures of Leo I and Gelasius I. At the same time, we will also see the extent to which Gregory developed new ways to harness the power of Peter—most notably in the promotion and implementation of Peter's shrine and relics as extensions of Gregory's own authority. Concerning the reception of Gregory's Petrine claims, the chapter offers four test cases (the Sicilian clergy, Germanic aristocracy, Eastern clergy, and Roman emperor) to show that Gregory's use of the topos was, at best, inconsistently effective in achieving its immediate goals.

The Absence of a Petrine Discourse in Gregory's Theological Works

Perhaps the most striking aspect of Gregory's handling of the Petrine legacy is the sharp contrast between the lack of emphasis on Peter's authority in Gregory's theological works and the treatment of Peter's authority in Gregory's correspondence.[4] Gregory's theological corpus is substantial: in addition to the ever-influential *Book of Pastoral Rule* (*Liber regulae pastoralis*), he authored a collection of Italian saints' lives, known as the *Dialogues*, and numerous biblical commentaries, including select passages from the Gospel lectionary (*Homiliae in Evangelia*), a partial commentary on the book of Ezekiel (*Homiliae in Hiezechihelem prophetam*), and a massive treatment of the book of Job (*Moralia in Job*), which runs to a dizzying 1,800 pages in the modern critical edition.[5] For our purposes, what is perhaps most surprising is that there is no extended theological justification of Peter's authority anywhere within Gregory's voluminous theological corpus. That is not to say, of course, that Peter goes unnoticed—Gregory employs the biblical figure repeatedly—but Peter functions in Gregory's theological works as a historical and literary resource in the service of pastoral rather than ecclesiological or diplomatic objectives.[6]

In his biblical commentaries, Gregory most often uses Peter as a saintly exemplar, someone whose actions encapsulate the Christian life. For example, in the opening chapters of the *Moralia*, Gregory extols Peter's willingness to proclaim his faith in Christ publicly.[7] Later in the text, the pontiff stresses the aspects of Peter's character that enable him to offer inspired spiritual direction, such as his discernment in pastoral matters[8] and his humility in the face of opposition.[9] In his commentary on the prophet Ezekiel, Gregory likewise lauds Peter's ability to remain humble after performing miracles, and extols the apostle's repentance following his denial of Christ.[10] Similar examples exist in his *Homilies on the Gospels*, where Gregory is particularly keen to promote the depth of Peter's faith.[11] In short, Peter's function in Gregory's biblical commentaries is exclusively one of saintly imitation. For the average Christian, Peter serves as an example of Christian piety, someone all Christians should imitate. For Gregory's clerical readers, Peter also serves the pontiff as a proof text for a particular type of Christian leadership, drawn from ascetic models, that Gregory famously advocates throughout his career.

It is this second function, of course, that Gregory employs for the surprisingly few references to the apostle in the pope's famous *Book of Pastoral Rule*.[12] There are, in fact, only two significant engagements with the "historical" Peter in the text. The first well demonstrates Gregory's nuanced understanding of both Peter's authority in the Church and the authority of a spiritual leaders in general. Emphasizing the need for a pastor to retain humility while leading a community, Gregory notes:

> But we will more fully understand this power of discernment if we study the example of the first shepherd [*pastoris primi*]. For Peter, who by God's authorization held the position of leadership [*principatum tenens*] in the holy Church, refused immoderate veneration from Cornelius (though the latter had acted well by humbly prostrating himself before Peter), but Peter recognized him as an equal, saying: "Arise, do not do this, for I am also a man." . . . He had a self-awareness that he was the head of the Church in the battle against sin [*summum se intra Ecclesiam contra peccatum recoluit*], but

he did not acknowledge this honor when he was in the presence of upright brethren.[13]

Gregory of course affirms Peter's authority in the apostolic community, but for the explicit purpose of emphasizing his humility. Peter is saintly not because he is the leader of the Christian community, but because he leads the faithful with no concern for his personal prestige. While several scholars have noted Gregory's advocacy of the monastically inspired virtue of humility, the extent to which Peter functions in that pastoral discourse has yet to be fully developed.[14]

The second example of Peter in the *Book of Pastoral Rule* is quite brief and simply notes that because of his pastoral humility, Peter accepted the censure of Paul concerning the debate over circumcision (Gregory compares this to David's reception of the rebuke of Nathan).[15] Perhaps most interesting about the passage is that it begins with the affirmation that "no one lives who does not occasionally sin."[16] Thus, Gregory shows no qualms about identifying Peter's sinfulness, precisely because it is the apostle's humility that Gregory wants his priests to imitate. Had Gregory, in this context, been concerned to link the historic Peter to papal authority, he might not have been so quick to affirm Peter's flaws.

Indeed, one element that dramatically distinguishes the theological works from the correspondence is Gregory's willingness in the former to mine Peter's shortcomings for a greater pastoral purpose. In the *Moralia* alone there are nearly a dozen occasions where Gregory exposes one of Peter's various faults for the purpose of emphasizing a theological point about the value of vigilance, humility, or pastoral leadership. Gregory rather cavalierly suggests that Peter has a carnal mind,[17] misunderstands the purpose of the transfiguration,[18] fails to comprehend why the Gentiles do not need circumcision,[19] and, of course, denies Christ three times.[20] Similar examples fill the commentary on Ezekiel and the homilies on the Gospels. Gregory's purpose, of course, is not to denigrate Peter specifically, but to use the apostle's failings (and his rehabilitation) as an opportunity to promote Gregory's own larger pastoral goals.

In one of the most interesting examinations of the consequences of Peter's denial, in the twenty-first homily on the Gospels, Gregory notes that the reason the women at the empty tomb were instructed to tell the disciples "and Peter" that Jesus has risen (Mk 16.7) was because Peter would not have

gone with the other apostles to the tomb unless he had been named specifically by the angel, because he was too embarrassed about having denied
Christ. Gregory argues that God put these words into the mouth of the angel
so that Peter, who would eventually become a shepherd of the Church, would
know (having received compassion from the angel) to have compassion on
those under his care.[21] In short, Gregory uses the error of Peter's denial and
subsequent despair to instruct those engaged in pastoral leadership about the
importance of compassion.

Gregory's handling of the altercation between Peter and Paul over the
circumcision of the Gentiles is equally illuminative of the pontiff's willingness to employ Peter's shortcomings as a lesson for pastors. In his examination of the matter in the *Moralia*, for example, Gregory explains that even
those who have great faith receive only partial theological understanding during this life, and that is why Peter, despite his faith, erred when he first
devised his policy for initiating Gentile converts.[22]

In the commentary on Ezekiel, Gregory offers a different, longer examination of the confrontation between Peter and Paul.[23] Here Gregory moves
from criticism to praise as he utilizes the Galatians text to extol Peter's humility in the face of Paul's rebuke. With an impressive rhetorical flourish, Gregory lists eight reasons that Peter was Paul's superior. Gregory notes, however,
that Peter humbly accepted correction from his lesser brother.[24] The pontiff
concludes the section with a more general exhortation to humility before
moving on to admire Paul's boldness in preaching. What is noteworthy about
this passage is that Gregory is obviously able to identify each of the biblical
proof texts that constitute Peter's leadership of the apostolic community. But
Gregory does not attempt here (or elsewhere in the biblical commentaries)
to use these arguments to bolster the authority of the Roman Church, nor
does he make any direct reference to his own position as Peter's heir.[25]

This does not, of course, mean that Gregory ignores Peter's authority
among the apostles altogether. That, too, provides the pontiff with certain
pastoral opportunities. For example, in his twenty-fourth homily on the Gospels, Gregory examines the story of Christ's post-resurrection appearance to
the apostles while they are fishing (Jn 21.1–14). Noting that it is Peter who
ultimately brings the catch of fish to Christ, Gregory reflects:

> I believe that you, beloved, perceive why it was that Peter brought
> the net to land. Our holy Church had been entrusted to him; it was
> to him alone that it was said "Simon, son of John, do you love me?

Feed my sheep [Jn 21:17]." . . . Because the Church's preacher would separate us from the waves of this world, it was necessary that Peter bring the net full of fish to land. He dragged the fish to the firm ground of the shore because by his preaching he revealed to the faithful the stability of our eternal home. He did this by both words and letters and he continues to do this daily by his miraculous signs. Is it not like we are fish caught in the net of faith and brought to shore every time that he separates us from earthly concerns and returns us to a desire for eternal stillness?[26]

For Gregory, St. Peter plays a critical role in the history of salvation. His leadership, teaching, and humility not only built the foundation of the apostolic community but remain as examples for the faithful and their leaders. The continuation of Peter's miracles and the lessons that can be learned from his mistakes contribute further to the pastoral and exegetical importance that Peter has for Gregory. Absent is any sense that Gregory, at least in his biblical commentaries, wants or needs to link Peter's authority to that of the Roman Church or to himself as Peter's heir.

Peter as Agent of Papal Authority in the West I: The Sicilian Clergy

As we move from Gregory's theological works to his correspondence, we see a dramatic shift in both Gregory's presentation of Peter and the way Peter functions as a tool for asserting either Roman or pontifical authority. Because the pope's surviving correspondence is so wide-ranging (over eight hundred letters), the subsequent sections of this chapter will focus on the particular communications that are most extensive and/or most illuminative of his correspondence as a whole.[27] We begin with an assessment of Gregory's engagement with the clergy of Sicily and the ways he asserted Roman authority there. As we will see, Gregory's interventions in the Sicilian Church well attest to his nuanced understanding of his own authority outside Rome and to new ways the Petrine legacy could be leveraged to assert that authority.

As noted, Leo had made the Roman Church's first jurisdictional claim over the churches of Sicily. By the middle of the sixth century, it would appear that the Sicilian episcopate had essentially consented to that claim. In large part, the spread of Roman influence in Sicily can be explained by the appropriation of vast estates that had been gifted to the Roman Church by the landowning aristocracy. As papal landholding in Sicily grew, so too did papal influence in local ecclesiastical matters. By Gregory's tenure, Sicily was the location of approximately four hundred agricultural estates owned by the Roman Church—farms that provided vital income for the bishop of Rome and a steady supply of grain for the urban poor of the Western capital.[28]

Nearly one quarter of all Gregory's letters were sent to or concerned the island of Sicily—a fact that clearly indicates the importance of the Sicilian patrimony to the Roman Church.[29] It was Gregory who cemented the division of the Roman patrimony in Sicily into two administrative centers, by separating the governance of the Sicilian Church into two archdioceses (Palermo and Syracuse).[30] As elsewhere, the papal farms were administered by a *rector* (Gregory's term), who was responsible for funneling both the income and the produce from these farms to Rome. Before Gregory's tenure, the patrimonial administrators (often identified as *defensores ecclesiae*) were typically appointed from Rome, but they were often local aristocrats or, in some cases, local bishops.[31] Beginning with Gregory's tenure, however, the administrators were always Roman clerics, holding various ecclesiastical ranks.[32] The duties of Gregory's rectors were certainly legal and financial, but he, like some of his predecessors, employed his administrators to institute his ecclesiastical policies as well.[33] The degree to which Gregory could truly rely on his rectors varied, but the pontiff tried to insure their cooperation by introducing a new element into the long history of the discourse of Petrine authority—he made them swear an oath of allegiance at the tomb of St. Peter before embarking on their commission.

The significance of this development in the Petrine story should not be understated. Not only was it a powerful symbolic mechanism by which Gregory could demand obedience from his agents (at times, he reminded them of their oath), but employing the physical space of Peter's tomb also represented an important expansion of the way that the Petrine discourse could be used as an instrument of papal control and exclusion.[34] Whereas Popes Leo and Gelasius had loaded their Petrine arsenals with mostly rhetorical weapons, Gregory added the ritualistic exercise of public submission at the very locus of papal power—the tomb of St. Peter.[35] As we will see, this was one of Gregory's most important contributions to the expansion of Petrine authority.

Because Gregory's correspondence to Sicily is so extensive, it provides the most complete evidence of his attempts to effect clerical reform (what I have elsewhere described as his "asceticizing of spiritual direction") and the extent to which his policies were accepted or resisted by the local clergy.[36] It should be noted at the outset, however, that Gregory did not employ the rhetorical features of the Petrine topos in his letters to Sicily with the same regularity or the same force that he did with other correspondents. For example, he almost never resorted to Rome's connection to St. Peter as a justification for Roman intervention in the Sicilian Church.[37] This is not to say that he failed to employ any of the rhetorical options of his predecessors—he did regularly refer to his see as the "Apostolic See"—but that he rarely turned to the Petrine topos to assert his influence over Sicilian affairs.

With so much material at our disposal, there are a number of ways that we could explore Gregory's Sicilian involvement. For brevity's sake, we will focus on two specific aspects of Gregory's interaction with the Sicilian Church: his prosecution of miscreant bishops and his intervention in local episcopal elections. Indeed, the making and unmaking of a regional episcopal court was the most deliberate way that a Roman bishop could assert his authority over other churches—in the case of Sicily, Jeffrey Richards has suggested Roman intervention was a systematic "Gregorianization" of the episcopate.[38]

Scrutinizing Episcopal Behavior

At the outset of his pontificate, Gregory commissioned his first Sicilian rector, the subdeacon Peter, to investigate the local churches to see if any church was lacking in spiritual leadership (due to immorality or simple vacancy). If so, Peter was to fill the position with a member of the lower clergy, or, if possible, with a candidate from a local monastery.[39] In less than eighteen months, Peter charged four bishops with various crimes.[40] Over time, Gregory's agents on the island would bring a total of six of Sicily's thirteen bishops to trial. But even those bishops who were not brought to trial were censored, in one way or another, from Rome. In fact, Gregory criticized the actions of every Sicilian bishop on at least one occasion, including those bishops closest to him. The details of the alleged crimes need not detain us, but there are certain elements in the prosecution and resolution of the most extreme cases that are directly relevant to Gregory's exercise of Petrine authority and the extent to which Gregory's interference in Sicily met with the approval of the local populations.

The case of Leo of Catana is especially illuminating. Leo, along with two other accused bishops, was sent to Rome for trial. Although Gregory ultimately determined that Leo was innocent of the charges against him, the pontiff made Leo take the extra step of swearing an oath of innocence at the tomb of St. Peter.[41] In other words, even though Leo had been exonerated, Gregory made him submit to the most potent symbol of Roman ecclesiastical authority—Peter's tomb. When Gregory wrote to the imperial *praetor* in Sicily, Justin, informing him that Leo was innocent of the charges that had been made against him, the pope instructed Justin that he would need to protect Leo against those persons who had perpetrated and/or believed the rumors against the innocent bishop. Gregory stressed that Justin should accept the Roman verdict, do everything in his power to protect the bishop's dignity, and honor him in a way befitting his episcopal rank.[42] While we do not have any direct record of how the people of Catana viewed Leo's arrest, trial, or exoneration, we might infer from Gregory's letter to Justin that the Sicilian resistance to Rome's intervention was not directed at Leo's incarceration—but at his exoneration.

Of the six bishops that Gregory or his agents brought to trial, only two were deposed (Agatho of Lipari and Lucillus of Malta). Of course the mere investigation of provincial bishops by Roman officials constitutes an exercise of authority. Apart from the *Life of Gregory of Agrigentum*, which was written at least a generation after Pope Gregory's death (and will be examined in the Postscript), no evidence survives of any form of lay or clerical resistance to Roman intervention in these cases. Thus, we might conclude that Gregory was able to discipline the Sicilian bench as he saw fit. But Roman jurisdiction in Sicily cut both ways: it gave Rome not only the ability to censure or even depose unresponsive clerics, but also the ability to exonerate men who had been condemned by members of their local communities—as in the cases of Leo of Catana and Gregory of Agrigentum.

The Lack of Roman Intervention in Local Episcopal Elections

According to the two scholars who have looked most closely at the Sicilian story, Jeffrey Richards and John Martyn, by 595 the Sicilian episcopate had been, to use Richards' phrase, "completely Gregorianized."[43] This means, according to Richards, that the local Greek-speaking Sicilian episcopate had been replaced by Roman clerics, typically monks, who had been hand-selected by the pontiff. It would seem, however, that this position is over-stated. With the exception of the See of Syracuse, there is no contemporary evidence that Gregory ever imposed Roman candidates on the Sicilian Church. In fact, he often argued that candidates for episcopal vacancies should be selected from among the local clergy, which would imply that they may well have been Greek.

The two cases in Syracuse in which Gregory did get involved are illuminating: the election of Maximian in 591 and the election of John in 595. There is no question that Gregory had a hand in Maximian's election.[44] Maximian was, in fact, one of Gregory's closest advisers, and his election to the See of Syracuse certainly advanced the pope's plans for the island.[45] But Maximian died a few years later, and the election of an appropriate successor required deft statesmanship on the part of Gregory's second rector, Cyprian.

In February 595, Gregory wrote to Cyprian acknowledging that the people of Syracuse desired the election of a local priest, Trajan.[46] Gregory argued, however, that Trajan was "unsuitable," and he instructed Cyprian to work quietly for the election of an archdeacon, John, from a neighboring see.[47] Ultimately, John was elected, but we know nothing about him. If we follow Richards and Martyn, we will assume that John was a Latin rather than a Greek, that he possessed the monastic pedigree that Gregory preferred, and that he was a cleric of the Roman Church. But there is no surviving evidence to support any of those conclusions. All we know for certain is that John was serving the See of Catana, which, without other evidence, suggests that he was a native Sicilian. And given the fact that Catana is located on the eastern coast of the island, which had the largest Greek population, John's principal language and liturgical tradition would likely have been Greek.

Key to Richards's thesis of a Gregorianization of the Sicilian bench is the idea that the pope deposed those bishops he did not like and replaced them with men he could trust. According to Richards, Gregory deposed Agatho of Lipari and Paul of Triocala. While it is true that he deposed Agatho, there is no record of a Paul of Triocala in any of our surviving sources or that Gregory deposed a bishop from that see.[48] What is more, there is no evidence that Gregory was directly involved in either of these replacements. In fact, we do not even know the name of the bishop who succeeded Agatho in Lipari or the circumstances of the election.[49] While we do know that the See of Triocala was filled by a man named Peter, we do not know anything for certain about him and even less about the circumstances of his election.[50] Richards also asserts that the replacement for Felix of Messina was orchestrated from Rome. But, even though Gregory had repeatedly threatened Felix with canonical punishment, there is no evidence in our sources that the pontiff had any involvement in the election of Felix's successor.[51]

In short, of the nine episcopal elections on the island of Sicily that occur during Gregory's tenure, the only two in which he openly interfered were those involving the Archdiocesan See of Syracuse, whose officeholder served, for a period of time, as papal rector. Of the seven other cases (Lilybaeum, Lipari, Malta, Messina, Palermo, Triocala, and Tyndari), contemporary sources reveal nothing about the elections in four of them (Lipari, Messina, Triocala, and Tyndari) apart from the fact that Benenatus, the bishop of Tyndari, had been a priest in the diocese before his election—thus, he too was likely a native Sicilian.[52] In the final three cases (the Sees of Lilybaeum, Malta, and Palermo), Gregory instructed his agents to encourage the clergy and people to select a candidate from among the local clergy.[53] He never promoted a specific candidate. Remarkably, the candidate selected by the people of Malta in 598 was the same Trajan that Gregory had rejected for the See of Syracuse in 595. It is worth noting that even in this case, Gregory did not do anything to oppose the will of the local population.[54]

Gregory's willingness to support a local candidate in Palermo is especially noteworthy. The vacancy was created by the death of Victor, who had been one of the bishops initially brought to trial by Peter in 591. Although exonerated at the time, he was a frequent recipient of Gregory's criticism, and we might expect that his death would have provided an opportunity for Gregory to place a close associate in this important See. And yet, Gregory insists— more strongly here than in any other Sicilian election—that Victor's replacement must be selected from among the local clergy.[55] We know from Gregory's correspondence with a long-time friend and local aristocrat that one local faction had been advocating for the election of Urbicus, the abbot of St. Hermes, which was one of the monasteries Gregory personally endowed when he abandoned his secular career in the 570s. We might expect the pontiff to have jumped at this possibility, but, instead, he informed his friend that he should not pursue Urbicus' election.[56] According to Richards, Urbicus represented the papal party and was therefore unpopular among the local community. Gregory instructed his friend to investigate the other candidate, a deacon named Crescens, that the majority supported. If he was satisfactory, then Gregory would not intervene.[57] In the end, however, a third candidate was selected—John. Our sources reveal nothing about him. Richards speculates that Crescens was found to be unworthy, and so Gregory appointed someone from Rome who could be trusted. Given Richards' own description of resistance to Rome in Palermo, and given the fact that Gregory was criticizing John within months of his election, Richards' conclusion seems untenable.[58]

So why would Richards, Martyn, and others conclude that Gregory completely transformed the Sicilian episcopate when he was involved in only two of the nine elections, and both of those were for the same see? As it turns out, their position is informed, in large part, by the partisan testimony of John the Deacon, a ninth-century biographer of Gregory. According to John the Deacon, both Donus of Messina and Peter of Triocala had been Roman clerics (Donus a priest and Peter a subdeacon) before their election as bishops in Sicily.[59] But John's reliability in this matter should be questioned for at least three reasons. First, he wrote nearly three hundred years after the events he claims to chronicle, without providing any source for his information. Second, the thesis of John's biography was that Gregory was a heroic figure because he had effectively purged the Western episcopate of Simoniac priests and spread the influence of the Roman Church as a counterweight (two important concerns for the ninth-century Roman deacon). But the only evidence the biographer provides in support of Gregory's efforts is a list of the names of several deacons, priests, and monks "from Rome" that Gregory raised to the episcopate. Without any independent attestation, we have no credible evidence that John did not simply exaggerate his numbers and mine Gregory's correspondence for appropriate names. What is more, in the case of Peter of Triocala, supposedly a subdeacon from Rome, John the Deacon may very well have confused him with another subdeacon of the same name, who served as the first rector of the Sicilian patrimony and then later as the interlocutor of the *Dialogues*.[60] But even if we accept the suspect testimony of John the Deacon that Donus and Peter were Roman appointees (as Martyn and Richards clearly do), that would still amount to Gregory's direct involvement in only four of the nine elections, with only three of the nine having been appointed from the Roman clergy. In short, the contention that Gregory stacked the Sicilian bench with Latin-speaking members of the Roman Church is unsustainable. Revising our estimation of Gregory's efforts in Sicily has broad implications. Most important, the fact that Gregory was not inclined to dominate episcopal elections in Sicily (a region traditionally receptive to Roman involvement) suggests that this pontiff was not nearly as keen as Leo and Gelasius to maximize his control over the suburbican Italian clergy.

Additional Considerations

While Gregory did not routinely employ the rhetorical features of the Petrine discourse in his Sicilian correspondence, and while he did not actively interfere in the majority of episcopal elections in Sicily, there were still other ways he employed the Petrine legacy to maintain Roman jurisdictional authority on the island. For example, according to a letter that Gregory presented the rector Peter at the beginning of his commission to Sicily in 590, the pontiff ordered the annual gathering of Sicilian bishops to occur on the feast of St. Peter. As the letter attests, it had, by that time, become customary for the bishops of Sicily to gather, under the supervision of the papal rector, on the anniversary of the pope's election (a tradition that Leo had helped to promote). Clearly the gathering functioned as a symbolic ritual, designed to reinforce Rome's super-jurisdictional rights and by meeting on the anniversary of the pope's election it reinforced the individual pontiff's personal authority over the regional bishops.[61] Interestingly, Gregory instructs Peter that the Sicilian bishops should gather on the feast of St. Peter, rather than the anniversary of his own election, because, the pontiff reasons, "unnecessary vanity gives me no pleasure."[62] Ostensibly, this was a mild critique of Gregory's predecessors, even though the net result was the same—Sicilian bishops would gather annually under the direction of a Roman agent. But one might, in fact, argue that shifting the date to the feast of St. Peter was a clever way for Gregory to aggrandize his authority by hiding it behind a mask of humility. In other words, although Gregory's stated instruction was to remove a symbol of his personal authority from the occasion for the gathering, the selection of the feast of St. Peter simply transferred that symbol in that it reinforced for the Sicilian bishops the implicit connections between St. Peter, the See of Rome, and Gregory himself.

In addition to the annual gathering of bishops in Sicily, we learn of an "old tradition" in which the bishops of Sicily were to journey to Rome every third year, on the feast of St. Peter, to take part in a Roman gathering of bishops.[63] Here too, the occasion of the feast of St. Peter provides an obvious symbolic affirmation of Roman prestige. Interestingly, Gregory acknowledges that this triennial gathering of Sicilian bishops in Rome has never taken place during his pontificate (now in its seventh year). Owing to the difficulty of travel, Gregory proposes that future gatherings should occur only every fifth year.[64] But Gregory instructs his rector that a meeting of Sicilian bishops in Rome will take place at the upcoming "nativity" of St. Peter, just one month away.[65]

In the following section, we will explore Gregory's use of the Petrine discourse among Western rulers (namely the leaders of the Germanic tribes), but it is worth noting here that the pontiff employed several features of the discourse in his correspondence with the lay leaders of Sicily as well. For example, he invited one correspondent to "visit St. Peter"—by which he meant Rome—so that the two of them could read scripture together.[66] He informed an imperial official that if he "devoted himself to the cases of St. Peter," he could expect to be "compensated" both here and in the future.[67] And for the interim *praetor*, Leontius, Gregory took the extra step of sending him a relic of St. Peter—another expansion of Petrine authority that will be taken up in detail in the following section.[68]

The record of Gregory's involvement in the Sicilian Church affirms his perpetuation, even his extension, of the Petrine topos as a means to assert papal authority over ecclesiastical affairs in regions beyond the immediate reach of Rome itself. But, at the same time, Gregory's Sicilian correspondence also demonstrates the extent to which Gregory typically did not maximize the resources of Petrine rhetoric or some of the traditional prerogatives of Roman super-jurisdiction (such as interference in local elections). Never, for example, did Gregory justify his intervention in Sicily by reciting the scriptural basis for Petrine authority; never did he claim that an uncontrollable bishop was guilty of insulting Peter's *principium*; and never did he avail himself of the canonical grounds for his Petrine authority. In other circumstances (with both the Germanic rulers and the leaders of the East), Gregory readily employed each of those strategies. If nothing else, the evidence from Sicily shows Gregory to have employed the Petrine legacy in creative ways, but that he did so to maintain, rather than to extend, Roman influence.

Peter as Agent of Papal Authority in the West II: The Aristocracy

It has long been observed that Gregory's diplomatic efforts among the Merovingian, Visogothic, and Saxon aristocracy marked a significant expansion of papal engagement with the Germanic kingdoms. Not surprisingly, scholars have proposed divergent interpretations about whether these embassies constitute an effort by Gregory to extend Roman ecclesiastical jurisdiction and/or his authority.[69] In this section we will look at one particular aspect of that debate—the opportunities provided by the Petrine discourse—in Gregory's Germanic correspondence. Because his objectives were different, the thrust of Gregory's Petrine appeal in this correspondence was different from what it was in Sicily or, especially, with his Eastern correspondents.

Peter as Guarantor of Orthodoxy

As we have seen in previous chapters, one of the most important rhetorical opportunities the Petrine discourse afforded Roman bishops was the possibility of linking their theological opinions to the supposedly incontestable orthodoxy of St. Peter. To the extent that any pontiff could persuade his audience that his particular theological vision had been Peter's or could link his theological authority to Peter's, Gregory hoped his cause would prevail in his correspondence with the Germanic leaders of northern Italy and Gaul.

Gregory's bid to convince the Lombard queen Theodelinda of the orthodoxy of the *Three Chapters* condemnation provides an excellent case in point. One consequence of the Lombard intrusion into northern Italy was that it created a safe haven for the bishops who continued to reject the condemnation of the *Three Chapters*. Lombard rulers, sensing the political advantages of a fractured Italian episcopate, aligned themselves with those bishops who were theologically divided from both the imperial position and the bishop of Rome. Theodelinda was such a ruler, and in anticipation of her resistance to orthodox overtures, the pontiff chose to emphasize the Petrine topos.[70]

In September 593, Gregory sent a letter to Queen Theodelinda, *Epistle* 4.4, through his ally Constantius, bishop of Milan, who was then residing in exile in Genoa.[71] Gregory begins his letter to the queen sensibly enough by implying that her commitment to the *Three Chapters* was the consequence of her having been betrayed by schismatic bishops who have given her poor theological advice.[72] He goes on to defend the "council in the time of Justinian" (i.e., the Fifth Ecumenical Council) as a faithful continuation of the Council of Chalcedon.[73] Subsequent letters reveal, however, that Constantius chose not to pass along this letter to Theodelinda because he believed that it would not achieve its intended purpose.[74] In other words, Constantius had learned from experience that the path to peace in the *Three Chapters* controversy was paved by ambiguity and obfuscation rather than direct recognition of the schism, and it was equally important to avoid any mention of Justinian's council.[75]

So nearly a year later, Gregory sent a revised letter, *Epistle* 4.33, which conveyed a similar desire for reconciliation but deployed an entirely different set of rhetorical strategies. Whereas *Epistle* 4.4 makes no mention of the early ecumenical councils or of St. Peter, *Epistle* 4.33 begins with an affirmation of the councils from Nicaea to Chalcedon and offers a concise summary of the achievements and villains of each gathering. Concluding the letter, Gregory proclaims that Theodelinda should now have no reservations about the "Church of St. Peter, prince of the apostles."[76] Gregory then adds the following: "but persist in the true faith, and establish your life on the rock of the Church, which is to say, on the confession of St. Peter, the prince of the apostles."[77] Not only did Gregory add these two references to Peter, but he also withdrew any direct mention of Justinian and the council of 553.

The change in rhetorical strategy demonstrates a pastoral sensitivity characteristic of the author of the *Book of Pastoral Rule*.[78] But the insertion of the twin appeals to Petrine authority seems more than an added pastoral maneuver. Rather, it appears designed to be a powerful rhetorical affirmation that Gregory—as the representative of St. Peter, the de facto human representative of orthodoxy—is fully qualified to know the difference between orthodoxy and heresy and could, therefore, be trusted to represent the correct faith.

Gregory similarly harnessed Peter's orthodox integrity, in combination with other efforts, as he sought to pressure the Merovingian rulers of Gaul to suppress simony in the Gallic Church. For example, in the first of two letters to Childebert II, Gregory implores the king to put an end to simony and concluded his request with a simple "for the sake of God and St. Peter, prince of the apostle."[79] Simony, of course, was not the only matter that concerned Gregory in Gaul. Among other things, he was also keen to reestablish a reliable stream of income from the Roman patrimony in Childebert's realm. In subsequent letters, Gregory cleverly ties the two concerns together and increasingly employs the Petrine topos in those efforts. Emphasizing the importance of the patrimony, Gregory's second letter to Childebert notes: "because you preserve sincerity of faith both in mind and deed, the love that is within you for St. Peter, prince of the apostles, shows manifestly in that his property [i.e., the papal patrimony in Gaul] has so far been well governed and preserved for the sake of the Christian faith, beneath the power of your leadership."[80] Rather cleverly, Gregory's defines the patrimony, for which he needs help, as belonging directly to St. Peter.

In the same dispatch of letters, Gregory wrote to Childebert's mother, Brunhilde, even more candidly. He begins with a request for the patrimony with the phrase "on behalf of the love of St. Peter, prince of the apostles, whom we know you love with all your heart."[81] This was innocuous enough. But shifting his concern to the prevalence of simony in her realm, Gregory offers a far more daring statement:

> And so, let your Excellency agree to apply yourself willingly to our request in such a way that St. Peter, the prince of the apostles, to whom the power of binding and loosing was granted by our Lord Jesus Christ, may allow your Excellency to rejoice here over your offspring and after many years have run their course, may find you guiltless of any evil before the sight of the eternal judge.[82]

In other words, Gregory here implies that the health and happiness of Brunhilde's family depends on the intercession of St. Peter. And the granting of that intercession is linked directly to the cessation of simony in Gaul and to Brunhilde's commitment to act according to the wishes of Peter's church (the Church of Rome) and its bishop (Gregory). Only Peter could protect Brunhilde's children and forgive her sin. And Peter will do this, Gregory suggests, only if the queen does what Gregory asks of her. In this way, Gregory shows himself to be the sole arbiter of Peter's intercession and, as such, employs this aspect of the Petrine legacy as a potent tool for achieving his goals.[83]

Relics and Power

In addition to the obvious rhetorical reasons for employing the Petrine topos with his interlocutors, it is quite clear that Gregory believed that Peter remained mysteriously active in the Church and performed miracles through his tomb and relics.[84] This not only helps to explain why the tomb was used for the swearing of oaths, but also provides a theological rationale for the distribution of the saint's relics, a practice that Gregory repeatedly employed.[85]

Over the course of his tenure as pope, Gregory sent "relics" of St. Peter to a little more than a dozen persons, including Childebert, Brunhilde, and Reccared (Visigothic king of Spain).[86] These relics consisted of filings from the chains that had supposedly bound Peter during his imprisonment in Rome.[87] These filings were placed inside of a small key, symbolic of Christ's granting of the keys of heaven to St. Peter. As he distributed the relics to his select group of patrons and clients, Gregory issued various instructions concerning their care. Recipients were often told to wear the relic around their neck. Some were informed that it would cure illness, others that it had the power to release them from sin or protect them from evil. For example, he instructed Childebert that "whenever he wears it around his neck he will be protected from all evils."[88] This distribution of relics was more than a transmission of sanctified objects; it was an act of diplomacy designed to achieve ecclesiastical goals for the Church of Rome.

By being placed within a key, these relics symbolized the link between the historic authority of Peter and his contemporary arbiter, the bishop of Rome. Christ's granting of the keys of heaven to Peter (Mt 16.18–19), more than anything else, provided the biblical justification for Peter's leadership among the apostles and, as a consequence, Rome's privilege in the Church of Gregory's day. Gregory no doubt hoped that the recipients of these gifts would be reminded of this connection every time they viewed the key or called on it for help. As bishop of Rome, Gregory was the contemporary steward of the gates of heaven—another point subtly reinforced by his distribution of the keys.

It is significant that Gregory distributed the relics of Peter to three of the most important Germanic leaders with whom he corresponded. Not only were these rulers powerful in their own right, but the exchange of relics also corresponded directly to Gregory's diplomatic efforts. For Reccared, the Visigothic king, the relic functioned as a kind of reward for the king's renunciation of Arianism and conversion to the Catholic faith.[89] For Childebert, the relic was linked to Gregory's concerns for the Roman patrimony in Gaul and his desire to rid the Gallic Church of simony.

The relic exchange with Brunhilde, like so many things in the pontiff's correspondence with the queen, did not follow normal patterns. Whereas Gregory's gifts to Reccared and Childebert came at the beginning of his correspondence with those kings, Gregory did not send a gift to Brunhilde initially. It was only after Brunhilde requested a relic (obviously noting that one had been granted to her son) that Gregory determined to send her one.[90]

And in the letter accompanying the gift, Gregory warned her vigorously about the need to care for the relic properly, lest it "be rendered useless and idle in the service of God."[91] Although he consented to share his spiritual treasure with the queen, he appears to have had little confidence that the exchange would affect the pastoral or diplomatic goals that normally accompanied the distribution of Petrine relics. Nevertheless, we see in this exchange (as in the others) the ways the encouragement of specific practices and use of material objects could help to define and perpetuate the Petrine narrative and its connection to the See of Rome.

Gregory's diplomatic initiatives among the Germanic rulers of Italy, Gaul, and Spain were both similar and dissimilar to his efforts with lay rulers elsewhere. The pontiff's application of the Petrine topos also functioned in typical and atypical ways. At its most basic level, the figure of Peter was employed as one component in a multidimensional diplomatic effort. Here as elsewhere it was designed to convey Roman privilege in the adjudication of orthodoxy and to harness the still-viable mystical power of Peter's relics. Even allowing for the letter to the Lombard queen, Gregory's Germanic correspondence was decidedly devoid of theologically sophisticated arguments, so the appeals to Peter and Peter's authority never reached the elevated form or content that they did in Gregory's disputes with the East. But even for the quasi-Christian leaders of the Germanic tribes, Gregory hoped that the figure of Peter would prove strategically advantageous for the promotion of orthodoxy and the projection of his own authority.[92]

The Crisis of the Ecumenical Title

Of all Gregory's international efforts, none tested his ecclesiological perspective or his diplomatic skills more completely than the showdown with the patriarch of Constantinople over the latter's use of the title "Ecumenical Patriarch."[93] As I have argued elsewhere, Gregory objected to the title for myriad reasons, but the common theme among them was a fear that traditional Roman rights were being usurped by patriarch and emperor alike. Thus, Gregory's stand against the title served as a proxy for all his frustrations with the Eastern Church.[94] Rather than review the entire affair, we will focus on the shifting ways Gregory employed the Petrine topos in his efforts to rebuff the patriarch personally and attempt to build a consensus against his title. As we will see, these efforts ultimately proved futile, but they reveal the extent to which Gregory, like his predecessors, turned to the rhetorical possibilities provided by the Petrine discourse when all other diplomatic efforts had failed and Roman international prestige sunk to its nadir.

Although Gregory's diplomatic attempt to repress the title had begun as early as 593, his first public critique came in June 595, when he dispatched three letters: *Epistle* 5.37 to the emperor Maurice, *Epistle* 5.41 to Eulogius of Alexandria and Anastasius of Antioch, and *Epistle* 5.44 to John of Constantinople. While the letters share a common goal (i.e., the suppression of the title), and while each letter employs the Petrine topos, the thrust of each letter is unique, as are the specific ways Gregory leverages the Petrine theme. For example, in the long letter to Patriarch John, Gregory underplays Petrine privilege. St. Peter is mentioned only once explicitly and functions as an example of apostolic collegiality, despite his privileged position. Emphasizing the idea of a "universal Church" rather than a "universal bishop," Gregory notes: "Certainly Peter, the first of the apostles [*apostolorum primus*], is a member of the holy universal Church. What are Paul, and Andrew and John but leaders [*capita*] of individual communities? And yet all were members under the one head [Christ]."[95] The closest Gregory ever comes to asserting Roman or Petrine privilege is several paragraphs later when he asserts:

> As your fraternity knows, was it not at the venerable council of Chalcedon that the predecessors of this Apostolic See, which I serve by the dispensation of God, were called "universal" as an honor? But not one of them has ever desired to be called by this title, not one has seized such an audacious name for himself because in seizing the glory of an episcopal singularity for himself he might appear to deny the glory due to all of his brothers.[96]

This passage illuminates Gregory's initial strategy with John. He subtly asserts that Rome deserves the title, that Rome alone is an "apostolic see," but through a tradition of pontifical humility (the chief characteristic of authentic leadership according to Gregory), Roman bishops have refused the ecumenical title even when it has been offered to them by ecumenical councils.

Gregory's approach with the emperor and Eastern patriarchs was notably different. With the emperor Maurice, Gregory went straight to the biblical justifications for Roman privilege:

> Therefore, it is clear to all who read the Gospels that the care of the whole Church [*totius ecclesiae cura*] was committed by the voice of

the Lord to the Apostle Peter, prince of the apostles. Because to him
it was said: "Peter, do you love me? Feed my sheep" [Jn 21.16–17].
To him it was said: "Behold, Satan has desired to sift you all like
wheat but I have prayed for you, Peter, that your faith may not fail,
and when you are converted strengthen your brethren" [Lk 22.31–
32]. To him it was said: "You are Peter and upon this rock I will
build my Church, and the gates of Hell will not prevail against it. I
will give you the keys of the kingdom of Heaven, and whatever you
shall bind on earth shall be bound in Heaven, and whatever you
shall loose on earth shall be loosed in Heaven." [Mt 16.18–19][97]

Following these scriptural proof texts, Gregory cuts right to the point:
"Behold, [Peter] received the keys of the heavenly kingdom, he was granted
the power to bind and loose, and the care of the entire Church and the
empire was committed to him, and yet even he is not called the universal
apostle."[98] As we see, Gregory is far more explicit with Maurice than he had
been with John: if the title is too grand for Saint Peter, it is certainly too
grand for the bishop of Constantinople—a See that, in Gregory's era, made
no claim to apostolicity (Constantinopolitan identification with Saint
Andrew was not popularized until the following century[99]) and, instead, was
all too often administered by heretics.[100]

With the patriarchs of Alexandria and Antioch, Gregory took yet another
approach. Instead of recounting the biblical justifications for Roman authority, he simply begins the letter by recounting the history of the crisis. At its
earliest stage, Gregory notes, his predecessor, Pope Pelagius II, had annulled
the acts of the Constantinopolitan synod that had been convened to autho-
rize the title. Pelagius did this, Gregory tells his Eastern colleagues, "on the
authority of St. Peter the Apostle [*ex auctoritate sancti Petri apostoli*]."[101] This
is the only reference to Peter in the entire letter. Rather than emphasize
Petrine authority as he had with the emperor, or even Petrine humility as he
had with Patriarch John, Gregory's initial strategy with the Eastern patriarchs
is to play off of their own sense of entitlement and to stress for them the
extent to which John's ecumenical claim is a usurpation of episcopal dignity
everywhere.

But Gregory learned all too quickly that he had overestimated the extent
to which the Eastern patriarchs shared his concerns regarding the title. Anastasius, the patriarch of Antioch, responded that the title was a non-issue, and
that the pope would be better off to drop the matter entirely.[102] Perhaps even

more deflating was the fact that by the summer of 596, Patriarch Eulogius of Alexandria had not even bothered to respond to Gregory's lengthy letter of the previous summer. Exasperated, the pontiff wrote again to Eulogius, employing the Petrine card forcefully and insisting that his colleague in Alexandria pay closer attention to their common bond and common threat:

> There is something that binds us in a unique way to the Alexandrian Church and compels us in a special way to love it. For as everyone knows, the blessed Evangelist Mark was sent to Alexandria by his teacher Peter; and so we are bound by this unity of teacher and disciple to the extent that it appears that I am to preside over the see of the disciple in accord with [my relationship to] the teacher, and you are to preside over the see of the master in accordance with [your relationship to] the disciple.[103]

What is interesting here is the way in which Gregory is able to achieve three distinct but interrelated goals through the Petrine topos: (1) he links Alexandrian apostolic authority to Peter; (2) he establishes a hierarchy of Petrine authority that places Rome above Alexandria; and (3) based on this common link, he is able to imply that the ecumenical title is an affront to both Rome and Alexandria because it is an affront to Peter. With this letter, Gregory signals a shift in his strategy, one that relies heavily on a specific version of the Petrine narrative.

By June 597, Gregory's diplomatic efforts had moved farther still, most notably in a hardening of his rhetorical stance. He told Anastasius of Antioch that the title was the invention of the devil, a charge he would repeat in subsequent letters.[104] He also reinforced an older line of argument that he had not fully developed in 595—that calling one bishop universal links the fate of the universal Church to a single man. But if that man falls, as anyone can, then the universal Church falls with him. From Gregory's perspective, this was an untenable position, not only because the fate of the Church could not be linked to a single individual, but also because such a claim compromised the autonomy of individual bishops.[105]

Then, in July 597, Gregory offered the most pronounced assertion of Petrine authority in his entire corpus. Eulogius had finally responded to Gregory about the question at hand.[106] In doing so, the patriarch of Alexandria had embraced the long-standing Roman assertion that Peter continued to sit on his throne in the person of his successors. Acknowledging Eulogius' love for Peter, the pope offered a brief exegesis of Matthew 16 and other select passages, because they endorse what was for Gregory a new claim—that the Sees of Rome, Alexandria, and Antioch are the three most important in the Christian world because they alone have special ties to St. Peter. Gregory writes:

> Therefore, while there are many apostles with respect to preeminence, the See of the Prince of the Apostles has alone become valid in authority, which, in three, is unified as one. For [Peter] exalted the see in which he deigned to rest and complete the present life [i.e., Rome]; he adorned the see to which he sent his disciple, the Evangelist [i.e., Alexandria]; and he established the see in which he sat for seven years, though he would eventually leave it [i.e., Antioch].[107]

Thus, Gregory further elaborates the strategy he had employed in his previous letter to Eulogius. Whereas his initial tact of 595 had been to suggest that the title was an affront to all episcopal authority, here he argues that the title is especially an affront to the three preeminent sees of Christendom that have a special link to Peter. Because Antioch, Alexandria, and Rome alone have Petrine authority, they alone have a special claim to super-jurisdictional authority. As a consequence, the ecumenical title is especially a challenge to the authority of those three apostolic Sees. Gregory is quite consciously linking preeminence among the episcopal body to the Apostle Peter. By doing so, his intention is clear: he seeks to undermine the authority of Constantinople, which (from Gregory's perspective) is based on imperial, not apostolic, credentials.[108] Gregory concludes the letter by acknowledging the various gifts exchanged between Rome and Alexandria. Notably he describes this exchange as a transaction not between Eulogius and himself but between St. Mark and St. Peter.[109] In subsequent years, that same appeal to apostolic authority became a permanent feature of Gregory's letters to Eulogius.[110]

Gregory's efforts to influence Eastern bishops were not restricted to the Sees of Antioch and Alexandria, but the way in which he employed the Petrine topos with respect to other sees was decidedly different. In 599, Patriarch Cyriacus convened an Eastern synod in Constantinople. In anticipation of this meeting, Gregory wrote to Eusebius of Thessalonica and six other Eastern bishops warning them not to accept any attempt by Cyriacus or the emperor to have the council affirm the ecumenical title.[111] Not surprisingly,

Gregory employs the argument that if one bishop is the universal bishop, then all other bishops are deprived of their dignity.[112] He also notes: "when our predecessor, Pelagius of blessed memory, became aware of all of this, he annulled by an entirely valid censure all the acts of the synod [of 587], except those related to the cause of Gregory, the bishop of Antioch of venerable memory."[113] In 595 Pope Gregory had reported the same thing to Eulogius and Anastasius. The difference this time is that Gregory now promises that he will annul the impending council in Constantinople if it confirms the ecumenical title.[114] This is the strongest assertion of personal privilege in Gregory's corpus, and it belies his previous statements suggesting that synods are more authoritative than individual bishops.[115] Gregory concludes with further threats that if any one of these seven bishops should endorse the title, he will be severed from communion with Peter, prince of the apostles.[116]

From Gregory's perspective, the promotion of the ecumenical title was especially threatening because the emperor seemed to endorse it and Gregory's Eastern colleagues could not be convinced of its significance. Thus, it was in his bid to defend the traditional rights of Rome that Gregory maximized Petrine authority by investing Alexandria and Antioch with the same apostolic capital. This was a calculated move designed to undermine Constantinopolitan arrogance. By affirming the apostolic credentials of Alexandria and Antioch, the pontiff, just as Leo before him, implicated the imperial foundations of Constantinople's authority. It is noteworthy that it was late in the controversy before Gregory employed this argument. The principal strategy of his initial campaign had been that the title undermined the authority of other bishops. Only after that position failed to convince the patriarchs of Antioch and Alexandria did Gregory dig deep into the annals of papal rhetoric to assert further the Petrine privilege and to distinguish apostolic sees from those with lesser credentials.

Peter and the Subversion of Imperial Privilege

In her masterful work, *Christianity and the Rhetoric of Empire*, Averil Cameron demonstrates how Christian leaders in late antiquity were able to overcome opposition to the Christian message by developing a particular and totalizing Christian discourse in which they could both appropriate and critique the Roman world in which they were operating.[117] I would like to build on her insights here by offering a brief example of how Gregory similarly co-opted and transformed elements of the imperial discourse to subvert them in his promotion of Petrine authority. Specifically, I will consider how Gregory employed the language of empire, imperial privilege, and imperial obligation in his bid to compel the emperor to suppress the ecumenical title. As we will see, Gregory leaned on and gestured toward imperial sensibilities for the very purpose of undermining imperial sovereignty by re-inscribing Peter as the "imperial"—that is, the "authoritative"—voice.

Gregory subverts imperial authority in a number of ways in his eight surviving letters to the emperor Maurice.[118] For example, in the first letter, which objects to a new imperial law forbidding soldiers to leave their posts to pursue the life of monasticism, Gregory affirms the divine sanction for Maurice's rule but does so in a way that actually usurps imperial privilege and warns the emperor of dire political and spiritual consequences should he not rescind the law.[119] Elsewhere, Gregory solicits imperial obligation in religious matters by linking the emperor's temporal success, and the success of his armies, to his willingness to do what Gregory deems necessary.[120] In this regard, *Epistle* 5.37, the letter in which Gregory beseeches Maurice to intervene in the controversy over the ecumenical title, is especially illuminating. Among all the arguments that Gregory musters to condemn John's supposed arrogance, perhaps the most provocative is the evaluation that imperial armies are failing to halt the barbarian incursions (coupled with a prediction that they will continue do so) for no other reason than that the patriarch of Constantinople has insisted on calling himself "Ecumenical Patriarch." The following three excerpts from the letter clearly demonstrate the connection between the title and the emperor's lack of military success:

> My most serene Lordship, what human virtue, what strength of
> arms would presume to raise its irreligious hands against the glory
> of your most Christian empire, if the minds of priests devoted them-
> selves to beseech their Redeemer as one, on your behalf, and as was
> proper of your merits? Or what sword of a most ferocious race would
> proceed violently and so cruelly to destroy the faithful, unless the
> lives of us who are called priests, but are not priests, were not
> weighed down by most wicked deeds? But while we leave what is
> appropriate for us and consider what is inappropriate for us, we
> associate our sins with barbarian forces. Our sin has sharpened the
> enemy's swords, which burdens the strength of the republic. . . .

For when you press down [the arrogance of priests] you raise up the republic and when you cut away [arrogant presumption] you drag it from the width and breadth of your kingdom. . . .

I am compelled to exclaim and say: "What Times, What Immorality!"[121] Behold, in parts of Europe everything has been handed over to the barbarians: cities have been destroyed, army camps overwhelmed, provinces depopulated, and no farmer inhabits the land. The cults of idols run riot and daily the faithful are dominated. And, yet, priests, who should have humbled themselves with ashes and with tears in their eyes, seek out names for themselves full of vanity, and boast of new and profane titles.[122]

Such direct statements hardly require a complex analysis. Gregory boldly connects John's arrogance to recent military defeats. The implication is that the emperor's failure to suppress the title is more than an ecclesiastical failure; it has political consequences. Also implicit in Gregory's critique is the promise that Maurice's military fortunes will change as soon as the emperor takes a stronger hand with the patriarch John.

In the previous section, we noted how Gregory's initial public efforts to suppress the ecumenical title involved three letters in June 595 (to the emperor, to John, and to the patriarchs of Alexandria and Antioch). With respect to Gregory's use of the Petrine discourse, the element that most differentiated the letter to the emperor from the others was Gregory's inclusion of the many scriptural proof texts for Peter's authority. Those passages were capped by Gregory's rhetorical question to the emperor, which essentially asked "if so much honor is due to Peter and the See of Rome, but neither Peter nor any pope has ever asked for an arrogant title like it, then how can the patriarch of Constantinople, who has no such basis for the claim, assert the title?" One element that deserves further analysis here is the extent to which the same letter elides the symbols and ideology of imperial stature in order to assert Petrine authority.[123]

While there are multiple passages in the letter that could be assessed in this way, two examples will suffice. The first is a passage we have already examined:

Therefore, it is clear to all who read the Gospels that the care of the whole Church [*totius ecclesiae cura*] was committed by the voice of the Lord to the Apostle Peter, prince of the apostles [*apostolorum*

principi]. Because to him it was said: "Peter, do you love me . . ."
To him it was said: ". . . I will give you the keys of the kingdom of
Heaven, and whatever you shall bind on earth shall be bound in
Heaven, and whatever you shall loose on earth shall be loosed in
Heaven." Behold, Peter received the keys of the heavenly kingdom,
he was granted the power to bind and loose, and the care of the
entire Church and the empire was committed to him [*cura ei totius
ecclesiae et principatus committitur*], and yet he is not called the "universal" apostle [*universalis apostolus*].

The second passage is similar in argument to one that Gregory had made in
Epistle 5.44 to John:

> It was certainly due to the eminence of St. Peter, the prince of the
> apostles, that [the ecumenical title] was offered to the Roman pontiff
> [*Romano pontifici*] through the venerable synod of Chalcedon. But
> none of [the popes] ever consented to use this title of singularity, in
> case, while a personal honor was given to one person, universal
> priests might be deprived of their due honor.

For our purposes, there are at least three things to note about these twin
passages. First, whatever Jesus' listeners might have imagined when they
heard him use the phrase "kingdom of heaven," it is extremely unlikely that
a sixth-century aristocrat of the Roman Empire could have conceived of the
"kingdom of heaven" without some mental recourse to the imperial signs
and symbols of the empire. However transcendent and ethereal the heavenly
kingdom might be in comparison to the earthly one, in the late sixth century
the earthly empire was the only real referent for a kingdom in which Peter
had received the keys.

Second, Gregory's repeated designation of Peter as "prince," the "prince
of the apostles," likely reinforced (rather than weakened) the connection
between a heavenly and an earthly kingdom. To be sure, Gregory was not
the first pope to advance Peter's status as a *princeps*,[124] but there is absolutely
no reason to believe that the significance of the term was lost on him. Indeed,
apostolorum princeps simultaneously provided a subtle but authoritative imperial purchase for papal privilege and transferred a key imperial term, *princeps*,
to the Church.[125]

Third, the first passage in particular offers a sophisticated play on the
words *oikoumenikos, universalis*, and *totus*. The Greek word *oikoumenikos* is

the adjectival form of the noun *oikoumenē*, meaning "the inhabited earth." The Byzantines, drawing from their Roman predecessors, understood the borders of the empire to constitute the entire inhabited earth. As I have argued elsewhere, there are a myriad of ways to interpret the specific jurisdictional claims embedded in the assertion of the ecumenical title.[126] And, as is well known, Gregory rather famously took the Greek word *oikoumenikos* to be the equivalent of the Latin word *universalis* when he publicly challenged John's use of the title in 595. What is significant here is that in addition to making a series of comparisons between the "universal" Church, Peter's "total" authority, and John's "ecumenical" title, Gregory is also doubly asserting the "totality" of Peter's jurisdictional authority throughout the *oikoumenē*—in other words, the empire. Indeed, the passage concludes: "to him the care of the whole Church and *of the empire* is committed and, yet, he is not called the 'universal' apostle." Thus, we see, once again, how the language and symbols of empire are appropriated and put in the service of a specifically Christian discourse—in this case, it is a discourse of Petrine authority, which Gregory obviously develops to protect what he believes to be traditional papal prerogatives vis-à-vis the patriarch of Constantinople.

As we conclude this final section, let us note that it has not been our purpose to discern, in any comprehensive way, Gregory's understanding of empire or his understanding of the relationship between empire and Church.[127] Either of those analyses would require a different method and would obviously require a much wider reading of Gregory's corpus than just a single letter. Rather, in this final section we have simply tried to expose and examine the extent to which one dimension of Gregory's use of the Petrine topos involved the co-option and subversion of imperial discourse. In this particular case, we see that Gregory in some ways mimicked and in other ways mocked imperial signs and symbols for the purpose of enlisting the emperor's help in suppressing the ecumenical title. While it is true that Gregory's efforts in this regard did not achieve their intended goal, an analysis of this function of the pontiff's imperial correspondence nevertheless illustrates Gregory's theological nuance and rhetorical sophistication.

Conclusion

The preceding analysis has demonstrated the extent to which Gregory was familiar with, but typically stretched in different ways, the Petrine discourse that he inherited from his predecessors. Gregory's biblical commentaries, especially, evince the extent to which the figure of Peter functioned for Gregory as a theological and pastoral resource, which show little concern for Roman or papal authority. In these texts, Gregory frequently reflected on Peter's faults as a means to advocate the virtues of humility and repentance for his clerical readers. Moreover, large sections of Gregory's clerical correspondence (as represented by two hundred letters concerning the Sicilian Church) reveal little interest in promoting the traditional staples of the papal application of the Petrine topos, such as the biblical justifications for Peter's authority or the link between St. Peter and his papal successors.

Those traditional elements, however, were certainly a part of Gregory's most tense diplomatic initiatives, especially those concerning the controversy over the ecumenical title. Like Leo and Gelasius before him, Gregory was able to emphasize Peter's biblical authority, the link between Peter and the Roman See, and how that connection guaranteed theological orthodoxy. Also like his predecessors, Gregory usually advanced those positions in times of international weakness, when all other avenues had been exhausted. While Gregory was able to maximize the rhetorical force of the Petrine topos, it was not his default mode, and he seems to have gravitated toward it only when all else failed him.

Perhaps the most intriguing element of Gregory's use of the Petrine tradition is the extent to which he added to it by introducing the ritualistic exercise of the swearing of oaths at Peter's tomb and through the dissemination of Peter's relics. Whereas previous popes had employed Peter in their diplomacy as a purely rhetorical instrument at the level of language and/or text, Gregory transformed the Petrine legacy into a multidimensional resource constituted in terms of space, time, and memory. Papal agents and recalcitrant clerics swore oaths, in Gregory's presence, before Peter's tomb. Synods of bishops, both local and regional, gathered on the anniversary of Peter's death. And a select group of elite lords and bishops received Peter's relics as personal gifts from their pope. More than simply disseminate Peter's relics, however, Gregory offered specific advice for how the relics should be used and treated. While Gregory may have employed the rhetorical elements of the Petrine discourse more subtly than his predecessors, he nevertheless creatively stretched its possibilities in new ways that would be perhaps even more important in the centuries to come.

Postscript: The *Life of St. Gregory of Agrigentum* as a Seventh-Century Petrine Critique of the Papacy

Gregory of Agrigentum was a Greek-speaking native of Sicily who was elected to the See of Agrigentum, on Sicily's southern coast, at roughly the same time that Pope Gregory I was elected to the Roman See in 590. His *vita* was probably produced in the 630s by Leontius, a monk of the St. Savas monastery in Rome.[1] If this date is accurate, it would fix the composition to a time shortly after the death of Bishop Gregory and roughly thirty years after the death of Pope Gregory.[2] The author, like Bishop Gregory, was a Greek-speaker and composed the *vita* in Greek. This *vita* is significant for our study for two reasons. First, it confirms that the Petrine discourse had permeated Christian apologetics (papal or otherwise) by the early seventh century—the text links its hero to Petrine miracles and Petrine authority in multiple ways. Second, it testifies to the fact that as late as the seventh century, constituencies that found themselves in opposition to the bishop of Rome could still leverage the Petrine topos for their own purposes.

In brief, the *vita* chronicles its hero's journey as a young man from Sicily to the East, where he visits the holy shrines of Antioch, Jerusalem, and Constantinople. During a protracted stay in Constantinople, Gregory, now a deacon and monk, befriends both the patriarch and the emperor and, somewhat surprisingly, sits in for an absentee bishop during a regional council, which had been called to adjudicate a charge of heresy.[3] At the conclusion of the synod, Gregory begs permission of the emperor to complete his pilgrimage by traveling to Rome, where he desires to venerate the relics of the apostles.[4] Once in Rome, Gregory settles into the Greek-speaking monastery of St. Savas (the same monastery as Leontius, the author of the *vita*). Shortly thereafter, the bishop of Rome (with the assistance of a miraculous vision) selects monk Gregory to fill the vacant see of his native Agrigentum in Sicily.

The *vita* does not mention which pope oversees the election, but given other factors, it would seem that Martyn is correct in concluding that Gregory's election to the see would have come during the tenure of Pope Gregory.[5]

Soon into his tenure as bishop, Gregory is falsely accused of both adultery and witchcraft by two men who had themselves coveted the see. The rector of the papal patrimony in Sicily determines that there is enough evidence for Gregory to stand trial, and so the rector sends the bishop to Rome in chains. Once he arrives in Rome, Pope Gregory is said to look on the saintly bishop with utter contempt and orders him cast into prison while he awaits a trial.[6] This accusation of brutality is significant because, if true, it would be contrary to both canonical prescription and Pope Gregory's typical practice (which would dictate that an accused cleric be confined to a monastery while he awaited his trial, not a prison).[7] As if the victim of a bureaucratic mistake, Bishop Gregory languishes in prison for more than a year before Pope Gregory finally remembers he needs to act on the case. Rather than decide the matter by himself, however, Pope Gregory is advised by Bishop Gregory's former abbot, at St. Savas, to call a general synod to adjudicate the case. The abbot instructs Pope Gregory that both the patriarch of Constantinople and the emperor should be represented at the trial. Pope Gregory is said to consent without hesitation. Bishop Gregory is finally vindicated and after additional trips to Constantinople and then back to Rome, eventually resumes his governance of the See of Agrigentum. The narrative concludes with Bishop Gregory's construction of a new cathedral dedicated to Sts. Peter and Paul.

The legendary nature of these details notwithstanding, we will focus our literary analysis of the *vita* on the author's presentation of Pope Gregory. Although the pontiff appears frequently in the *vita*, four episodes will suffice for our purposes. The first concerns the pope's role in the election of Bishop Gregory to the See of Agrigentum. The *vita* states that a large contingent of lay and clerical rulers traveled from Agrigentum to Rome to lobby Pope Gregory regarding the selection of their next bishop. This detail is interesting in itself because it suggests both a Sicilian deference to Roman authority and a measure of Gregorian supervision in the episcopal elections of Sicily that is not borne out by other contemporary sources.[8] According to the text, Pope Gregory is dismissive of the two candidates put forward by some members of the delegation, and after a few days of being troubled over the matter, he receives a vision in which "two men in apostolic attire" instruct him to elect the Sicilian monk Gregory, who was currently hiding in a Roman monastery.[9] In this initial encounter, Pope Gregory is described as being respected by the Sicilian delegation, as being discerning in the selection of bishops, and as being worthy to receive and properly interpret a miraculous vision.

Such a positive characterization stands in stark contrast to a subsequent encounter between Pope Gregory and Bishop Gregory that occurs when Bishop Gregory arrives in Rome in chains. According to the *vita*, Pope Gregory was "filled with anger and was unwilling to be looked at by him." He then ordered that Bishop Gregory be thrown into prison, "with his hands and arms bound to a wooden beam with a heavy iron chain."[10] A few lines later, the author laments: "Oh the folly, oh the cruelty, oh the evil that filled the man who held the first throne of the Apostles, and should be looking after those who do wrong with comfort and prayers, rather than driving them to despair. But in this case, he had not asked questions to find out exactly what happened and to learn the truth."[11] The author then concludes: "But anyway, anger destroys even the intelligent, and this confusion came upon him from the ancient and evil enemy."

This is a fascinating passage. Despite being the man who "holds the first throne of the apostles," Pope Gregory is described as "filled with evil" and as susceptible to the "ancient and evil enemy." But perhaps the most interesting charge against the pope is that he failed to be pastoral—interesting, because Pope Gregory is the author of what is widely regarded as the most sophisticated treatise on pastoral care in patristic literature, the *Book of Pastoral Rule*. As I have argued in multiple venues, Gregory consistently put the theories of his *Book of Pastoral Rule* into practice in his dealings with both lay and clerical interlocutors.[12] Thus, we must consider whether Leontius' charge is deliberately designed as a subtle but powerful critique of Gregory's legacy—an attempt to undermine the very thing for which the pope was best known.

In the next chapter of the *vita*, the criticisms of Pope Gregory continue; only this time they are put into the mouth of two of the apostles. According to the text, on the first evening of Bishop Gregory's imprisonment in Rome, two men "dressed in apostolic garb" appear to the bishop and say: "Greetings, Gregory, servant of God, Christ has sent us to free you from your chains, since the pope wrongly bound you."[13] After instructing the saint that it would be necessary for him to perform many miracles during his stay in Rome, the two apostles remove the bishop's shackles and then mystically depart. Just as in the case of the miraculous vision that Pope Gregory received earlier in the story, the two men "in apostolic garb" are not named. There can be little doubt, however, that the two visitors are intended to represent

Peter and Paul—indeed, the two apostles are explicitly named elsewhere in the text, and it is with these specific saints that the text ends, when Bishop Gregory dedicates a church in their honor.

Although it is significant that heavenly agents are sent by Christ to unshackle Bishop Gregory, because the pope "wrongly bound him," it is even more telling that the author employs the most powerful symbols of papal authority to right a papal wrong. The use of Sts Peter and Paul, I would argue, is intended as a counter to contemporary claims that the bishop of Rome is the principal arbiter of the saints' miraculous powers. Given Pope Gregory's efforts to stretch the Petrine discourse in new ways (particularly through the tomb and relics of St. Peter), Leontius' use of Peter and Paul to critique Pope Gregory is arresting. By advancing the notion that the apostles can and do intervene on behalf of those who are wronged by the pope himself, the author is challenging the most potent of contemporary papal claims to ecclesiastical authority.

One final interaction with Pope Gregory is worth exploring—the dialogue between the pontiff and the abbot Mark. According to the *vita*, Mark convinces Pope Gregory that both the patriarch of Constantinople and the emperor should be represented at Bishop Gregory's trial. Not only is Mark portrayed as being more discerning than Gregory, but the author clearly places limits on Pope Gregory's right to adjudicate the matter for himself. It would seem unlikely that Leontius is disputing that the bishop of Rome has some jurisdiction in Sicily—he had already reported that a delegation from Agrigentum had gone to Rome in order to obtain a new bishop.[14] Rather, I believe, Leontius is suggesting that Bishop Gregory (whether because of his friendship with Eastern rulers or because of his saintliness) deserves the legal and spiritual protection that can be provided only by the emperor and the patriarch of Constantinople.[15] This is confirmed by the fact that both the emperor and the patriarch are described as not being able to trust that Pope Gregory would handle the case fairly.[16] By including the patriarch and the emperor in the story, Leontius, in effect, offers an additional challenge to Pope Gregory's spiritual and legal authority. The suggestion in this text that Eastern rulers must be consulted before the pope can judge a Western bishop is, to my knowledge, unique among our surviving documents from the period.

What makes this text all the more intriguing is that, despite all of this, many of the actors in the story, including Bishop Gregory, show considerable deference to the pontiff. For example, when he is first brought to trial in

Sicily, Bishop Gregory actually asks that his case be heard in Rome. Once he is there, he never criticizes Pope Gregory or his handling of the case—all criticisms of Pope Gregory are put into the mouths of others.[17] The emperor, likewise, even though it is said that he cannot trust that Pope Gregory will treat Bishop Gregory fairly, nevertheless instructs his delegation to depart for the "holy synod as commanded by the most holy pope, the common father of our city there so dear to God."[18]

How then are we to interpret this ambivalence? Morcelli, the original editor of the text, argued that the antagonism toward Pope Gregory was likely influenced by and/or drew on anti-Gregorian pamphlets that are believed to have circulated in Rome at the time of the *vita*'s composition. It is certainly true that following the pontiff's death in 604 there was a lengthy polemical campaign between the supporters and the opponents of Gregory's asceticizing program. It is also true that the *Life of St. Gregory of Agrigentum* includes several anti-Gregorian statements. But what is interesting about these two forums for criticism is that they are distinct. Apart from this text, the post-mortem Roman criticism of Pope Gregory for which we have evidence was almost entirely related to his attempt to remove the clerical establishment in Rome and replace it with monks from his monasteries. In other words, the dispute was between the ascetic and nonascetic parties within the Roman clergy.[19] The criticism of the *vita*, however, relates almost entirely to Pope Gregory's handling of Bishop Gregory. Although Pope Gregory is accused of lacking pastoral depth, the question of the pontiff's asceticism and his administration of the Roman Church are nonfactors in the *vita*.

Even more problematic, however, is the question of whether or not the *vita*'s criticisms of Pope Gregory are intended as personal or institutional critiques. We can be confident that the author of the *vita* was a Greek-speaking monk living in a Greek monastery in Rome, that he held the patri-arch of Constantinople and the emperor in high regard, and that he fre-quently questioned Pope Gregory's judgment and portrayed him as being susceptible to the intrigues of the devil. But what, if anything, is this author saying about Roman ecclesiastical privilege?

At the very least, the *Life of St. Gregory of Agrigentum* serves as an impor-tant caution against anachronistic readings of papal history and papal claims. Despite all the attempts by individual pontiffs and those sympathetic to them in the late ancient period to inscribe a narrative of papal primacy upon the Christian consciousness and to do it through its most effective marketing tactic—the promotion of the Petrine legacy—this text clearly demonstrates that it was still possible in the seventh century for clerics within the city of Rome itself to accuse a pope of having fallen victim to the wiles of the devil. Even if the most salacious of the accusations in the *vita* were against Gregory himself (and not the See of Rome more generally), that they exist at all is an important reminder that there were clerics in Rome who did not believe individual popes were beyond reproach. What is more, the text offers a direct challenge to the idea that the bishops of Rome were the sole arbiters of the sacral power of St. Peter. Indeed, the *Life of St. Gregory of Agrigentum* testifies to the ability of others to employ the legacy of Peter's primacy as a weapon against the papacy.

Before we turn to our concluding analysis, it is important to recall an important element of papal historiography that we identified in the Introduction—namely, that so much of the way we think about the early papacy and the individual bishops of Rome has been shaped by later papal activists who were eager to spread Roman influence in their own period. For example, the eighth- and ninth-century archivists and historians carefully selected and preserved the sources that would be the most beneficial in advancing a record of the past that most suited their needs in the then present. They allowed the rhetorical claims of papal authority (claims, as we have seen, that were almost always born of insecurity and weakness) that had been offered by Leo, Gelasius, and Gregory to masquerade as the truth of a papal past. They selected those authors and particular texts within their *corpora* because those texts offered models of papal strength and often did so through a medium that was still powerful in the ninth century—the Petrine topos.

But let us consider how our collective appreciation for the early papacy would be different if those same editors had emphasized a Petrine tradition more consistent with that found in the *Life of St. Gregory of Agrigentum*. In other words, what if the kinds of texts that survived, and the traditions of thinking about those texts, had been shaped by Petrine rebukes of papal actors rather than by Petrine affirmations of papal authority? What would we think about Gregory (and Leo and Gelasius as well) if the purveyors of Gregorian materials in the Middle Ages had been predisposed to emphasize the limits of papal sovereignty via Peter rather that its confirmation?

Conclusion: The Invention of Peter

In *Christianity and the Rhetoric of Empire*, Averil Cameron demonstrates the value of examining the ascendancy of Christianity in an otherwise unfavorable Roman context by seeking to understand the "articulation" and "ideology" of Christianity as dynamic factors in and of themselves.[1] In doing so, she offers a prime example of how the field of early Christian studies can benefit from the critical resources provided by discourse analysis. In the current study, I have sought to elucidate a more specific form of early Christian discourse than Cameron pursued, the "Petrine discourse," and, in the process, I have maintained that this analysis forces us to reconsider the traditional narratives of the early papacy.

Among the several aspects of early Christian discourse Cameron identifies as having played a role in the religion's ascendancy in the Roman world, at least three of the same elements are found to be central to the Petrine discourse. First, Cameron argues that because early Christianity was multiform (i.e., there are variations within its belief and practice), the religion could present itself in different ways at different times, effectively altering its discursive emphases for an ever-shifting Roman audience. Second, Cameron stresses the "totalizing" nature of Christian discourse and ideology, which offered an all-encompassing vision and differentiated it from Greco-Roman religion. Third, Cameron emphasizes the importance of Christianity's narrative emphasis, represented in both the apocryphal acts of the second and third centuries and in the creation of Christian biography beginning in the fourth. Biography, she argues, was central to the creation of a particular mythic universe in which the stories and practices of the saints, particularly the martyrs, conveyed meaning and invited participation.

As we conclude our analysis of the "invention" of Peter, I would like to suggest that these very same features were contained within the Petrine discourse and contributed similarly to the eventual ascendancy of the See of Rome over other authoritative voices in the medieval West. First, concerning the multiform and elastic qualities of the Petrine discourse, we should recall the extent to which the pontiffs and their supporters in this period emphasized different aspects of the Petrine legacy in their bid to secure and promote Roman episcopal authority. In different times and for different reasons, Peter filled any number of roles: founder of the Church, sole dogmatic authority, originator of baptismal rituals, mystical patron of the city of Rome, chief heretic hunter, source of episcopal authority, *primus* of the episcopate, and leading citizen of the empire. His shrine and relics also served multiple functions: a place of pilgrimage, a barricade against rival factions, a host site for secular and ecclesiastical dignitaries, the locus for the swearing of oaths, the vehicle for disseminating spiritual talismans, and, of course, the symbol of papal power. The most creative of pontiffs and their literary and editorial supporters were able to employ multiple combinations of Petrine attributes and effectively link them to the See of Rome and its many causes. The malleability of the biblical Peter in these distinct roles and symbols—or perhaps the rhetorical sophistication of those early popes that was able to render the biblical Peter so malleable—was of fundamental importance to the discursive presentation of the papacy's hegemonic claims and the ultimate willingness of other Christians to authenticate those claims through their own use of them.

Second, there is little denying the papal efforts to present Petrine authority in a "totalizing" fashion—not only the completeness of Peter's authority, but a vision in which all Christian meaning flows from Peter and his heirs. While it may be true that many of the claims to total authority (whether dogmatic, ecclesiological, legal, or otherwise) were in no way based on actualized or actualizable authority at the time they were offered, the discourse of primatial ecclesiastical authority fit within the discursive parameters of the age and therefore became an important rhetorical and polemical feature of all subsequent papal and Petrine narratives. While we have not delved deeply into the preexisting discursive possibilities that enabled such statements (be they derivative of an imperial and/or Christian discourse more broadly), it is important to recognize that the Petrine discourse was not a unique late ancient formulation of an all-encompassing narrative.

Finally, concerning the importance of narrative, we might recall that one of the most significant advances in this period of the way that Petrine authority could be connected to the papacy was the creation of papal biography that drew on earlier apocryphal traditions linked to St. Peter. This literary form helped both to insulate particular bishops from accusations of misconduct and to provide a comprehensive account of papal sovereignty that began with Peter's tenure in Rome and continued unabated from pope to pope, down to the then present. The use of narrative, of course, made it possible for papal biographers to weave aspects of Peter's story into the story of their own subjects and, in the process, to reinforce the papal link to the "prince of the apostles."

The papal narratives about Peter himself combined biblical and apocryphal elements but, equally important, possessed a certain fluidity that enabled individual pontiffs to showcase the elements of the Petrine story that best suited their needs—recall, for example, the difference in the extent to which Leo was not but Gregory was willing to mine Peter's "faults," or the different ways Gelasius and Gregory defined which bishops had a share in Peter's apostolic capital. Let us also note in the context of narrative, the extent to which the location of Peter's tomb in Rome allowed late ancient pontiffs to articulate further the connections between Peter's spiritual authority and their own ability to access and distribute that authority, particularly through the narration of Petrine miracles.

In the end, the success of papal actors in harnessing the Petrine topos to their own ends lay in their capacity to invent and perpetuate an epistemic horizon for Christian teaching and Christian leadership through the careful articulation of a Petrine legacy that was tied directly to the city of Rome and, most importantly, to the Roman bishop, "Peter's heir." To the extent that the development and control of discourse can be seen as a key to social power, then the papal expansion and promotion of the Petrine discourse along self-interested lines should certainly be seen as one of the critical factors that contributed to the papacy's ascendancy over other power structures in Western Europe in the later Middle Ages.

What is so fascinating about the period between Leo and Gregory is that the development of the Petrine discourse was typically not accompanied by actual papal strength—the escalations in rhetoric did not match actualized or actualizable authority—but instead often occurred because of frustration, humiliation, and internal dissent. It is indeed one of the great ironies of the papal story that its most significant rhetorical and narrative advances were designed to mask its most troubling problems. With time, the papacy was able to minimize and ultimately suppress those humiliations through a combination of self-perpetuating papal biographies and editorial erasure. But it was the invention of a decidedly Roman, ecclesiologically sovereign, dogmatically orthodox, and inherently malleable Peter that ultimately enabled the ascendancy of the See of Rome.

Pope Gelasius to Augustus Anastasius

1. O my son, when the servants of Your Piety, the Illustrious Faustus Magister and Irenaeus, had returned to the city after fulfilling their public embassy, they said that Your Clemency had asked why I had not sent formal greetings to you after my election as Bishop of Rome. I must say that it was not my intention to avoid sending you a letter. However, because new representatives from the East made it known throughout the whole City that *on your orders* I was not allowed to see them, I decided that I ought to refrain from writing you because I was afraid that if I were to write I would be burdensome rather than dutiful to you.

And so you can see that this situation did not arise from a desire to conceal my election from you, but rather from my precaution: I did not want to annoy one who rejects me. But when I discovered, as the aforementioned persons indicated to me, that Your Serenity's goodwill had already mercifully asked a word of my humility, then I clearly realized that I would be acting unjustly if I were to remain silent, because, o glorious son, I, as one Roman-born, love, cherish, and highly esteem you both as a Roman Prince and as a Christian, alongside him who has zeal for God, desire that you have that zeal according to the knowledge of truth, and I, the vicar of the apostolic see, for whatever it is worth, fight in my own little way by timely suggestions if I find that anything of the full catholic faith is lacking anywhere. Indeed, the stewardship of the divine word has been imposed on me: woe to me if I do not proclaim the Gospel![1] Now, since the blessed Apostle Paul trembled to call himself a vessel of election, how much more ought I fear to subtract from the divinely inspired ministry of preaching that has been handed down to me by fatherly devotion?

2. I beg Your Piety not to consider my obedience to the divine economy to be arrogance. For I think that a Roman prince should not consider the truth that he knows in his heart to be an offense. For, as you know, Emperor, there are two primary means by which this world is ruled: the hallowed authority of the pontiff and royal power. Now, if we were to compare the two of them, the sacerdotal burden is as much heavier as the responsibility [for priests] is more serious for they will render an account even for the kings of men at the divine judgment. Of course, as you know, Most Merciful Son, you have been allowed to preside over humankind in dignity. However, devoutly incline your head[2] to those who rule in the divine sphere, wait for your source of salvation from them, and recognize that you should be placed under the rule of religion rather than rule over it when the question concerns receiving or setting aside heavenly mysteries. Furthermore, you know that these affairs depend on those ruling in the divine sphere and they are certainly not willing to be reined in by your will. Now, regarding the sphere of public discipline, those bishops know that *imperium* has been taken from the ends of the earth and given to you by a heavenly arrangement.

Now then, the bishops who are the leaders in the sacred sphere obey your laws in such a manner that their opinions concerning the world (and these opinions are distinct from the world) do not seem to be opposed to those laws. How much more, I ask you, should you lovingly obey those who have been assigned to administer the venerable mysteries? So it is right for the pontiffs to have kept silent, because a heavy judgment rests on them because of their place in the divine cult. However, there is a great danger to those who (God forbid!) despise the pontiffs when they ought rather to obey them. If all the priests are essentially handling divine affairs correctly and it is deemed appropriate that the faithful submit their hearts to them, how much more should everyone follow the opinion of him who presides in the chair, he whom the most high God desired to preside over all the other priests, whom the whole pious Church has celebrated without ceasing?

3. Your Piety ought to consider that it is clear that no one has ever been able to elevate himself by any human counsel whatsoever to that acknowledgment or confession which the voice of Christ has brought to the whole world, which the venerable Church has always confessed and faithfully considered to be of chief importance. Although those prerogatives that have been established by divine decision can be attacked by human presumption, they cannot be conquered by anyone's power. But those who struggle against those

prerogatives are destroyed by their own arrogance! But that which has been established by the very author of holy religion cannot be overcome by any power whatsoever. Indeed, God's support remains firm.[3]

For is it not true that when religion is troubled by certain persons, however much it might be overpowered by their novelty of doctrine, nevertheless it also remains unconquered to the same degree to which it was judged it would fall? So I beg you, at least in your reign, make these men cease from hasty canvassing (which they are not even allowed to do) on account of an instance of ecclesial difficulty. Make them stop, I ask, so that they do not attain those things that they maliciously desire and, furthermore, so that they do not have their way in front of God and man.

4. And so, I beg you in purity and sincerity, and testify and exhort Your Piety in the sight of God that you not receive my petition with resentment. Furthermore, I ask that you hear my petition in this life rather than, God forbid!, you see me accusing you at the divine judgment. For, Emperor Augustus, the zeal of your devotion in your private life has not been hidden from me. You have always desired to become a participant of the eternal promise. So do not, I beg you, get angry at me if I love you so much that I desire you to have eternally the kingship that you have obtained in time and for you, who rule in this temporal world, to also reign with Christ. For certainly, Emperor, in your laws you neither allow anything to be destroyed, nor do you allow the Roman name to be diminished. Thus is it not true, o Distinguished Prince, you who desire not only the present benefits of Christ but also future ones, that in your rule you would never allow anyone to cause loss to religion, truth, and the wholeness of Catholic faith and communion? On account of what fidelity, I ask you, will you seek his rewards there, since you did not prevent his getting robbed here on earth?

5. I ask you, are not the things said for the sake of your eternal salvation very serious? You have read what is written: "Better are wounds from a friend than kisses from an enemy."[4] So I ask Your Piety to receive these words in the affection with which they are said by me. Let no one deceive Your Piety. What the scripture figuratively witnesses to through the prophet is true: "My dove is one, my perfect dove."[5] Christian faith is one and it is the catholic faith. That faith is truly catholic, however, which, separated from the fellowship with all traitors and their successors, remains whole, pure, and immaculate in communion. Otherwise there will not be a divinely mandated division,

but a pitiful confusion. If we allowed contagion in any one, there would be no reason why we would not open wide the doors and gates to all the heresies *en masse*. He who offends in one matter is responsible for everything,[6] and he who despises the smallest affairs soon falls.[7]

6. This is what the apostolic see strenuously guards against: that the Church be split by no fissure of evil nor stained by any contagion. The apostolic see has this duty because the glorious confession of the apostle[8] is the pure root of the Church. Now, if some such thing were to happen, God forbid! (and we do not believe that it could happen anyway), but if it were possible, how would we dare to resist an error, or whom could we ask for correction for those who wander? Furthermore, if Your Piety denies that the people of one city can be organized, what are we to make of the whole world if, God forbid, it has been deceived by our lie? If the whole world has been healed from the profane and despicable teaching of its fathers, why will not the people of just one city be corrected if they receive a faithful preaching after having had [Eutyches' teaching]. So, you can see, Emperor, that I desire the peace of the Church, and I will embrace that peace even if my blood must be spilled in order to attain it. But, I beg you, let us be clear that this peace ought not be of just any kind, but truly Christian. Indeed, how could we have true peace without pure charity? The kind of charity that it ought to be is clearly preached to us by the apostle: "charity from a pure heart and a good conscience and unfeigned fidelity."[9] How, I ask you, will that charity be from a pure heart if any foreign contagion is added to it? How will it be from a good conscience if it is deformed and mixed with evils? How, finally, "from unfeigned fidelity" if it remains associated with traitors?

Although we have said this many times already, it bears repeating incessantly, and we will not be silent for the sake of "peace." We do this because it is not our duty to make peace, as is enviously bandied about, but so that we might teach *that* peace which we desire. We do this in order that this peace, which is the only true peace, and besides which there is no other peace, might be shown.

7. Certainly if it is believed that Eutyches' teaching (against which the apostolic see has been vigilant) can agree with the salvific truth of the catholic faith, then his teaching ought to be promoted, supported, and encouraged by all possible means so that not only may it be shown how much it is, in and of itself, an enemy to the Christian faith, but also so that we might show

how many and how deadly are the heresies that it holds in its cesspool. If however, and we have more confidence that you will take this course of action, you judge that the teaching ought to be excluded from catholic minds, I ask you, why do you not also at the same time decree that the contagions of them who demonstrate themselves to be polluted by Eutyches' teaching are to be refuted? For the apostle says: "Rather is it not the case that not only those who do unlawful deeds are guilty, but also those who give their consent to those who do them?"[10] Furthermore, just as the carrier of iniquity cannot be accepted without simultaneously approving the iniquity, so too an iniquity cannot both be refuted and at the same time a closely connected follower of that iniquity accepted.

8. Certainly according to your laws those aware of crimes and those harboring thieves are bound by the same sentence. One who has received the friendship and alliance of a criminal would not be considered to be without culpability for the crime, although he has not committed the deed himself. Therefore, since the council of Chalcedon, celebrated on account of its truth and communion of the catholic and apostolic faith, has damned Eutyches as the author of that detestable madness, it must likewise strike down his associate Dioscorus and the others.

So, just as when judgment is passed on a heresy, so it is passed on everyone who follows that heresy, in the same way in this case the successors of Eutyches, namely Timothy, Peter, and the other Peter from Antioch, have not been struck down man by man, each of them in a new council called to deal with them individually, but they have been struck down all together as a consequence of the Acts of the synod that was performed once for all. So why is it not evident that all the others are bound in a similar sense as well, all those, that is, who have been communicators and abettors of them, and that all of them are entirely and appropriately cut off from the catholic and apostolic communion? We declare that this Acacius by right also ought to be removed from our fellowship because he preferred to move across to the fellowship of evil rather than remain in the sincerity of the Catholic communion, even though for three years he had been rightly instructed by letters from the apostolic see not to enter into the evil fellowship.

However, after he had been made part of a foreign communion, he had to be cut off from the society of the catholic and apostolic communion. For if we had backed off just a little, we would also have seemed, through his mediation, to have gotten infected by the evil contagions. But truly, even when he was struck by such a punishment, did he come to his senses, promise correction, and fix his error? Or rather did he, who could not even feel the harsh blows, not desire to be treated leniently? However it may be, because he died in evil and damnation, his name cannot be added to the ecclesial recitation[11] because the contagion of external communion ought not to be admitted. For this reason, it needs to be clear that the sincere penitent either ought to be removed far from participation with those heretics in whose communion he has dallied, or he will not be able to avoid being shunned alongside them.

9. The bishops of the East, however, have been grumbling because the apostolic see has not written these things to them, as if either they would make the apostolic see more secure concerning the legitimate reception of the Petrine authority with their letters or as if they have not already shown themselves to be equal participants of his disordered reception. Just as they cannot teach that Acacius has been cleansed from heretical depravity, so they will not be able to in any way make up an excuse for their fellowship with heretics. But if by chance they should add that they all had unanimously reported back to the apostolic see on the question of the acceptance of Peter by Acacius, then through Acacius they would by the same token see for themselves that he had been rescripted. Indeed, the authority of the apostolic see, because it has been given in all Christian ages to the universal Church, is strengthened both by the series of canons of the fathers and a multifaceted tradition.

But indeed if anyone, contrary to the constitutions of the Nicene Synod, should dare to take some authority for himself, this should be made plain to the assembly of one communion rather than opened to the minds of the outside world. If anyone among them is confident in himself, let him come out into the open and refute and instruct the apostolic see on both questions. Therefore, let that name,[12] which operates so distantly from the judgment of the churches and the Catholic communion, be taken out of its midst, so that the sincere peace of faith and communion, and unity moreover, might be revived. And then if one of us should either rise up or try to rise up against venerable antiquity, he will be competently and legitimately investigated. And then it will be clear who gently conserves the form and tradition of our ancestors, who irreverently attacks those traditions, and who considers himself able to become an equal by theft.[13]

10. But if the person of the Constantinopolitan people is put forward, he who says that the name of the scandal (that is, of Acacius) cannot be removed,

I am silent because, both when, at one time, the Macedonian heretic was expelled and when Nestorius had just been ejected, the Constantinopolitan folk chose to remain catholic rather than be held back by their affection for their condemned ancestral leaders. I am silent because those who had been baptized by those very same damned leaders, inasmuch as they remained in the catholic faith, have not been disturbed by any agitation. I am silent because the authority of Your Piety also holds back, at this time, the popular commotions for ridiculous matters. Therefore the multitude of Constantinople will all the more submit to you for the necessary salvation of their souls, if you, their prince, should lead them back to the catholic and apostolic union.

However, Emperor Augustus, if by chance, and God forbid, someone were to try to do something against the public laws, you would in no way be able to allow it. Do you not think that it is of concern to your conscience that the *plebs* who are placed under you and subject to you be brought to a pure and sincere devotion for the Divinity? If the mind of the people of a single city is considered unharmed as long as divine affairs are reformed, how much more is it true that we are not able to harm the faith of the universal catholic name in preventing offense to divine affairs?

11. And yet these same people ask to be cleansed by our will. Let them, therefore, accept the possibility of their being cured by the appropriate remedies! Otherwise (God forbid!) by crossing into their destruction we could perish with them, because, really, we are not able to save them. I submit to your conscience, under divine judgment, what course ought to be followed in this case: either, as we desire, let us all return together to certain life or, as they demand, let us all head toward obvious death.

12. But they vehemently declare this apostolic see haughty and arrogant simply because we are suggesting a cure for them. Indeed, it is characteristic of the ill to accuse doctors of malpractice when they coax them back to health by appropriate treatment, instead of agreeing with the doctors' recommendations to set aside or condemn their own habits that are unhealthy for them. If we are arrogant because we minister the appropriate remedies to souls, what should they who resist us be called? If we who say that the commands of our fathers ought to be obeyed are arrogant, what should we call them who oppose those commands of our fathers? If we who desire that godly

worship be preserved with a pure and intact union are haughty, let them say how they should be named who opine against the Divinity? In this way others who are in error also think of us because we do not agree to their insanity. Nevertheless, truth herself makes clear the place where a spirit of arrogance truly stands and fights.

Tract VI

Against Senator Andromachus and the other Romans who have decided that the Lupercalia ought to be celebrated in the old way.[1]

1. Some people sit in their houses unaware of what they say or of what they approve of, judging others even though they do not judge themselves and preferring to accuse rather than to understand, and to teach before they learn. And so, although this question has not been discussed, and the cases have not been investigated, and there has not been an inquiry into the rationale of the affair, nevertheless they pour out without thinking and vomit forth whatever comes to their mouths, expressing their opinion not on the basis of a declaration of the truth that has been brought forward, but instead argue (in their zeal for shitty words) for things which they do not know. And they have come so far that they are trying to mangle good deeds in their resolute commitment to malevolence.

If they were sensible, they would not rush forward with just any argument, but they would present a case based on a prior examination of the matter. But because they argue that we are sluggish censors of those vices of the Church that ought to be kept in check, they should also learn from us that there is a kind of fornication and adultery that is much worse than the sin of corporeal adultery that is rightfully struck down and punished by law. This other kind of adultery ought to be conquered appropriately in any Christian, since every Christian is a member of the Church. Indeed the crime of sacrilege is that much the greater because fornication of the soul is so much worse than that of the body; for through fornication of the soul one is cut off from God, and so by a kind of spiritual adultery one crosses over towards unclean spirits.

2. But why doesn't this guy sneak off into a corner? He wishes to seem a Christian, and claims that he is one, but he does not shrink from, does not hide from the prospect of, does not grow pale at the very idea of saying in front of everyone that people are getting sick because the demons are not worshiped and the god Februarius is not propitiated? I see where he has come up with these delusions. How can the one who rushes into this unholy blasphemy not be a sinner? How can he not be considered sacrilegious? He has abandoned the providence and power of the one God that he earlier confessed and is now seduced to prodigious superstitions and empty products of his imagination. Indeed according to the Apostle, the one who deserts the truth that he once confessed is a far worse criminal and more deserving of condemnation than he would be if he had never believed in that truth.[2] Furthermore, although the stories that he tells are ridiculous, his character[3] and will are involved in the crime, and his public profession and declaration ought to justly be condemned. So this guy who wants somebody else to be condemned immediately should know that he is condemning himself by that very request.

3. Now should the pontiff punish those who commit adultery in the body but not judge those who commit sacrilege, that is, spiritual fornication and adultery? Did not the Lord himself say to the accusers when an adulteress was brought to him, "If any of you is without sin, let him be the first to throw a stone at her"?[4] He did not say, "if any of you is not an adulterer in the same way," but rather, "if any is without sin." Therefore, he who is fettered by any sin should not dare to throw a stone against one who is guilty of another sin. While those people were leaving because of their conscience, the Savior of the world added, "Woman, where are your accusers? Has nobody condemned you? Neither do I condemn you but go now and sin no more."

Hold and you are held, force and you are forced, bind and you are bound. You demand an examination of the pontiff and you ask for vindication: remember that every charge will be brought back against you. Don't even the human laws say that the defendant cannot bring a charge against someone else? "You see the splinter in your brother's eye; don't you see the log in your own eye?"[5] Do you who accuse adulterers yourself commit adultery? Do you, the spiritual adulterer, attack the bodily adulterers? You ask for an examination. As an esteemed man who has come of age and is devout, you desire that no one in the Church should sin. You want the sinner to be cut off and that he thereby be punished. Whatever you say against another you are also compelled to bring forth against yourself. He does this in order that an accusation might not be brought against the pontiff's sloth and the Church not be stained. For the pontiff's solicitude and severity with respect to all evil deeds ought not be lacking, and the reputation of the Church should be altogether cleansed.

4. But perhaps you will say that you are a layman and that he is a minister of the Church, and thus you will say that his crime is greater. You speak truly, nor do I deny that: he ought to be much more seriously examined because he is nearer [to the center of the Church]; and he is much more guilty because he is established in that ministry, and he ought not to have done these things at all. So look, he's not lacking censure: once the case is heard and if he's sentenced, then he'll be punished. But let's take a look at your situation. What do you think of yourself? Just because you're not in the sacred ministry, are you not among the holy people? Or are you not aware that even you are a member of the most high pontiff?[6] Or are you not aware that the whole Church is called a priesthood? Finally, if he who comes forward to the ministry of the Church and commits an offense is a criminal, are you then not a criminal who, after having made a confession of truth, are led back to depraved, perverse, profane, and diabolical images, which you professed to have renounced? Indeed, you ought also, after you openly and publicly poured out blasphemies, to abstain completely from the sacred body. You cannot participate in the table of the Lord and the table of demons, nor can you drink the cup of the Lord and the cup of demons, nor can you be the temple of God and the temple of the devil: light and darkness cannot be present at the same time in you.[7] I have seen clearly how you demand and urge that a misdeed be punished in another's case. Nevertheless, you will not be able to escape from the weight of your evil deed: and just like you will not allow another's crime to go unpunished, so too we will hold you accountable for your actions.

5. Indeed, you are rightly punished for your blasphemies. Further, you should acknowledge your lack of experience in this area. Your case is just like the one he describes: "You're willing to lie, but you're not clever enough to deceive."[8] Your mind is so warped and your intention to apostatize so perverse that you don't even have the means to deceive, nor are you even able

to contribute what you have conceived in your heart and have uttered with your mouth.

Tell me, since one reads many times in Livy's Roman history that often when a plague had arisen in this city untold thousands of men died and that it has frequently reached such a pitch that there was scarcely any reserve of manpower left from which an army could be conscripted in those warlike times. Now, in that ancient time, was Februarius insufficiently appeased? Or did even that cult provide no benefit at all at that time in which the Lupercalia was celebrated? You can't say that these sacred pagan rites had not yet begun at that time, which are reported to have been brought to Italy by Evander even before Romulus.[9]

In his second decade, Livy speaks about the institution of the Lupercalia and what we know about the fabrications of this superstition.[10] He does not say that the Lupercalia was instituted in order to check the spread of disease, but rather that it had to be maintained—or so it seemed to him—because of the sterility of women, which had then struck the Romans. So, if this rite is at all effective toward the end for which it was originally instituted, which was for the fertility of women, and it has been taken away, then women, according to your logic, should be infertile. But we do not see this, and the disease that we do see is not caused by the removal of the Lupercalia.

What are you going to say about the plague, about bad crops, about the continual storm of wars? Do these things also happen because the Lupercalia has been removed? But it was not for that reason that it was instituted in the first place and so any diseases that are spreading around now are not due to the abeyance of the rites. Yet still you complain about pestilence, bad crops, and continuous wars. But isn't it true that these things happened even while the Lupercalia was conducted? But if the Lupercalia wasn't instituted in order to stop these things, why are you all worked up about them? What would you say about Tuscany, Aemilia, and the other provinces where hardly a man survives because they have been destroyed by war? Is this destruction because of the Lupercalia? But those places were devastated long before the rites of the Lupercalia were interrupted. When the Emperor Anthemius came to Rome,[11] the Lupercalia was going on everywhere, and yet such a great pestilence crept in that it could hardly be endured! Finally, wasn't the Lupercalia being celebrated in Campania, which endured sickness and pestilence?

6. But you'll say that everything pertains to Rome like the head, and since it was not done here, it injured her various provinces. But why, then, did these

provinces flourish by their own resources without the Lupercalia back when they weren't subject to Rome? Did the Lupercalia, once removed from these lands, cause sterility to continue, or was it because of our sins, concerning which it was once said: "whatever the Romans gain, they will lose because of their morals"?

Sterility of women certainly ought to have resulted, as it was to remove this that they say that the Lupercalia was instituted and not the sterility of the fields, for which it wasn't. Where does the sterility in Africa come from? Where does it come from in Gaul? Have the Lupercalia caused these things, or have our lack of morals, thefts, murders, adulteries, injustices, iniquities, bribing for votes, lusts, perjuries, false testimonies, oppression of the poor, attacks against good causes and the simultaneous defense of evil ones, unheard of perversity in everything and finally, what is worse than all of that, false images and sacrileges against God, and magic arts that are horrifying even to pagans! So these are the things that cause everything that is harmful to us, not the Lupercalia, which was disbanded for your salvation!

7. But what do you yourselves say, you who defend the Lupercalia and propose that it ought to be done? You consider these things to be of little import and so you return to their vulgar and vile cult and festival. If the offense to the Lupercalia has brought evil to us, it's your fault, you who consider that this thing is a singular benefit for yourselves, namely that you instruct that these rites ought to be celebrated most thoughtlessly and with far less cult and devotion than that profane rite which your ancestors celebrated.

For in their day even nobles would run as *Lupercali* and strike the bodies of naked matrons in broad daylight. You, therefore, have committed the first offense against the Lupercalia: it would have been better not to conduct it than to celebrate it and change the rites; but you brought down the cult, which you thought venerable and salutary to yourselves, to the level of the base and common people, those who are the abject dregs of society.

If you truly declare that this rite (or rather, this piece of shit)[12] is salutary for you, then celebrate it yourselves according to the custom of your ancestors and run naked yourselves, with just your whip[13] in hand, so that you might solemnly complete this mockery of your salvation. If these things are great, divine, and salutary, if the soundness of our life depends on these rites, why are you ashamed to celebrate such things in your own persons? If it shames you and is embarrassing, is it truly salutary, divine, and profitable, this thing that you yourselves confess to be a disgrace? No one professes a religion that he is ashamed to follow in every way and from which he flees; your own bashfulness ought itself to teach you that the Lupercalia is a public crime, not salvation and the cult of the Divinity, regarding which no wise man would blush. Rather, the Lupercalia is an instrument of depravity, which your mind, bearing testimony against itself, blushes to fulfill.

8. Why have your Dioscuri[14] (from whose cult you have refused to desist) rarely granted you calm seas during the winter? If they did, ships might come here with grain and the city then suffer less from a lack of food. Or does this not rather happen in the days of summer that follow?[15] The gift has been established by God, but the vain opinion regarding the Dioscuri has not.

   Tell us, you who are neither Christians nor pagans yet altogether dishonest and never faithful, altogether corrupt and not at all pure, you who are not able to hold either side as much as each side is opposed to you: tell us, I say, you patrons of the Lupercalia who actually are defenders of mockery of the Divinity and of dirty old songs, worthy teachers of madness, you who, for good reason, are insane, you who are worthy of this religion that is celebrated with the voices of obscenities and outrages: have you yourselves seen what kind of salvation this religion offers you, this religion that brings about so much destruction and ruin for public morals? Nor is it the case that souls are, as you claim, deterred by doing these things and by making known the evil deeds of each person from committing such crimes and that they are held back by shame so that their crimes aren't announced in public. Rather, it is just as that famous man says: these mockeries "don't seem to deter as much as encourage"[16] souls, and just as that other man said, "their anger and wrath comes from guilt."[17] In the end they are made more unashamed because the crime is known and the disgrace has been exposed! Then there is nothing left at all that would shame them. And so, not having anything that he would fear to become known, he now confidently uncovers himself. Such a person, whoever he is, who publicly without coercion but rather through a certain happiness and a celebration of the gods, is praised and trusts that he excels in religion: and thus it is that wherever the solemnities of the divinities are celebrated, they are not celebrated except by the praises of crimes.

9. So tell us, you who have the desire for profanity whose causes you cannot defend, you who have the intention of safeguarding lies that you cannot protect: what will you say concerning droughts, hail-storms, tornadoes, tempests and various other disasters which arise according to the character of our

morals? Isn't it the case that all of these things were connected with the removal of the Lupercalia or that they were given as a just recompense to correct evil habits?

So it's no wonder that people prefer to think that they happen not because of divine judgment but because of the assault of "deceitful superstition," those same people who, in order to cover up their crimes and evil deeds, claim that the authority of the consulted stars shows that they sin by necessity and that their crimes do not proceed from the perversity of their own heart, but depend on heaven as their author.

So, tell us: for the removal of what evils or the promotion of what goods was your Lupercalia established? Tell us so that we might see those good results that came when the Lupercalia was being celebrated and what evils followed when it seemed to have been discontinued. Establish your position, o worthy sirs who celebrate some damned part-man, part-goat monster (whether created naturally or the figment of human creation I know not). What evil thing was happening when these prodigies were discovered?[18] If the Lupercalia was established in order to take away pestilence, even if I ignore ancient history, behold! There is no doubt that, before the Lupercalia was removed during my tenure, there was a pestilence striking both man and beast that was as severe in the city as it was in the countryside. If you're so concerned about sterility, why does it strike Africa and Gaul where there never was a Lupercalia and, clearly then, it was never discontinued? Why does the East now abound and overflow with a wealth of foods of all kinds, which has never celebrated the Lupercalia in the past nor does so now? Or are you going to say that it is harmful in that place where it had been celebrated for centuries and then was suddenly taken away? Let's see, then, if in those times in which you say that the Lupercalia was conducted religiously and completed with all appropriate devotion (at least as it seems to you), there was never any famine or pestilence at all. If, however, these disasters repeatedly brought extreme danger, it would seem that the Lupercalia was never able to bring about the removal of these evils during that time in which, as was said, you think that it was conducted properly. So, if we agree that every single problem (for which you said the Lupercalia was established) did not even go away when the Lupercalia was properly celebrated, then this supposed remedy is shown to be completely ineffective.

10. Why not try now and see if they are good for anything even when conducted according to rite? And so go ahead, run around in this mockery

according to the way of your ancestors so that, as you claim, by more devoutly celebrating this divine and salutary rite, you might be able to provide more and more for your health. So [according to your understanding], Rome wasn't captured by the Gauls while this was being celebrated and the city didn't frequently come to the worst straits? Did not Rome fall into civil wars during the celebration of Lupercalia? Had the Lupercalia ceased, then, when Alaric overthrew the City? And more recently when the civil disturbance of Anthemius and Ricimer was overturned, had the Lupercalia ceased? Has this helped even a little bit? Certainly, if it is divine, if it brings safety to you, why should you not carry it out yourselves as your forefathers did? Why do you diminish the causes of your salvation? Why do you disgrace, destroy, and cheapen everything? Why do you blame us, when you yourselves trample upon your remedies? It is better not even to try it, than to carry it out outrageously. Certainly if your ancestors thought that they were carrying out a rite badly, they would have reformed that rite. Since you have reduced it to a vicious cult by carrying it out through the agency of certain unworthy persons, why don't you too reform the rite so that you can more fully and perfectly work for the source of your safety? Why blush to do these things if it saves you? If it is divine, what disgrace could there be in conducting it yourselves?

11. But, you say you are only keeping up the external rite and not its substance. But if it is beneficial, if it saves, how can you claim that it's just the image and not the reality? Or certainly, if it was of no use to our ancestors when they conducted the rite in (what you call) its completeness, why do you seek the image of a thing whose very reality you perceive not to have been of any use?

12. But, you say, a thing that has been conducted for so many centuries ought not be cancelled. Nonetheless, pagan superstition has surfaced at many times: "Let there be sacrifices in the temples of the demons and profane deception be celebrated on the Capital!" Why do you defend only a part and overlook the things that are greater? If the vast majority of those kinds of deceptions that have been conducted for centuries have been rightly taken away, why can't a portion that arises at any time be taken away? If it is prescribed for certain times, blame your ancestors who, although they did not follow this temporal prescription, indicated that that which is superfluous both can and should be removed, so long as those greater and more destructive [rites] were taken away.

13. But you say that these things were even done in Christian times. Indeed, they were even celebrated for a considerable part of the Christian era. Is it the case then that those things that were not taken away under the rule of the first Christian leaders must not be taken away by their successors? There are many things that were taken away by individual pontiffs at different times because they were harmful or abject. For the medical art does not cure all of the diseases in the body at the same time but it looks at that which is more dangerously threatening. Medicine does this because the material of the body is not strong enough to endure the treatment or because, on account of its mortal condition, it is not able to turn away all the diseases at once. So which is it? How would you deal with this? If it is good, divine, and healthy it ought not ever have been taken away; if it is neither healthy nor divine, you must make your case more urgently as to why a rite should be removed slowly, a rite which everyone knows is superstitious and empty and which certainly does not harmonize with a Christian profession of faith.

14. Finally, for my part, no baptized person or Christian is to celebrate the Lupercalia, and it is only to be carried out by the pagans, whose rite it is. It is right that I pronounce that this is absolutely pernicious and polluting for Christians. What would you accuse me of if I pronounce that this Lupercalia that is claimed by pagans to be hardly harmful at all ought to be taken away from those who are members of the Christian confession? Let them who have neglected to obey just admonitions see that I certainly have absolved my conscience. I do not hesitate about that which my predecessors seem to have done. I mean, they may have tried to have these rites removed by whispering to the Emperor. It is evident that they were not heard because these evil rites are still going on, and as a result the empire itself failed and even the name of the Romans came to its end because the Lupercalia had not been taken away.[19] And thus I now urge that these rites be taken away and because I know that they have never done any good, I pronounce them to be noxious, on the grounds that they have always been hostile to true religion. Finally, if you think that something ought to be written about the person of my predecessors, each one of us will give an account of his administration just as you shall see happen among public dignitaries. I do not dare accuse my predecessors of negligence but would rather believe that perhaps they tried to take away this depravity but that some causes and contrary wills arose which impeded their intentions just as now you yourselves do not even consider ceasing your insane attempts.

NOTES

INTRODUCTION

1. The document is available on the Vatican website, http://www.vatican.va/roman_curia/ congregations/cfaith/documents/rc_con_cfaith_doc_20070629_responsa-quaestiones_en.html.

2. As an introduction to the constitutive elements that came to comprise the Petrine discourse, Chapter 1 will provide a survey of the multiple legends, rituals, and material representations of Peter that emerged between the second and fourth centuries.

3. For example, when Pope Gelasius proclaims that it is "x," it might well be worth our while to presume that he fears or is embarrassed by the "not-x." It is precisely for these reasons that he proclaims "x" rather than "not-x." By pursuing this aspect of my investigation in this particular way, I am indebted to a methodological approach often dubbed the "hermeneutic of suspicion," typically understood to mean that a reader attempts to remain ever aware of a text's worldview, its embedded hierarchies, and the extent to which the text will reflect and reinforce that worldview by employing rhetorical strategies that openly reinforce it or by marginalizing and silencing alternative perspectives.

4. In different times and for different reasons, Peter would be used to fill any number of roles: founder of the Church, sole dogmatic authority, originator of baptismal rituals, mystical patron of the city of Rome, chief heretic hunter, source of episcopal authority, *primus* of the episcopate, and leading citizen of the empire. So, too, his shrine and relics would serve multiple functions: a place of pilgrimage, a barricade against rival factions, a host site for secular and ecclesiastical dignitaries, the locus for the swearing of oaths, the vehicle for disseminating spiritual talismans, and, of course, the symbol of papal power.

5. This idea of a "totalizing" discourse in early Christianity was informed by Averil Cameron, *Christianity and the Rhetoric of Empire: The Development of a Christian Discourse* (Berkeley: University of California Press, 1994).

6. The inclusion of ritual and institution within the matrix of discourse will prove to be an important element of our discussion, especially for our investigation of Gregory I (bishop of Rome 590–604), who, more than his predecessors, emphasized certain Petrine rituals associated with his tomb and relics.

7. Rather than simply describing the world as it is, as if language mediates truth directly, a discourse constructs the objects of reality and the ways they are perceived and understood.

8. Elizabeth Clark, *History, Theory, Text: Historians and the Linguistic Turn* (Cambridge, Mass.: Harvard University Press, 2004), esp. 158–59. I take Cameron's *Christianity and the Rhetoric of Empire* as an exemplary, if subtle, model for how historians can benefit from considering the development of early Christianity from the perspective of "discourse."

9. Perhaps the best representative of this type of approach to the subject is the account by Michele Maccarrone, "Sedes Apostolica-Vicarius Petri: La perpetuità del primato di Pietro nella sede e nel vescovo di Roma (secoli III–VIII)," in *Il primato del vescovo di Roma nel primo millennio: Atti del Symposium storico-teologico* (Vatican City: Libreria editrice vaticana, 1991), 275–362.

10. Put another way, the connections between Peter and the papacy were not unspeakable or alien to the possibilities of the age, or such connections would not have been tenable when Leo made them. Thus, when Leo first speaks about himself as Peter's heir, the terms "Peter" and "heir" and "bishop" must have operated in similar enough ways to be brought together by him.

11. For an alternative approach that seeks to chronicle every Christian statement linking Peter to Rome, see studies such as Roland Minnerath, "La tradition doctrinale de la primauté pétrinienne au premier millenaire," in *Il primato del succesore di Pietro* (Rome: Città del Vaticano, 1998), 117–43. See also Maccarrone, "Sedes Apostolica-Vicarius Petri." For a synopsis of similar material, see Walter Ullmann, "Leo I and the Theme of Papal Primacy," *Journal of Theological Studies* n.s. 11 (1960): 25–51, esp. 29–33.

12. Discourse analysis allows us to consider within a single framework the actions, non-actions, inclusions and exclusions, and any other set of performances that fit within the epistemic horizon of the discourse. Whereas this study will emphasize textual and ritualistic examples of this discourse, other scholars (more qualified than I) could easily examine the exercise of the Petrine discourse operating in other registers, including art, architecture, and liturgical dress.

13. Because our goal is to uncover the epistemological and hermeneutical structures that give meaning to the discursive statements linking Peter the apostle to the papal institution (rather than a grand narrative of the institution or an intellectual history of a particular text or author), discourse analysis allows us to take into account the multiple constitutive elements of the Petrine legacy.

14. For an inspired examination of the ways in which the discipline of history has evolved to include theoretical analysis (including an assessment of why some historians have resisted this move), see Clark, *History, Theory, Text*.

15. This is because, however much there was a discrete set of conditions that made possible a particular iteration or action, the individuals who acted or spoke in that moment in time often did so in a way that purposely brought Peter, Rome, and the papacy together to achieve a specific goal. To the extent that I am able to find instances where tying them together was deliberate, I will describe it as a purposeful "use" or

"employing" of the Petrine discourse. In other places in my analysis, however, I will speak more to the matrix of possibilities that enabled speech and action, which better reflects the Foucauldian sense of the term "discourse."

16. One note of caution in this regard: the Petrine discourse, the discursive register through which various authors advanced a link between Peter and the papal institution for the advancement of that institution, in and of itself does not convey a papal ideology. Instead, it consists of what Foucault called the "enunciative space" in which ideologies can be developed, transformed, and employed. As we will see, there were many individuals who spoke about Peter and did so for purposes related to the authority of the See of Rome. Not all those speakers, however, had the interests of Rome in mind. They may, in fact, have employed the Petrine topos for purposes alien to the interests of the papal institution. But that does not mean they did not operate in the same discursive formation as those who employed Peter in a manner consistent with papal ideology.

17. In the early part of the twentieth century, there was a lively debate about who was the first early Christian author to link the Matthew 16 passage to a special authority of the bishop of Rome. For our purposes, we can simply note that it began sometime in the early third century.

18. Though difficult to date with any certainty, the basilica of St. Peter was built on imperial property during the reign of Constantine (313–337).

19. Erich Caspar, *Geschichte des Papsttums*, 2 vols. (Tubingen: J.C.B. Mohr, 1930–33).

20. See especially Walter Ullmann, *The Growth of the Papal Government in the Middle Ages: A Study in the Ideological Relation of Clerical to Lay Power*, 3rd ed. (London: Methuen, 1970). For an excellent overview of the flaws in Ullmann's apologetical methods, see Marios Costambeys, "Property and Ideology of the Papacy in the Early Middle Ages," *Early Modern Europe* 9 (2000): 367–96, esp. 383–96. For a more complete dismantling of the Ullmann thesis, see Francis Oakley, "Walter Ullmann's Vision of Medieval Politics," *Past and Present* 60 (1973): 3–48.

21. For example, during the reign of Pope Hadrian I (772–795), it has been asserted that papal scribes condensed more than 20,000 papyri letters dated to the reign of Gregory I into two volumes of parchment manuscripts containing only 700 letters. See Ernst Pitz, *Papstreskripte im frühen Mittelalter: Diplomatische und rechtsgeschichtliche Studien zum Brief-Corpus Gregors des Grossen* (Sigmaringen: Thorbecke, 1990). I came to know of Pitz's work through Marios Costambeys and Conrad Leyser, "To Be the Neighbor of St. Stephen: Patronage, Martyr Cult, and Roman Monasteries, c. 600–c. 900," in *Religion, Dynasty, and Patronage in Early Christian Rome, 300–900*, ed. Kate Cooper and Julia Hillner (Cambridge: Cambridge University Press, 2007), 267–68.

22. Charles Pietri, *Roma christiana: Recherches sur l'église de Rome, son organisation, sa politique, son idéologie de Miltiade à Sixte III* (Rome: École Française de Rome, 1976).

23. Ibid., 271–401.

24. Pietri's argument works best when one ignores theological concerns and emphasizes instead the material culture and social dimensions of papal activity in the period. But if one were to measure Leo by his aptitude for theology, he would clearly be shown to be unlike any of his predecessors. Pietri, *Roma christiana*, 1413–1654.

25. See, for example, Charles Pietri, "Aristocratie et société cléricale dans l'Italie chrétienne au temps d'Odoacre et de Théodoric," *Mélanges de l'École Française de Rome* 93 (1981): 417–67; P. V. Aimone, "Gli autori falsificazioni simmachiani," in *Il papato di San Simmaco (498–514)*, ed. G. Mele and N. Spaccapelo (Cagliari: Pontificia facoltà teologica della Sardegna, 2000), 53–78; and especially the critical edition of apologetic texts from the period made available by Eckhard Wirbelauer, *Zwei Päpste in Rom: Der Konflict zwischen Laurentius und Symmachus (498–514)* (Munich: Tudov, 1993).

26. For example, see Marianne Sághy, "*Scinditur in partes populous*: Damasus and the Martyrs of Rome," *Early Medieval History* 9 (2000): 273–87; and Dennis Trout, "Damasus and the Invention of Early Christian Rome," *Journal of Medieval and Early Modern Studies* 33 (2003): 517–36. See also Cooper and Hillner, eds., *Religion, Dynasty, and Patronage*.

27. Kristina Sessa, *The Formation of Papal Authority in Late Antique Italy: Roman Bishops and the Domestic Sphere* (Cambridge: Cambridge University Press, 2012).

28. Cooper and Hillner, "Introduction," in *Religion, Dynasty, and Patronage*, 1–18.

29. Ibid., 5.

30. Unless otherwise noted, the reader can assume that all translations from Greek or Latin are my own. The two obvious exceptions to this are the two treatises by Gelasius I that appear as appendices to this volume. Those translations are by Matthew Briel.

CHAPTER I. PETRINE LEGENDS, EXTERNAL RECOGNITION, AND THE CULT OF PETER IN ROME

1. This is true of all the letters attributed to Paul.

2. Naturally, this would suggest that Paul does not think Peter is in Rome at the time of his writing to the Roman community.

3. Otto Zwierlein, *Petrus in Rom: Die literarischen Zeugnisse* (Berlin: De Gruyter, 2010), 7–13. The scholarly reception of such a radical reinterpretation has been mixed. See, for example, the reviews by James Dunn, *Review of Biblical Literature* (2010) and Pieter van der Horst, *Bryn Mawr Classical Review* (2010).

4. On the current scholarly consensus regarding authorship, see John Elliot, "Peter, First Epistle of," in *Anchor Bible Dictionary*, vol. 5, ed. David Freedman (New York: Doubleday, 2001), 269–78, esp. 277–78.

5. In addition to Zwierlein, see Michael Goulder, "Did Peter Ever Go to Rome?" *Scottish Journal of Theology* 57 (2004): 377–96.

6. Clement's name does not appear in the letter; its association is one of tradition. Because we do not know who authored the text, we cannot say with any certainty what role the author had with respect to the Christian community in Rome. Some see him as a kind of recording secretary. See Andreas Lindemann, *Die Clemensbriefe* (Tübingen: Mohr Siebeck, 1992); and O. B. Knock, "Im Namen des Petrus und Paulus: Der Brief des Clemens Romanus," *Aufstieg und Niedergang der römischen Welt* 2, 27 (1993): 3–54.

7. Zwierlein (*Petrus in Rom*, 30), of course, rejects the idea that Clement knew of Peter's martyrdom.

8. "Let us set before our eyes the good Apostles. There was Peter who, by reason of unrighteous jealousy, endured not one but many labors and, thus, having born witness, went to his appointed place in glory." *1 Clement* 5.4. The passage continues with a longer description of Paul's labors.

9. For Zwierlein, there is no information about Peter and Paul not otherwise found in the New Testament.

10. The question circulates around the phrase οὕτω μαρτυρήσας and whether it is to be interpreted as referring to the apostles' death or their "bearing witness," which would be more in line with the conventional way to understand μαρτυρία in the New Testament. See Goulder, "Did Peter Ever Go to Rome?" 388–89.

11. See Lindemann, *Die Clemsbriefe*, 60. Robert Grant interpreted the passage as testifying to Peter's martyrdom in Rome. Robert Grant, *The Apostolic Fathers*, vol. 2 (New York: Thomas Nelson, 1964), 25. I would like to thank Larry Welborn for his counsel in understanding this passage.

12. This is the argument of Zwierlein and Goulder. It is also possible, of course, that the passage could evince the author's general knowledge that Peter had been martyred, but that he did not know anything specific about that martyrdom. If this is the case, then we could reasonably conclude that such a martyrdom did not occur in Rome.

13. See Zwierlein, *Petrus in Rom*, esp. 30 and 245–331.

14. Ignatius, *Letter to the Romans* 4.3.

15. Yet another possibility is that Ignatius believes Peter and Paul to have been leaders of the Christian community that traveled to Rome but were never permanent leaders of the Roman Church. Indeed, he refers to them not as *episcopoi* (a critical designation for him), but as *apostoloi*. I would like to thank Michael Peppard for his consultation on this passage.

16. See Zwierlein, *Petrus in Rom*, 31–33 and 183–205. In addition to the passage in Ignatius' *Letter to the Romans*, there is a reference to Peter in his *Letter to the Ephesians*.

17. Zwierlein, *Petrus in Rom*, 128–33.

18. Ibid., 160–62.

19. Likely the earliest example stems from a tradition related to what Dionysius of Corinth had written to Rome. Not only does Dionysius further ground the tradition of Peter and Paul having suffered martyrdom in Rome, he claims the authority of the apostles for his own community in Corinth by claiming that both of them had planted orthodoxy in his city as well. The letter no longer survives but is quoted by Eusebius, *Church History* 2.25.

20. The sixth-century Latin manuscript (Codex Vercellensis 158) comes from Vercelli, Italy, and was edited and printed in R. A. Lipsius and M. Bonnet, eds., *Acta apostolorum apocrypha*, vol. 1 (Leipzig, 1891–1903), 45–103. For the complications in linking this manuscript to the original, see Hans-Josef Klauck, *The Apocryphal Acts of the Apostles: An Introduction*, trans. Brian McNeil (Waco, Tex.: Baylor University Press, 2008), 81–112. For more on the manuscript itself, see Anton Hilhorst, "The Text of the Actus Vercellenses,"

in *The Apocryphal Acts of Peter: Magic, Miracles, and Gnosticism*, ed. Jan Bremmer (Leuven: Peeters, 1998), 148–60.

21. Zwierlein, *Petrus in Rom*, 36–40.

22. The Latin manuscript comprises 41 chapters. Several Greek manuscripts of the *Martyrdom* section survive, but they begin at different sections with respect to the Latin text. Some begin with the final confrontation between Simon Magus and Peter (which corresponds to ch. 30 in the Latin *Acts of Peter*); others begin with the conspiracy to arrest Peter (which corresponds to ch. 33). For an overview, see Klauck, *The Apocryphal Acts of the Apostles*, 81–112; and James Keith Elliot, *The Apocryphal New Testament: A Collection of Apocryphal Christian Literature in an English Translation* (Oxford: Clarendon, 1993), 390–96.

23. Another significant textual issue that has drawn scholarly attention is the relationship between these texts, the *Acts of John*, and other late second-century apostolic *acta*, such as the *Acts of Paul* and the *Acts of Andrew*. See P. J. Lalleman, "The Relations Between the Acts of John and the Acts of Peter," in Bremmer, *The Apocryphal Acts of Peter*, 161–77; and Klauck, *The Apocryphal Acts of the Apostles*, 2–5, 84. For his part, Zwierlein believes that the *Acts/Martyrdom of Peter* predate all others. See Zwierlein, *Petrus in Rom*, 75–127.

24. For an overview of the possibility that Nero had been responsible for the persecution of Christians, see Peter Lampe, *Christians at Rome in the First Two Centuries: From Paul to Valentinus*, trans. Michael Steinhauser (London: Continuum, 2003), 82–84.

25. For an overview of the early Christian accounts of Peter's martyrdom, see R. J. Bauckham, "The Martyrdom of Peter in Early Christian Literature," in *Aufstieg und Niedergang der römischen Welt: Geschicte und Kultur Roms in Spiegel der neueren Forschung*, ed. H. Temporini and W. Haase, vol. 26 (Berlin: De Gruyter, 1992), 539–95.

26. This portion of the text is contained in the Latin *Acts of Peter* (chs. 30–33) and the Greek manuscript from Athos but not the manuscripts from Patmos or Ochrid. For the confrontation between Peter and Simon in the *Martyrdom*, consult Lipsius and Bonnet, *Acta Apostolorum Apocrypha* (hereafter *Acts of Peter*). Zwierlein, *Petrus in Rom* (404–25) offers a critical edition of the *Martyrdom* (without the opening three chapters concerning the confrontation with Simon). Subsequent references to Zwierlein's text will be denoted as *Martyrdom of the Apostle Peter*.

27. *Martyrdom of the Apostle Peter* 6.4–5. In the Latin translation, Peter's question to Christ, "Where are you going (*quo vadis*)?" and Christ's reply "I am going to be crucified again (*Romam vado iterum crucifigi*)" took on a hagiographic life of their own in subsequent renditions.

28. *Martyrdom of the Apostle Peter* 8.1–3.

29. Ibid. 8.4–10.4. Klauck notes that the request to be crucified upside down does not mark an exhibition of humility but rather points to theological concerns related to humanity's fallen condition. He also notes a possible parallel passage in Seneca's *Consolatio ad Marciam*, which mentions upside-down crucifixions. Klauck, *The Apocryphal Acts of the Apostles*, 102–5.

30. *Martyrdom of the Apostle Peter* 11.1–4.

31. Ibid. 12.1–4.

32. Lipsius argued that these characteristics suggested a Gnostic origin for the text. Richard A. Lipsius, *Die Quellen der römischen Petrus-sage kritisch untersucht* (Kiel: Schwers, 1872). That position has been modified by scholarship that typically holds that the text reflects debates with Gnostics but does not necessarily have a Gnostic origin. See Elliot, *The Apocryphal New Testament*, 392.

33. Alternatively, it is possible the author was criticizing a developing cult of dead saints.

34. *Martyrdom of the Apostle Peter* 5.1–5.

35. Ibid., 6.4.

36. Ibid., 7.4.

37. Ibid.

38. *Acts of Peter* 33. The precise route of the Via Sacra is disputed and it probably changed over time, but it essentially extended from the summit of the Capitoline Hill to the Roman Forum.

39. The *Gesta Martyrum* is a collection of Roman martyr acts of multiple authorship and unknown date. The pioneering work on the *Gesta Martyrum* was completed by Albert Dufourcq, *Études sur les gesta martyrum romains*, 4 vols. (Paris: Fontemoig, 1900–1910).

40. See Christine Thomas, "The 'Prehistory' of the *Acts of Peter*, in *The Apocryphal Acts of the Apostles*, ed. Francois Bovon (Cambridge, Mass.: Harvard University Press, 1999), 39–62. See also Klauck, *The Apocryphal Acts of the Apostles*, 81–85; and C. H. Turner, "The Latin Acts of Peter," *Journal of Theological Studies* 32 (1931): 119–33.

41. For a summary, see Elliot, *The Apocryphal New Testament*, 390–96.

42. Eusebius, *Church History* 3.3.2. Later writers claimed that the *Acts of Peter* was heretical on the basis that it was used by Manichaeans. See Elliot, *The Apocryphal New Testament*, 390.

43. With good reason, some scholars doubt that this portion of the surviving Latin text was in the original Greek. Léon Vouaux, *Les Actes de Pierre* (Paris: Letouzey, 1922).

44. *Acts of Peter* 5.

45. Contained in chs. 9, 13, and 25–28 respectively.

46. *Acts of Peter* 3.

47. Ibid., 6.

48. Ibid., 28.

49. Ibid., 23.

50. When Peter first arrives in Rome, he learns that Marcellus (a convert who had given generously to the poor) has recently fallen under the sway of the evil Simon, currently residing in Marcellus' home. Many of Peter's initial miracles are performed for the benefit of Marcellus' faith, with the eventual conclusion that Marcellus expels Simon from his *domus*. Ibid., 8–19.

51. Ibid., 11.

52. Ibid., 23.

53. Klauck maintains that the emphasis on repentance (and the possibility that every-one, including Simon can be forgiven) suggests that the author is searching for a way to address the question of the "lapsed." Klauck, *The Apocryphal Acts of the Apostles*, 111–12.

54. In fact, the only time a bishop is mentioned at all is in ch. 27, when Peter foretells to an unnamed boy that the man who has just risen from the dead will one day serve the Church as deacon and bishop. *Acts of Peter* 27.

55. Concerning the *Acts of Peter and Paul*, which is derivative the *Acts of Peter*, see Klauck, *The Apocryphal Acts of the Apostles*, 107–9. Concerning the *Acts of Peter and the Twelve Apostles*, a text found among the Nag Hammadi collection and reflecting few of the concerns of the texts examined in this study, see Klauck, 181–92.

56. Irenaeus, *Against Heresies* 3.3.2–3. Tertullian, however, had held that Peter ordained Clement and led the Church of Rome immediately after him. Tertullian, *Prescriptions Against the Heretics*, 32.

57. Bernard Pouderon, "Flavius Clemens et le proto-Clément juif du roman pseudo-clémentin," *Apocrypha* 7 (1996): 63–79.

58. For an overview, see Klauck, *The Apocryphal Acts of the Apostles*, 193–229; con-cerning their supposed Arianism, see esp. 196. According to Klauck, there is the possibility of an Ur-text that served as a source for the present documents. He speculates that such a text was likely composed before 250.

59. The Latin translation of the *Recognitions* was completed by Rufinus. Though the *Recognitions* and the *Homilies* are distinct texts, there is considerable overlap between the two, and some scholars consider the *Recognitions* to be a subsequent, reorganized, and "sanitized" version of the *Homilies*. According to Klauck, we should assume that the texts derive from a common source and draw from it idiosyncratically. See Klauck, *The Apocryphal Acts of the Apostles*, 197. Critical editions were completed by Bernhard Rehm: *Die Pseudoklementinen*, vol. 1, *Homilien*, GCS 42; and vol. 2, *Rekognitionen in Rufins Übersetzung*, GCS 51 (Berlin: Akademie Verlag, 1992, 1994).

60. Rufinus translated the letter attributed to Clement, but as a separate work, not as part of his translation of the *Recognitions*.

61. Several scholars have noted the similarities between the *Pseudo-Clementines* and Greco-Roman novels. See, for example, M. J. Edwards, "The Clementina: A Christian Response to the Pagan Novel," *Classical Quarterly* 42 (1992): 459–74 and D. U. Hansen, "Die Metamorphose des Heiligen: Clemens und die Clementina," in *Groningen Colloquia on the Novel*, ed. H. Hofmann, vol. 8 (Groningen: Egbert Forsten, 1997), 119–29.

62. See, for example, Pseudo-Clement, *Homily* 3.38–57 and *Recognitions* 2.24–70.

63. Pseudo-Clement, *Homily* 5.7–6.25.

64. Ibid. 3.60, 62, 67, 11.36; and *Recognition* 3.66 and 6.15.

65. For example, in *Homily* 3, we find Peter making Zaccheus bishop of Caesarea as he plans to travel on to Tyre, hoping to thwart Simon and thereby spread the gospel among the Gentiles. The same events are chronicled in *Recognitions* 3.66. So, too, follow-ing Peter's establishment of churches in Tyre, Sidon, and Beirut, he appoints bishops before moving on to another city. Pseudo-Clement, *Homily* 7.5 (Tyre); 7.8 (Sidon); and

7.12 (Beirut). At the close of *Homily* 11 (ch. 36), we are told that Peter appoints Maros bishop of Tripoli (see also *Recognitions* 6.15). Similarly, he appoints a bishop for Laodicea at the conclusion of the final *Homily* (20.23) and in *Recognitions* 10.68.

66. See, for example, Pseudo-Clement, *Homily* 3.60–72 and *Homily* 9.2.

67. Pseudo-Clement, *Recognitions* 1.43.

68. Pseudo-Clement, *Homily* 11.35 and *Recognitions* 4.35.

69. Pseudo-Clement, *Recognitions* 1.68.

70. In fact, James issues directives to Peter, as in *Recognitions* 1.72, when James sends Peter to Caesarea to forestall the threat posed by Simon. For more on the traditions surrounding James' authority in the *Pseudo-Clementines*, see Wilhelm Pratscher, *Der Herrenbruder Jakobus und die Jakobustradition* (Göttingen: Vandenhoeck & Ruprecht, 1987), esp. 121–50.

71. Rufinus' solution to the conundrum is to say that Linus and Anacletus served as bishop while Peter was still alive, whereas Clement assumed the office on Peter's death.

72. Reed notes that the letter was included in Rufinus' translation and therefore suggests a date between 320 and 407. Annette Yoshiko Reed, "Heresiology and the (Jewish-)Christian Novel: Narrativized Polemics in the Pseudo-Clementine Homilies," in *Heresy and Identity in Late Antiquity*, ed. E. Iricinschi and H. Zellentin (Tübingen: Mohr Siebeck, 2008), 273. E. C. Brooks, "The 'Epistola Clementis': A Petrine Infusion at Rome, c. AD 385," in *Studia Patristica*, 15 1 (Berlin: Akademie Verlag, 1984), 212–16 suggests a date between 370 and 382 and Antioch as the site of the original composition.

73. Ullmann, "Significance of the Epistola Clementis in the Pseudo-Clementines," *Journal of Theological Studies* n.s. 11 (1960): 305.

74. He notes especially the connections to the *Liber Pontificalis* and the Pseudo-Isidorian *Decretals*. Ullmann, "Significance of the Epistola Clementis," 302–4.

75. I would like to thank Ashley Purpura for sharing an unpublished paper on ecclesial expectations of Pseudo-Clement's *Letter to James*.

76. Given the mid-fourth-century dating of the letter, the violent conflict between Damasus and Ursinus in 366 may well have been a concern for the author.

77. Irenaeus, *Against Heresies* 3.3.

78. Ibid.

79. Ibid.

80. As evidence that this was the "middle-road" approach, we might note that Cyprian's decision causes schisms on both sides. The rigorists were led by Felicissimus, who was ordained bishop by Novatus. The "laxists" were led by Fortunatus. See Jane Merdinger, *Rome and the African Church in the Time of Augustine* (New Haven, Conn.: Yale University Press, 1997), 36–49.

81. See, for example, *Ep.* 55, ed. W. Hartel, CSEL 3. Note that the numeration for the critical edition and the translation provided in the Ante-Nicene Fathers (ANF) series are not the same. See also Merdinger, *Rome and the African Church*, 39–41.

82. Cyprian, *On the Unity of the Church* 4. Cyprian's view is based largely on his reading of Matthew 16, in which Christ says the Church will be built on Peter as a consequence of his confession of faith that Jesus is the Christ, the Son of God.

83. Cyprian, *Ep.* 59.8. This important letter is numbered *Ep.* 54 in the ANF translation.

84. The debate over the meaning of Cyprian's Petrine language has been at the forefront of one of the many Catholic/Protestant battle lines. For an excellent summary of the way that Caspar's thesis fit within the historiographical and confessional debates of his generation, see Norman Baynes, review of *Geschichte des Papsttums*, by Erich Caspar, *English Historical Review* 47 (1932): 293–98.

85. See Merdinger, *Rome and the African Church*, 43–49.

86. See Maurice Bénevot, "Primatus Petro datur," *Journal of Theological Studies* n.s. 5 (1954): 19–35.

87. See, for example, Cyprian, *Ep.* 69 and 71.3.

88. See Hamilton Hess, *The Early Development of Canon Law and the Council of Serdica*, rev. ed. (Oxford: Oxford University Press, 2002), 185.

89. The letter is not extant but is summarized by Sozomen, *Ecclesiastical History* 3.8.5–8.

90. Although the letter to Julius does not survive, there are twenty-five canons, known as the "Antiochian Collection," that most scholars believe date to this synod. Several of these speak indirectly to Athanasius' and Julius' behavior, specifically seeking shelter in another diocese and reception of a condemned cleric from another diocese. See especially Canon 13, which forbids a bishop to go from one eparchy to another if he has been condemned. Charles Hefele, *A History of the Councils of the Church*, vol. 2, *326–429* (1896; Edinburgh: T & T Clark, 1972), 70–71.

91. For a thorough summary of the many details that follow, see Hess, *The Early Development of Canon Law*, 95–100.

92. The letter is contained in Athanasius' *Apologia contra Arianos* 35.4–5. See Hess, *The Early Development of Canon Law*, 186.

93. Athanasius, *Apologia contra Arianos* 35.4–5

94. The Petrine character of that assertion was not lost on Pietri. Charles Pietri, *Roma christiana: Recherches sur l'église de Rome, son organisation, sa politique, son idéologie de Miltiade à Sixte III* (Rome: École Française de Rome, 1976), esp. 187ff.

95. The Western bishops who convened at Serdica were sympathetic to both Athanasius and Julius, and it was for this reason, no doubt, that they authorized the appellate canons, which essentially justified both Athanasius' appeal to Julius and Julius' decision to issue a verdict. There is actually very little in the Serdican canons that explicitly links Rome's appellate authority to the see's historic link to St. Peter. In the appendix to his study (*The Early Development of Canon Law*), Hess provides transcriptions and translations of both the Greek and the Latin versions of the Serdican canons.

96. Hess, *The Early Development of Canon Law*, esp. 197–99, where he exposes the anachronisms of Caspar's argument. Cf. Erich Caspar, "Kleine Beiträge zur älteren Papstgeschichte: IV. Zur Interpretation der Kanones III–V von Sardica," *Zeitschrift für Kirchengeschichte* 47 (1928): 164–77.

97. Both elements are significant: (1) that Peter's confession of faith in Mt 16 is the basis for his authority among the apostles, and (2) that the episcopate draws its strength from this Petrine authority.

98. For our purposes, I distinguish the theology of martyrdom and eyewitness accounts of martyrdom from the subsequent cultic commemoration of the martyrs. For a recent account of the former in the context of Roman situation, see Candida Moss, *Ancient Christian Martyrdom: Diverse Practices, Theologies, and Traditions* (New Haven, Conn.: Yale University Press, 2012), 77–99.

99. Giovanni De Rossi, *Roma sotteranea cristiana, descritta ed illustrate*, 3 vols. (Rome: Cromo-litografia pontifica, 1864–77). Equally instrumental was Albert Dufourcq's four-volume study of the *Gesta Martyrum*, which he treated not as an accurate account of pre-Constantinian history (as it purports to be) but rather as a testament to the post-Constantinian concerns of the Roman Church. Dufourcq, *Étude sur les gesta martyrum*.

100. In the latter part of the twentieth century, the prevailing appropriation of this material fed a scholarly narrative that pitted the aristocratic households of Rome against an increasingly centralized institutional church. See Charles Pietri, "Aristocratie et société cléricale dans l'Italie chrétienne au temps d'Odoacre et de Théodoric," *Mélanges des Écoles Françaises de Rome et d'Athènes* 93 (1981): 417–67. More recently, scholars have challenged the clerical/lay binary to suggest that the competition between cultic sites likely drew coalitions of clerical and aristocratic parties. See especially Kate Cooper, "The Martyr, the *Matrona*, and the Bishop: The Matron Lucina and the Politics of Martyr Cult in Fifth- and Sixth-Century Rome," *Early Medieval Europe* 8 (1999): 297–317.

101. Kimberly Bowes, *Private Worship, Public Values, and Religious Change in Late Antiquity* (Cambridge: Cambridge University Press, 2008), esp. 8–15 and 63–65.

102. There is ample textual evidence for the trafficking of martyr relics by Roman aristocrats for private ownership. See, for example, Paulinus of Nola, *Ep.* 31 and 32.7–8, CSEL 29; and Gregory of Nyssa, *Life of Macrina* 24, SC 178:252. See also Bowes, *Private Worship*, 84–85.

103. Among other sites, Bowes examines a domestic chapel located within a Constantinian palace in Rome, the *sancta ecclesia Hierusalem* (now Sancta Croce), which likely included its own private reliquary. Although the church eventually became a public space under the supervision of the Roman bishop, Bowes argues that its original function was private and domestic. See Bowes, *Private Worship*, 85–87.

104. For an overview of the complex, see Richard Krautheimer et al., *Corpus Basilicarum Christianarum Romae* (Vatican City: Pontificio istituto di archeologia cristiana, 1937–77), vol. 1, 276–83.

105. For an overview, see Bowes, *Private Worship*, 88–90.

106. Concerning the laws forbidding *in urbe* burials, see Marios Costambeys, "Burial Topography and the Power of the Church in Fifth- and Sixth-Century Rome," *Papers of the British School at Rome* 69 (2001): 169–89, esp. 170–71. Concerning other domestic possessions of martyr relics, see Bowes, 92–96, who details the likely private possession

of relics of Saint Felix of Nola, Saints Gervasius and Protasius, and Saint Stephen the protomartyr.

107. Bowes, *Private Worship*, 93.

108. Ibid., 72.

109. Ibid., 72–73.

110. See Joseph Donalla Alchermes, "'Cura pro mortuis' and 'Cultus Martyrum': Commemoration in Rome from the Second through the Sixth Century" (PhD diss., New York University, 1989), 195–288.

111. See Alchermes, "Commemoration in Rome," 255–62.

112. For an excellent overview of Christian commemoration of the dead, see Alchermes, "Commemoration in Rome."

113. Alchermes, "Commemoration in Rome," 10–14.

114. The cult of Saint Agnes evinces the way Roman bishops could assert themselves into popular martyr cults through patronage. See Hannah Jones, "Agnes and Constantia: Domesticity and Cult Patronage in the *Passion of Agnes*," in *Religion, Dynasty, and Patronage*, ed. Kate Cooper and Julia Hillner (Cambridge: Cambridge University Press, 2007), 115–39.

115. See Michelle Salzman, *On Roman Time: The Codex Calendar of 354 and the Rhythms of Urban Life in Late Antiquity* (Berkeley: University of California Press, 1990), esp. 42–46. See also Pietri, *Roma christiana*, vol. 1, 617–24.

116. See Gitte Lonstrup, "Constructing Myths: The Foundation of *Roma Christiana* on 29 June," trans. Lene Ostermark-Johansen, *Analecta Romana* 33 (2008): 27–64, at 39.

117. According to a series of texts preserved in the *Collectio Avellana*, Damasus was implicated (through his surrogates) in the murder of a large number of his rival's supporters. Otto Günther, ed., *Epistulae imperatorum pontificum aliorum inde ab a. CCCLXVII usque ad a. DLIII datae Avellana quae dicitur collectio*, CSEL 35 (1898). After a series of violent conflicts between factions, Damasus attempted to sanitize these sites by inscribing lavish epigrams dedicated to the martyrs. Those epigrams frame the martyr narratives in specific pro-Damasine ways. See Marianne Sághy, "*Scinditur in partes populous*: Damasus and the Martyrs of Rome," *Early Medieval History* 9 (2000): 273–87, esp. 279–81. See also Jones, "Agnes and Constantia," 122.

118. See Sághy, "Damasus and the Martyrs of Rome"; and Dennis Trout, "Damasus and the Invention of Early Christian Rome," *Journal of Medieval and Early Modern Studies* 33 (2003): 517–36.

119. Damasus' renovation of the sites at the catacombs included architectural reconfiguration, artistic elaboration, and the commissioning of a series of inscriptions in Virgilian verse on large marble blocks. The inscriptions, in particular, allowed Damasus to retell popular stories in a specific way that suited the pontiff's particular interests. See Pietri, *Roma christiana*, vol. 1, 595–617; Sághy, "Damasus and the Martyrs of Rome," esp. 276–77; and Trout, "Damasus and the Invention of Early Christian Rome."

120. For a brief overview of the scholarly understanding of the original Constantinian basilica, see Joseph Donalla Alchermes, "Petrine Politics: Pope Symmachus and the Rotunda of St. Andrew's at the Old St. Peter's," *Catholic Historical Review* 81 (1995): 1–40,

esp. 3–6. See also Turpin Bannister, "The Constantinian Basilica of St. Peter at Rome," *Journal of the Society of Architectural Historians* 27 (1968): 3–32; and Richard Krautheimer, *Rome, Profile of a City, 312–1308* (Princeton, N.J.: Princeton University Press, 1980). In its early years, the basilica received lavish gifts from lay patrons, whose financial resources greatly outstripped those of the Roman bishops in the period.

121. Concerning the archaeological evidence for third-century activity, see Lonstrup, "Constructing Myths," 27–64; and Alchermes, "Commemoration in Rome," 64–125.

122. For a summary of the archaeological problem, see Henry Chadwick, "St. Peter and St. Paul in Rome: The Problem of the 'Memoria Apostolorum ad Catacombs,'" *Journal of Theological Studies* n.s. 8 (1957): 39–51. The "problem" identified by Chadwick is glossed over by Pietri in his *Roma christiana*. See also A. G. Martimort, "Vingtcinq ans de travaux et de recherches sur la mort de saint Pierre et de sa sépulture," *Bulletin de littérature ecclésiastique* 3 (1972): 89–98.

123. Leo Mohlberg, "Historisch-kritische Bemerkungen zum Ursprung der sogennanten 'Memoria Apostoloorum' an der Appischen Straße," in *Colligere fragmenta: Festschrift Alban Dold zum 70 Geburstag am 7.7.52*, ed. F. Fischer and V. Fiala (Beuron: Beuroner Kunstverlag, 1952), 52–74. See Cooper, "The Martyr, the *Matrona*, and the Bishop," 311–13.

124. Cooper, "The Martyr, the *Matrona*, and the Bishop."

125. See Sághy, "Pope Damasus and the Martyrs of Rome," 273–87. She argues that Damasus' cultivation of epigraphy (rather than other options) at the Constantinian shrines was, in part, a financial necessity, because he could not compete with the deep pockets of Rome's wealthy elite.

126. This particular epigram has been transcribed as *Epigrammata* 20. Damasus, *Epigrammata*, ed. Antonio Ferrua (Vatican City: Bibliotheca Apostolica Vaticana, 1942).

127. Damasus, *Epigram* 20. Scholarly discussion of this epigram is extensive; some scholars focus on the classical motifs, and others seek to interpret Damasus' phrasing to understand whether or not the inscription implies that a translation of relics has occurred. On the classical illusions, see Trout, "Damasus and the Invention of Early Christian Rome." For the questions surrounding the possibility of a translation, see Chadwick, "St Peter and St. Paul in Rome."

128. Leo was likely the first pope to be buried in the portico of St. Peter's, a location that may well have been his own choice. The burial is noted at the conclusion of the entry for Leo in the *Liber Pontificalis*. On Leo as the first pope to be buried there, see Louis Duchesne, ed., *Liber Pontificalis*, 2nd ed. (Paris: Boccard, 1955), vol. 1, 241 n. 15.

129. See Lucy Grig, "Portraits, Pontiffs, and the Christianization of Fourth-Century Rome," *Papers of the British School at Rome* 72 (2004): 203–30.

130. Charles Pietri, "*Concordia apostolorum et renovatio urbis*: Culte des martyrs et propagande pontificale," *Mélanges d'Archéologie et d'Histoire de l'École Française de Rome* 73 (1961): 275–322. Pietri's thesis was adopted and asserted even more forcefully by J. M. Huskinson, *Concordia Apostolorum: Christian Propaganda at Rome in the Fourth and Fifth Centuries; A Study of Early Christian Iconography and Iconology* (Oxford: B.A.R., 1982).

131. Grig, "Portraits."

132. Some of these portraits include Saint Paul and additional martyrs; others include men believed to have been in Damasus' circle of friends and associates. See Grig, "Portraits."

133. Concerning the problems of patronage, see Grig, "Portraits."

134. See especially Sághy, "Pope Damasus and the Martyrs of Rome." See also Pietri, "*Concordia apostolorum*"; and Huskinson, *Christian Propaganda*.

135. Scholars point to the so-called decretals of Siricius (bishop of Rome, 384–399), especially his *Letter to Himerius of Terragona*, as one of the earliest deliberate attempts to assert papal influence in dogmatic and moral matters.

CHAPTER 2. THE MANY FACES OF LEO'S PETER

1. The final chapters of the first volume of Erich Caspar's *Geschichte des Papsttum* (Tubingen: J.C.B. Mohr, 1930) famously seek to examine Leo's significant contributions to the ever-expanding ideology of the papacy. Recent monographs devoted to Leo's theology include J. M. Armitage, *A Twofold Solidarity: Leo the Great's Theology of Redemption* (Strathfield: St. Paul's, 2005), and B. Green, *The Soteriology of Leo the Great* (Oxford: Oxford University Press, 2008). Political and theological investigations, of course, need not be mutually exclusive, as Susan Wessel's biography successfully demonstrates. Wessel, *Leo the Great and the Spiritual Rebuilding of a Universal Rome* (Leiden: Brill, 2008), 2–4, 137–38, and 145.

2. Philip McShane, *La Romanitas et le Pape Léon le Grand: l'apport culturel des institutions imperials à la formation des structures ecclésiastiques* (Montreal: Tournai, 1979).

3. Walter Ullman, "Leo the First and the Theme of Papal Primacy," *Journal of Theological Studies* n.s. 11 (1960): 25–51. See also Ullmann, *A Short History of the Papacy in the Middle Ages*, 2nd ed. (London: Routlege, 2003), 20–21.

4. See Bronwen Neil, *Leo the Great* (London: Routledge, 2009), 39–40. For Leyser's development of themes surrounding the rhetoric of humility and vulnerability, see his *Authority and Asceticism from Augustine to Gregory the Great* (Oxford: Oxford University Press, 2000), esp. 133.

5. Trevor Jalland, *Life and Times of St. Leo the Great* (New York: Macmillan, 1941).

6. Wessel, *Spiritual Rebuilding*, 288–97. Wessel's contribution in this regard is to see the importance Leo placed on the idea of spiritual *condescensio* in the rendering of pastoral care and justice. See especially 293.

7. For an overview of how the fractured political situation in Italy relates to Leo's pontificate, see Wessel, *Spiritual Rebuilding*, 9–34.

8. Later biographers made a great deal of Leo's supposed encounter with Attila, who, according to legend, was so impressed by Leo's sanctity that he decided to leave Italy. The *Liber Pontificalis* provides a prime example of this. While there is no reason to doubt that Leo participated with other Roman aristocrats in an embassy to meet Attila, there is no mention of this encounter in Leo's surviving corpus. See Wessel, *Spiritual Rebuilding*, 44–47.

9. Both he and Prosper of Aquitaine claim that his *patria* was Rome. According to the *Liber Pontificalis*, however, Leo was of Tuscan origin.

10. Leo tells us he was "away on a long journey at the time of his election." Leo, *Sermones*, ed. Antonius Chavasse, CCL 138–138a (hereafter *Serm.*) 1. Prosper of Aquitaine is our source for why he was in Gaul. Prosper, *Epitome Chronicon* 1341, ed. Mommsen (1892), 478. See Neil, *Leo the Great*, 2.

11. There is no complete critical edition of the letters. Those dealing with Eastern heresies, especially as related to the Council of Chalcedon, have been edited by Eduard Schwartz (*Acta Conciliorum Oecumenicorum I–IV* (Berlin, 1927–1932)) and Carlo Silva-Tarouca (*S. Leonis Magni Epistulae* (Rome, 1932–1935)). For uniformity, I have kept the numbering in the *Patrologia Latina* series (vol. 54).

12. See Neil on the development of the four Roman fasting periods. Neil, *Leo the Great*, 23–24.

13. For a concise overview of the organizational structure of the sermons, see Neil, *Leo the Great*, 13–15, which follows the more detailed account of Antonius Chavasse, the critical editor.

14. Leo was the first Western bishop to institutionalize collections for the poor. See Neil, *Leo the Great*, 19–20. See also Wessel's comparison of Leo and other fourth- and fifth-century theologians on the issue of almsgiving. Wessel, *Spiritual Rebuilding* 179–207.

15. Of course, that Italian bishops would gather in Rome on the anniversary of Leo's election indicates a general respect for pontifical authority in the period. We do not know which bishops actually attended these gatherings. We can assume that all local bishops would have been present, along with leaders of a good number of suburbican sees. By the close of the following century, Pope Gregory I tried to institute a policy by which all Sicilian bishops would travel to Rome to attend the feast of Sts. Peter and Paul on every fifth year.

16. Leo, *Serm.* 2.

17. See Siricius, *Ep.* 1.1 (PL 13.1132f.). Ullmann believed Leo's introduction of the legal phrase "unworthy heir" offered a more tangible connection between the papacy and Peter than previous concepts, which were, according to Ullmann, mostly symbolic. Ullmann, "The Theme of Papal Primacy," 33.

18. Leo, *Serm.* 3.

19. Mt 16.16–19.

20. Leo, *Serm.* 3.

21. In the event that he had not been sufficiently clear regarding that point in the homily, Leo continues, attempting to make his position plainer: "When we present our exhortations to your holy ears, you should believe that you are being addressed by the one in the place of whom we exercise this duty." Leo, *Serm.* 3.

22. Leo, *Serm* 3.

23. This point only further serves to uproot Ullmann's interpretation of Leo's use of the inheritance language. For more on Leo's use of domestic language, see Kristina Sessa, *The Formation of Papal Authority in Late Antique Italy: Roman Bishops and the Domestic Sphere* (Cambridge: Cambridge University Press, 2012), esp. 70–72.

24. Only five of Leo's "anniversary" sermons survive. The first was actually delivered at the time of his elevation. These sermons date to 440, 441, 443, 444, and sometime after 445. Interestingly, the sermon he offered on the occasion of his ordination and the final one (for which we do not have a firm date) do not display pontifical insecurity or the need to assert Roman authority through Petrine means. The two sermons delivered on the feast of St. Peter and Paul (*Serm.* 82 and 83) are dated early in his career, 441 and 443.

25. "Beloved, this is what that confession has obtained. Since it was inspired by God the Father in the heart of the apostle, it has transcended all the uncertain opinions of human error and has received the sturdiness of rock that cannot be shaken by any pounding." Leo, *Serm.* 3.

26. "These are the men through whom the Gospel of Christ enlightened you, oh Rome, and you who had been the teacher of error were transformed by the disciple of truth. These men are your holy fathers and your true shepherds, who enabled you to be a part of the heavenly kingdom. They are far superior and more favorable than that one, who gave you your name, defiled you with the murder of his twin brother." Leo, *Serm.* 82.

27. Leo, *Serm.* 83.

28. I presume that bishops who would travel to Rome for Leo's anniversary or the feast of Sts. Peter and Paul were either those of the immediate district around Rome (and therefore likely appointed directly by Leo) or those well disposed to him. It is, in fact, a fascinating element of his development of the Petrine discourse that the pontiff would pronounce so forcefully to a gathering of bishops that should have been already well disposed toward his authority.

29. Leo's sermons on the Nativity fast are *Serm.* 12–20, and his homilies for the Nativity are *Serm.* 21–30.

30. Leo's *Serm.* 46 (a Lenten sermon delivered in March 453, in the midst of the Christological controversy) also offers an uncommonly thorough Christological digression. Here, too, however, there is no connection to Peter's confession of faith.

31. For an example of early Christian exegetical criticism of Peter, see John Chrysostom's eighty-fourth homily on Matthew.

32. "Blessed Peter, who followed the Lord with the most fierce loyalty and burned with the fire of a holy love, used his sword to cut off the ear of the servant of the high priest, a man who was himself threatening violence." Leo, *Serm.* 52.

33. Leo, *Serm.* 52.

34. Leo, *Serm.* 60.

35. "Productive are your tears, holy apostle, tears which had the power of holy baptism for cleansing the guilt of the denial. Indeed, beside you was the right hand of our Lord Jesus Christ. As you were slipping, it grabbed hold before you would fall. You were given strength to stand amid the danger of falling. Our Lord saw in you not a faith overcome, not a love turned away, but a troubled stability. Tears flowed out since love had not given way and the fountain of love washed away the words of fear. No, the remedy of cleansing did not come slowly since there had not been a decision of the will. Quickly the rock returned to its firmness, becoming so strong that he did not fear afterward in his own suffering what had so terrified him in the Passion of Christ." Leo, *Serm.* 60.

36. Kevin Uhalde, "Pope Leo I on Power and Failure," *Catholic Historical Review* 95 (2009): 671–88. Uhalde cleverly contrasts the spiritually enriching experience of Peter to the spiritual degradation of Judas. See also Uhalde, "The Sinful Subject: Doing Penance in Rome," *Studia Patristica* 44 (2010): 405–14.

37. See, for example, *Serm.* 62 and 67.

38. See, for example, Paschal sermons 52, 54, and 56, and the Lenten sermons (39–51), especially 39, 43, and 48. There is, perhaps, a vague reference to Peter in *Serm.* 49 in connection with penance: "[Satan] sees that the lapsed . . . are washed in the tears of penitence and admitted to the healing of reconciliation, when the key of the apostles has opened the doors of mercy."

39. "But this height of praiseworthy understanding had to be built up concerning the mystery of the inferior substance [i.e., the humanity], otherwise the faith of the apostle might be so overwhelmed in respect to the glory of confessing the divinity in Christ that he might judge that the assumption of our weakness would be unworthy of God." Leo, *Serm.* 51.

40. Leo, *Serm.* 51.

41. "But the Lord did not respond to this suggestion, signifying that what [Peter] sought was not only base but inordinate, for the world could not be saved except by the death of Christ." Leo, *Serm.* 51.

42. As we will see in Chapter 5, Gregory I was far more willing than either Leo or Gelasius to explore Peter's miscues for a larger pastoral objective.

43. Leo, *Serm.* 12, but repeated in similar form in *Serm.* 13, 15, 17, 18, 19, and several others.

44. I would like to thank Michele Salzman, who graciously shared her essay on the location of Leo's preaching with me before its publication. Salzman, "Leo's Liturgical Topography: Contestations for Space in Fifth Century Rome," *Journal of Roman Studies* (forthcoming).

45. We know, for example, that when they came to Rome, the emperor Valentinian, along with his wife and mother, visited the church of St. Peter for the explicit purpose of venerating Peter's relics. See Leo, *Ep.* 55–58.

46. In addition to the petition for Peter's intercession that concludes so many homilies, four of Leo's sermons actively promote the cult of Christian saints: *Serm* 82 and 83, delivered on the feast of Sts. Peter and Paul; *Serm* 84, which commemorates the anniversary of Alaric's attack on the city; and *Serm* 85, offered on the feast of St. Lawrence.

47. Leo, *Serm.* 84.

48. See Wessel, *Spiritual Rebuilding*, 156–65. On the use of precedent in Roman law, see Jill Harries, *Cicero and the Jurists: From Citizens' Law to the Lawful State* (London: Duckworth, 2006), esp. 236–38.

49. The canons granting this privilege originated from a need to justify, after the fact, Athanasius' seeking asylum in Rome during the tenure of Pope Julius (and Julius' support of him) following his condemnation at the Synod of Tyre.

50. The authoritative account of both the Council of Serdica and its subsequent interpretation and use in Rome is Hamilton Hess, *The Early Development of Canon Law*

and the Council of Serdica, rev. ed. (Oxford: Oxford University Press, 2002). The first pope to appeal directly to the Serdican privilege was Innocent I. See Hess, 128.

51. See Wessel, *Spiritual Rebuilding*, 174–75.

52. For a recent account of the development of the papal estates in central Italy, which is based on a broader collection of evidence than papal letters, see Federico Marazzi, *Patrimonia Sanctae Romanae Ecclesiae nel Lazio (secoli IV–X)* (Rome: Istituto Storico Italiano per il Medio Evo, 1998). For a *status quaestionis* of the development of the Roman patrimonies in general, see Dominic Morneau, "Les patrimoines de l'Église romaine jusqu' à la mort de Grégoire le Grand," *Antiquité Tardive* 14 (2006): 79–93. An older but still useful account, which includes information on the Sicilian and Sardinian estates: Jeffrey Richards, *The Popes and the Papacy in the Early Middle Ages: 476–752* (London: Routledge and Kegan Paul, 1979), 307–22.

53. The appointment represents an attempt by Leo to maintain Roman influence (and does so following certain imperial models of provincial administration), but the correspondence lacks any Petrine content. Concerning the creation of the vicariate in Illyricum, see S. L. Greenslade, "The Illyrican Churches and the Vicariate of Thessalonica, 375–395," *Journal of Theological Studies* n.s. 46 (1945): 17–30.

54. Leo encouraged the bishop of Aquileia to persecute Pelagianism (*Ep.* 1 and 2), but the Manichaeans, who were found to be in Rome itself, were among his greatest concerns. The Catholic clergy of Rome had attempted to purge the city of its Manichaean inhabitants from the beginning of the fifth century. Leo's sermons (esp. 9, 16, and 24) display a noticeable spike in attention to Manichaeanism in 453–454. Neil suggests the refugees fleeing Vandal North Africa may have included a number of Manichaeans (*Leo the Great*, 32). In *Ep.* 7, Leo informs us that he formed a tribunal consisting of local bishops and aristocrats that successfully purged Rome of the Manichaean sect, a development Wessel dubbed the "first inquisition at Rome" (*Spiritual Rebuilding*, 38). Wessel interprets Leo's success against the Manichaeans as an example of the "unquestioned authority" of the bishop of Rome in suburbican Italy. But she also argues that the "spectacle" of a show trial was orchestrated by Leo to justify an "ecclesiology of surveillance" among both the laity and the episcopate of Italy. Wessel, 121–25.

55. Lynn White, "The Byzantinization of Sicily," *American Historical Review* 42 (1936): 1–21.

56. Whereas the Roman Church's celebration of the Feast of Epiphany was primarily a commemoration of the arrival of the Magi, the Eastern Christian tradition was to celebrate the feast as a commemoration of Christ's own baptism by John the Baptist.

57. Leo, *Ep.* 16.

58. Ibid.

59. Leo is willing to grant the practice on Easter, but his preference is for Pentecost.

60. Leo, *Ep.* 16.

61. See Wessel's contention that Leo's efforts to effect liturgical change in Sicily were probably unsuccessful. Wessel, *Spiritual Rebuilding*, 129–31.

62. Irenaeus' much-disputed referent stems from book 3 of his *Against Heresies*. Concerning the limited interaction between the Gallic Church and Rome until the fifth century, see Ralph Mathisen, *Ecclesiastical Factionalism and Religious Controversy in Fifth-Century Gaul* (Washington, D.C.: Catholic University Press, 1989), esp. 9–11.

63. Innocent, in fact, encouraged Gallic bishops to appeal to Rome whenever they felt themselves the victims of ecclesiastical injustice. But, interestingly, there is no reference to a Petrine privilege in this letter. Innocent, *Ep. "Etsi tibi"* (PL 20.468–81). Perhaps the earliest example (for which we have ample evidence) of a Gallic bishop taking advantage of a "Serdican" appeal was in 424, when Victricius of Rouen traveled to Rome and won an exoneration of all charges of heresy by Pope Innocent I. See Mathisen, *Ecclesiastical Factionalism*, 45–47.

64. Mathisen, *Ecclesiastical Factionalism*, 11.

65. Many "graduates" of the Lérinian monastic community assumed powerful episcopal positions in the Gallic Church. On the impact of Cassian's ascetic theology on subsequent Latin traditions, especially in the area of pastoral theology, see Demacopoulos, *Five Models of Spiritual Direction in the Early Church* (Notre Dame, Ind.: University of Notre Dame Press, 2007), esp. 110 and 130–39.

66. Beginning with Pope Zosimus (417–418), the Roman Church became involved in the metropolitan border disputes that had divided the Gallic Church for more than a generation. In 417, Zosimus, likely under secular direction, sought to realign the metropolitan boundaries according to the new secular realities. While he appealed to several legendary traditions as the basis of his authority to alter these boundaries (particularly the apocryphal tradition of St. Trophimus who had, supposedly, been sent from Rome to evangelize Arles), Zosimus made no mention of Petrine authority. Mathisen, *Ecclesiastical Factionalism*, 25–26 and 48–60.

67. Among other things, Mathisen explores the wildly divergent accounts provided by Leo's letters and the *Vita Hilarii*. See Mathisen, *Ecclesiastical Factionalism*, 141–72; and Wessel, *Spiritual Rebuilding*, 58–80.

68. "The Lord desires that the [proclamation of the gospel] should be a shared task by all the Apostles, but he placed the principal responsibility on the most blessed Peter, the greatest of all the apostles." Leo, *Ep.* 10.1.

69. He argues, in fact, that the Lord renamed Peter "the rock" so that "the building of the eternal temple, by a miraculous gift of God's grace, might be built upon the foundation that was Peter." Leo, *Ep.* 10.1.

70. "Anyone who thinks that the primacy [*principatum*] should be denied [to Peter] cannot weaken the apostle's dignity." Leo, *Ep.* 10.2.

71. This was true of both his anniversary sermons and *Ep.* 16 to Sicily.

72. Leo effectively offers three arguments in his defense: (1) Peter's primacy as a basis for his own supervision of the entire Church; (2) the precedent of "ancient tradition"; and (3) the evidence that Gallic bishops had in the past asked Roman bishops for assistance with problems in the Gallic Church.

73. See, for example, *Ep. 66*, which denies full metropolitan rights to the See of Arles; and *Ep. 96*, which attempts to force the bishop of Arles to conform to the Roman dating of Easter.

74. Leo, *Ep.* 10.

75. Leo had, in fact, censured Hilary because he was imposing his metropolitan rights on diocesan bishops who were outside of his metropolitan territory. See Mathisen, *Ecclesiastical Factionalism*, 153–72.

76. On Hilary's nonconformity with Leo's injunctions, see Mathisen, *Ecclesiastical Factionalism*, 170–71.

77. Mathisen, *Ecclesiastical Factionalism*, 173–81.

78. This letter is preserved as Leo, *Ep.* 65.

79. Leo, *Ep.* 65.

80. Mathisen, *Ecclesiastical Factionalism*, 177–79. This interpretation rebuts previous interpretations that had read submission to Roman authority as a sincere capitulation. See especially Trevor Jalland, *The Church and the Papacy* (London: SPCK, 1946), 306.

81. Leo, *Ep.* 66.

82. Note, for example, the gushing submission to Roman authority in *Ep.* 68.

83. An up-to-date account of Leo's Christological vision and involvement in the controversy is provided by Wessel, *Spiritual Rebuilding*, 209–344.

84. Among others, Eutyches wrote to Peter Chrysologus, the archbishop of Ravenna, presuming that he might have significant influence because the Western court at that time resided in Ravenna, not Rome. Eutyches' appeal to Leo is transmitted as Leo, *Ep.* 21, and dated to December 448. Leo had actually written to Eutyches the previous summer, thanking him for his warning that Nestorianism was reasserting itself in Constantinople.

85. Leo, *Ep.* 23.

86. Leo's letter to Flavian dates to June 449. Interestingly, of the seven letters Leo wrote to the East in anticipation of the synod, there is only one brief appeal to Petrine authority, contained in the *Tome* itself. Leo, *Ep.* 26–32, which are all dated to spring/early summer 449.

87. His chief delegate was Julian, bishop of Cos, who had likely lived for a time in Rome and was Leo's most trusted colleague in the East. For his announcement of Julian's role, see *Ep.* 28–32, and 34–35.

88. Leo, *Ep.* 44, 45, 50, 51, and 54.

89. Preserved as Leo, *Ep.* 55–58. Theodosius' responses are preserved as Leo, *Ep.* 62–64. Wessel observes that Leo's ultimate success was, in large part, the result of his skill as a negotiator and as a builder of an important diplomatic network. This might best be demonstrated by his ability to convince the imperial officials in the West to write to their colleagues in the East in support of Leo's position and desire for a new council. See Wessel, *Spiritual Rebuilding*, 260–62.

90. Preserved as Leo, *Ep.* 73; confirmed in a subsequent letter preserved as *Ep.* 76.

91. Leo, *Ep.* 79–84.

92. Leo, *Ep.* 83 and 89.

93. The gathered bishops sent a joint letter to Leo, preserved as *Ep.* 98, which offered him the first indication of what was developing.

94. For Leo's acknowledgment that this was happening, see *Ep.* 117, 124, and 130.

95. Preserved as Leo, *Ep.* 110.

96. Leo, *Ep.* 114.

97. See, for example, *Ep.* 115, 116, 119, and 127.

98. The pontiff feared that the new emperor might not support Chalcedon, and so it was no longer strategically advantageous to offer partial support for the council. For evidence of Leo's concern that the new emperor might rescind Chalcedon, see *Ep.* 146, 149, and 150. Leo's letters to Leo the emperor, in which he pleads for support of Chalcedon, are *Ep.* 145 and 148.

99. Leo, *Ep.* 33.

100. Leo, *Ep.* 44.

101. Leo, *Ep.* 93. Interestingly, Leo explains his absence from the council in terms of there being no precedent for his attendance—no pope had ever attended an ecumenical council.

102. Leo, *Ep.* 105.

103. Leo, *Ep.* 106.

104. Ibid. As for Antioch, "It was in that Church where the blessed Apostle, Peter, preached and the name 'Christian' was in first use."

105. Leo, *Ep.* 119. Interestingly, Leo's correspondence with Maximus of Antioch and Proterius of Alexandria was not a wholesale sharing of Petrine capital as Gregory the Great would attempt at the close of the next century. Although he invested Petrine authority in the See of Antioch, Leo remained determined to assert his own authority over Antioch and Alexandria. See also Leo, *Ep.* 129 to Proterius.

106. *Ep.* 79 to Pulcheria, for example, still attempts to persuade the court that the council should be held in the West. Despite the fact that Leo senses a losing battle, his letter harbors no complaints and no Petrine discourse.

107. Leo, *Ep.* 85.

108. As it turned out, even this letter was edited before it circulated among Eastern bishops, to remove any reference to papal hesitation. We learn of this through *Ep.* 127.

109. Concerning Chrysostom's appeal to Western leaders, see Geoffrey Dunn, "Roman Primacy in the Correspondence between Innocent I and John Chrysostom," in *Giovanni Crisostomo: Oriente e Occidente tra IV e V secolo* (Rome: Insitutum Patristicum Augustinianum, 2005), 687–98.

110. Eutyches' letter to Leo has been transmitted as Leo, *Ep.* 21.

111. This derives from Leo's second letter to Flavian, *Ep.* 26.

112. It is true that Eutyches had written to Leo earlier, warning him of a fresh outbreak of Nestorianism in the city. Leo responded (*Ep.* 20) with appreciation for the warning but offered no explicit endorsement of Eutyches' Christological positions.

113. For a theological assessment of Theodoret's role in the Christological debates of the period, see Paul Clayton, *Theodoret of Cyrus: Antiochene Christology from the Council of Ephesus (431) to the Council of Chalcedon (451)* (Oxford: Oxford University Press, 2007).

For a more social and political assessment of Theodoret's involvement, see Adam Schor, *Theodoret's People: Social Networks and Religious Conflict in Late Roman Syria* (Berkeley: University of California Press, 2011).

114. Theodoret's letter has been transmitted as Leo, *Ep.* 52.

115. Leo, *Ep.* 52.

116. *Ep.* 73, in fact, is the letter that announces Marcian's rule of the Eastern Empire and the decision to hold a new council to solve the Christological question. It was dated to September 450. *Ep.* 77, dated to December 450, attempts to convince Leo of Anatolius' orthodoxy and does so by noting that the new archbishop has endorsed Leo's *Tome*.

117. Transmitted as Leo, *Ep.* 55.

118. Transmitted as Leo, *Ep.* 56.

119. See Wessel, *Spiritual Rebuilding*, 264–65.

120. Theodosius' letters are transmitted as Leo, *Ep.* 63 and 64.

121. See, for example, *Ep.* 83, 89, 90, and 95.

122. This letter has been transmitted as Leo, *Ep.* 98.

123. The authors knew well that Leo would object to Canon 28. Not only had his delegates vehemently opposed it at the council, but the Roman Church had also long objected to any Constantinopolitan privilege.

124. Leo, *Ep.* 98.1.

125. Ibid.

126. Leo, *Ep.* 98.4.

127. Ibid.

128. The Eastern bishops may have been willing to acknowledge some of Leo's rhetorical claims (e.g., that he was "Peter's mouthpiece"), but they simultaneously insisted that the bishop of Constantinople was Leo's equal.

129. See Charles Hefele, *A History of the Councils of the Church*, vol. 3 (Edinburgh: T & T Clark, 1883), 317.

130. The full citation reads: "That is the faith of the fathers, that is the faith of the Apostles! We all believe thus, the Orthodox believe thus! Anathema to him who believes otherwise! Peter has spoken through Leo: thus, Cyril taught! That is the true faith!" Hefele, *Councils*, 317.

131. Chalcedon had granted the title "patriarch" to the Sees of Constantinople, Alexandria, Antioch, and Jerusalem.

132. For an overview and analysis of the complicated interaction between the imperial court and the non-Chalcedonians in this period, see Patrick Grey, *The Defense of Chalcedon in the East (451–553)* (Leiden: Brill, 1979), esp. 25–44.

CHAPTER 3. GELASIUS' DOMESTIC PROBLEMS
AND INTERNATIONAL POSTURE

1. The Gelasian corpus survives in two overlapping critical editions: A. Thiel, ed., *Epistolae Romanorum pontificum genuinae* (1868), vol. 1, 285–613; and the *Collectio Avellana*, an eleventh-century manuscript collection containing papal documents from the

time of the Acacian schism that was edited and printed by O. Günther, *Epistulae imperatorum pontificum aliorum inde ab a. CCCLXVII usque ad a. DLIII datae Avellana quae dicitur collectio,* CSEL 35 (1898), 218–464.

2. See the Appendix for English translations of *Ep.* 12 and *Tractate* 6 by Matthew Briel.

3. Jeffrey Richards, *The Popes and the Papacy in the Early Middle Ages: 476–752* (London: Routledge, 1979), 251–52.

4. Louis Duchesne, ed., *Liber Pontificalis,* vol. 1, 2nd ed. (Paris: E. de Boccard, 1955), 255–57 (hereafter *LP*).

5. Richards, in fact, suggests that Gelasius effectively elected himself, having spent the latter part of Felix's career pulling the strings of the office.

6. *LP*, 256.

7. Richards, *The Popes and the Papacy,* 242–43.

8. Peter A. B. Llewellyn, "The Roman Clergy During the Laurentian Schism (498–506): A Preliminary Analysis," *Ancient Society* 8 (1977): 255. Llewellyn observes that the percentage of non-Roman candidates elevated to the priesthood doubled during Gelasius' tenure, and takes this to be evidence that Gelasius did not possess pro-Roman sympathies and, instead, emphasized other characteristics when scrutinizing candidates for the priesthood.

9. See J. A. North, "Caesar at the Lupercalia," *Journal of Roman Studies* 98 (2008): 144–60.

10. See ibid. and Gerhard Binder, "Kommunikative Elemente im römischen Staatskult am Ende der Republik: Das Beispiel des Lupercalia des Jahres 44," in *Religiöse Kommunikation: Formen und Praxis von der Neuzeit,* ed. G. Binder and K. Ehlich (Trier: Wissenschaftlicher Verlag Trier, 1997), 225–41.

11. The only book-length treatment of the Lupercalia in the Christian period is that of W. J. Holleman, *Pope Gelasius I and the Lupercalia* (Amsterdam: Hakkert, 1974), which argues that Gelasius transformed the festival into a syncretistic ritual of public confession (see 38–53, 117–18). Note, however, Neil McLynn's persuasive critique of this thesis. McLynn, "Crying Wolf: The Pope and the Lupercalia," *Journal of Roman Studies* 98 (2008): 161–75, esp. 165–66.

12. Thiel, *Epistolae Romanorum pontificum genuinae,* vol. 1, 598–607; *Coll. Avell.* 100, CSEL 35:453–64. It is worth noting that the paragraph designations differ in the two editions, which can lead to inconsistencies in the secondary literature. For an English translation, consult the Appendix by Briel who has followed Thiel's paragraph divisions.

13. The identification of Andromachus as the ringleader of the Lupercalia celebration goes back to the eleventh-century manuscript that serves as the basis for the *Collectio Avellana.* McLynn identifies Andromachus with a prominent member of Odoacer's administration, who served as both Magister Officiorum and Consiliarius in 489. McLynn, "Crying Wolf," 163.

14. This charge by Gelasius has led to a number of divergent interpretations. Most likely, it was meant sarcastically, to the effect of "if you think that this festival is really

important, then why don't you perform it according to the traditional form?" In antiq-uity, the aristocrats themselves ran the semi-nude race, whereas by Gelasius' time the patrons paid actors to participate in it. See McLynn, "Crying Wolf." See also Alan Cam-eron, *The Last Pagans of Rome* (New York: Oxford University Press, 2010), 170–71.

15. The charge of hypocrisy is followed by an appeal for Christian mercy and forgiveness.

16. Gelasius, *Tractate* 6.1.

17. Ibid.

18. Ibid.

19. Gelasius, *Tractate* 6.2.

20. Gelasius, *Tractate* 6.8.

21. Paragraphs 10–12 imply that Gelasius and Andromachus have had a previous conversation about the festival. Here, Gelasius presents Andromachus' arguments in defense of the festival only to counter them one by one.

22. Gelasius, *Tractate* 6.4.

23. Several scholars have come under the sway of Gelasius' rhetoric by concluding that his call for an end to the event led to the cessation of the festival. For a corrective reading, see Cameron, *The Last Pagans of Rome*, 170–71.

24. That Andromachus is a Christian is attested both internally and by other associa-tions that place him acting on behalf of the papacy in 489. He is even recognized by Gelasius in a letter dating to 492 as his "son." Gelasius, *Ep.* 10.7.

25. See McLynn, "Crying Wolf."

26. Ibid., esp. 174.

27. Gelasius, *Tractate* 6.4.

28. Bowes argues that weekday public liturgies were not practiced in Rome until the sixth century. Although Christians would attend public masses at meeting houses and the new basilicas on Sunday and feast days, the majority of communion acts necessarily took place in the home. Kimberly Bowes, *Private Worship, Public Values, and Religious Change in Late Antiquity* (Cambridge: Cambridge University Press, 2008), 76.

29. See Kristina Sessa, "Christianity and the *cubiculum*: Spiritual Politics and Domestic Space in Late Antique Rome," *Journal of Early Christian Studies* 15 (2007): 171–204, esp. 196–204; and Sessa, "Domestic Conversions: Household and Bishops in the Late Antique 'Papal Legends,'" in *Religion, Dynasty, and Patronage in Early Christian Rome: 300–900*, ed. Kate Cooper and Julia Hillner (Cambridge: Cambridge University Press, 2007), 79–114. For a more thorough discussion, see Sessa, *The Formation of Papal Authority in Late Antique Italy: Roman Bishops and the Domestic Sphere* (Cambridge: Cam-bridge University Press, 2012); Bowes, *Private Worship*, esp. 61–103.

30. Sessa, "Domestic Conversions," 84.

31. Sessa, *The Formation of Papal Authority*, 127–73.

32. See ibid., 27–73; and Sessa, "Domestic Conversions," 82–85.

33. Gelasius, *Tractate* 6.1.

34. Concerning construction and consecration of new churches, see Gelasius, *Ep.* 14.4, 25, 35, 41.

35. Gelasius, *Ep.* 25.

36. Examples of Gelasius' attempts to oversee ordinations throughout Italy include *Ep.* 14, 15, 20, 21, 22, 23, 29, 34, and 41.

37. See especially *Tractate* 6.9–10.

38. Paul Veyne's work, of course, was pioneering in this regard. See his *Bread and Circuses: Historical Sociology and Political Pluralism*, trans. Brian Pearce (London: Penguin, 1990). See also Peter Brown, *Power and Persuasion in Late Antiquity* (Madison: University of Wisconsin Press, 1992).

39. McLynn, in fact, argues that, in the wake of Theoderic's recent assassination of Odaocer, Andromachus and his fellow senators were keen to demonstrate their role in the production of the traditional forms of civic life as a way of showcasing their continued importance. McLynn, "Crying Wolf," 173.

40. *LP*, 255.

41. Richards provides the most exhaustive study of the papal patrimonies, see *Popes and the Papacy*, 307–21.

42. Dionysius Exiguus (ca. 470–544) also confirms Gelasius' benevolence, by noting rather pietistically that the pontiff so exhausted his personal funds on the poor that he died in poverty. Exiguus was a Scythian monk who moved to Rome around 500 and became an important ally of Roman bishops and editor of their correspondence. Dionysius' description of Gelasius is cited by Louis Duchesne, *LP*, 256 n. 5.

43. Aided by imperial money, Pope Sixtus III (432–440) undertook the largest ecclesiastical building campaign of the fifth century, and the extravagant mosaics at Santa Maria Maggiore attest to his desire to be known as one of the city's patrons. Note also the inscriptions attesting to Pope Hilary's (461–468) patronage for the baptistery of St. John Lateran.

44. The *LP* lists the dedication of a church to the martyr Euphemia in the town of Tibur, and three basilicas dedicated to St. Nicander, St. Eleutherios, and St. Andrew in the village of Pertusa.

45. Concerning Gelasius' attempts to legislate against churches at private villas, see Luci Pietri, "Évergertisme chrétien et foundations privées dans l'Italie de l'antiquité tardive," in *Humana Sapit*, ed. J.-M. Carrié and Rita Lizzi (Turnhout: Brepolst, 2002), 253–63.

46. Llewellyn, "The Roman Clergy," 254–58. See also Iiro Kajanto, *Onomastic Studies in the Early Christian Inscriptions of Rome and Carthage* (Helsinki: Tilgman, 1963), 60.

47. Llewellyn, "The Roman Clergy," 258. On the origins of the *tituli* churches of Rome and their connections to the senatorial elite, see the impressive essay by Julia Hillner, "Families, Patronage, and the Titular Churches of Rome, c. 300–c. 600," in Cooper and Hillner, *Religion, Dynasty, and Patronage*, 225–61. One implication of Hillner's work is that Llewellyn may have overstated the divide between the titular priests and the papacy.

48. The text ends with the attribution "I, Sixtus, the notary of the Roman Church by the order of my lord most blessed Gelasius, gave this from my desk on the third day before the Ides of March [495]."

49. *LP*, 255.

50. According to the *LP*, the two envoys had succumbed to bribes (which is a common motif in the *LP*, used to explain behavior with which the editors find error). Interestingly, there is no mention of bribery in *Ep.* 30, which, instead, describes Misenus' acknowledgment of having previously held heretical views.

51. *LP*, 255.

52. While there is little direct evidence that Gelasius had a controlling hand in Felix's international policies, scholars have almost universally believed that Gelasius did and may even have authored several letters on Felix's behalf. This presumption is likely based on the similarity of their postures toward the Eastern Church and the forcefulness of Gelasius' character.

53. J. N. D. Kelly, *The Oxford Dictionary of Popes* (Oxford: Oxford University Press, 1986), 48.

54. Richards, *The Popes and the Papacy*, 66.

55. Ibid. Llewellyn, imagining a rather different scenario, attributes some missing priests to a clerical shortage brought on by a lack of episcopal ordinations. Llewellyn's thesis, though not inconceivable, is mostly born of silence. Llewellyn, "The Roman Clergy," 253.

56. Richards, *The Popes and the Papacy*, 66

57. For an alternative reading of *Ep.* 30 as indicating "authentic" and unbiased courtroom events, see Justin Taylor, "The Early Papacy at Work: Gelasius I (492–496)," *Journal of Religious History* 8 (1975): esp. 322–23.

58. Gelasius, *Ep* 30.6.

59. Gelasius, *Ep* 30.15.

60. An interesting element of the text is the protracted (and rather strained) justification the author must give for overturning a previous synodal decision. See *Ep* 30.11–14. Is this, perhaps, one of the reasons the local clergy objected to Misenus' rehabilitation?

61. As noted in the Introduction, I am deliberately employing "discourse" in two overlapping senses. In the Foucauldian sense, discourse refers to an all-encompassing range of enabling conditions that make possible any use of the Petrine theme. In this sense, discourse allows papal actors to act, but, through their actions, the realm of speech options can itself be stretched or expanded. It is to this Foucauldian idea of discourse that I refer when I suggest Gelasius stretches the possibilities for Petrine speech.

62. Gelasius, *Ep* 30.5.

63. As we will see in Chapter 5, Gregory the Great routinely made priests and other officials swear oaths before the tomb of St. Peter as a way of ritualizing their pledge to God. The act, of course, simultaneously enhanced Gregory's leverage as the one who made such pledges possible.

64. Gelasius, *Ep* 30.7. In this chapter, the Apostolic See is the repeated subject of a series of sentences supposedly spoken by Gelasius himself. In other words, when Gelasius speaks, rather than referring to himself, he speaks of the Apostolic See as that which forgives Misenus:

65. Gelasius, *Ep.* 30.10.

66. Gelasius, *Ep.* 30.11–14.

67. Gelasius, *Ep.* 14.6.

68. Gelasius, *Ep.* 14.4 and 14.25. The second example, in fact, is the most aggressive of his entire corpus, likening the consecration of unauthorized churches to Satanism and barbarism. *Ep.* 14.25. See Pietri, "Évergertisme chrétien et foundations privées."

69. Gelasius, *Ep.* 14.6.

70. Gelasius, *Ep.* 14.26. This is one of the oldest extant restrictions on the female deaconate, a practice that Gelasius found to be particularly offensive, and is repeated in several other letters including *Ep.* 21, 22, and 33.

71. Gelasius, *Ep.* 14.2 and 14.14. As we will see in Chapter 5, Gregory I took a decidedly different approach to both situations, welcoming slaves and soldiers into the monastic life. Gelasius acknowledges here that his rules are in conformance with an imperial interdict.

72. Jeffrey Richards, in fact, characterizes the whole of Gelasius' pontificate in terms of an extreme traditionalism. See Richards, *The Popes and the Papacy*, 20–25.

73. Gelasius, *Ep.* 14.9.

74. Gelasius, *Ep.* 14.9.

75. Gelasius begins the letter by noting that war and famine have upset the healthy rhythms of the Church and its discipline, and it is for that reason that he is writing. Gelasius, *Ep.* 14.1.

76. The letter is addressed to bishops Martyrius and Justus. Although their sees are not identified in the letter itself, Thiel notes that the two men match the names of bishops who participated in the Symmachan synods a few years later, which would render them local bishops.

77. *Ep.* 25 explicitly claims that Gelasius' promotion of these regulations stems from a local Roman synod.

78. Gelasius, *Ep.* 14.16.

79. Gelasius, *Ep.* 19.

80. Taylor makes a brief comment to this effect. Taylor, "The Early Papacy at Work," 317.

81. See John Moorhead, *Theoderic in Italy* (Oxford: Clarendon, 1992), 9. See, however, Sessa's rejection of Odoacer's involvement. Sessa, *The Formation of Papal Authority*. Either way, Gelasius attempted to downplay Odoacer's involvement in the Church, styling the Goth's non-intervention as a preferred alternative to the emperor Zeno's interference in ecclesiastical affairs. Gelasius, *Ep.* 26.11.

82. The premier study on the multiple and competing allegiances and identities (e.g., "Goth," "Roman," "Italian,") in sixth-century Italy is Patrick Amory's *People and Identity in Ostrogothic Italy, 489–554* (Cambridge: Cambridge University Press, 1997). Especially relevant to the current study are ch. 6 and 7 (195–276), which explore the complexities of religious identity. Amory argues compellingly that Gelasius' ecclesiastical policy concentrated on the threat by the Eastern Greeks and not by the Arian Goths, thus dispelling any reason to believe Gelasius was in any way "anti-Goth" or "anti-barbarian."

83. Whereas Ullmann attributes Gelasius' indifference to the cultural divide between Romans and barbarians (presuming that Gelasius could not be bothered with barbarian things), Amory argues that Theoderic posed little threat to Gelasius' political theology because he was not an emperor, and therefore not a real threat to papal autonomy or the Catholic community as a whole. Walter Ullmann, *Gelasius I (492–496): Das Papsttum an der Wende der Spätantike zum Mittelalter* (Stuttgart: Anton Hiersemann, 1981), 217–18; Amory, *Identity in Ostrogothic Italy*, 197–98.

84. In addition to his protracted campaign against the Eastern Monophysites (Eutychians, as Gelasius typically styled them), he persecuted Manichaean communities in Rome and sought to expunge Pelagian sympathizers throughout Italy. Concerning his pursuit of Pelagians, see *Ep.* 4, 5, 6, and *Tractate* 5. Concerning Manichaeans, see *Ep.* 37 and *LP* entry for Gelasius.

85. Writing to the bishops of Dardania (in the Balkans), Gelasius referred to the recently murdered Odoacer as "that barbarian heretic." Gelasius, *Ep.* 26.11.

86. This collection of letters was edited by Mommsen and is contained in MGH AA 12. (389–91), the so-called *Epistulae Theodericianae variae* series. Three letters are addressed to Theoderic (*Ep.* 1, 3, and 6—the last replicated by Thiel's frag. 12). Ullmann dismisses the collection entirely, both because he believes that they are later forgeries and because of his contention that the pope would have not pursued any contact with an Arian or a barbarian ruler. Ullmann, *Gelasius I*, 217–18 and 225–26. Both Moorhead and Amory believe them to be authentic. Moorhead, *Theoderic in Italy*, 12, 27–28; Amory, *Identity in Ostrogothic Italy*, 200. Apart from *Ep.* 6, the letters are not contained in Thiel, the *Collectio Avellana*, or *Patrologia Latina*.

87. *Epistulae Theodericianae variae*, *Ep.* 4 and 5.

88. As we will see in the following section, Gelasius was quite happy to accuse the entire Eastern Church of heresy and threaten the emperor that his personal salvation and the fate of the empire itself would be placed in great jeopardy should he not resist the Acacian heresy and return to the Catholic fold. Gelasius' altogether different posture toward the Ostrogothic rulers is remarkable by contrast, and the only sensible explanation for the difference is to be found in the proximity of the Ostrogothic army to the city of Rome itself.

89. Amory's argument that Arianism was an "old" and Monophysitism a "new" heresy is not convincing.

90. Both the Senate and the Church suffered bitter internal disagreements about what course should be pursued vis-à-vis the Ostrogoths and the Eastern emperor. With respect to the Senate, the civil war between Odoacer and Theoderic certainly exacerbated those internal divisions.

91. See Moorhead, *Theoderic in Italy*, 35–39.

92. Ibid., 38.

93. Gelasius, *Ep.* frag. 12.

94. *Epistulae Theodericianae variae*, *Ep.* 5.

95. Gelasius, *Ep.* frag. 13.

96. For example, see Gelasius, *Ep.* 6, 14, and 19.

97. Note, for example, Erich Caspar's treatment in volume 2 of his *Geschichte des Papsttums* (Tubingen: J.C.B. Mohr,1930).

98. Gelasius, *Ep.* 12.2, trans. Briel; see Appendix I. In Thiel's edition, the letter comprises twelve paragraphs and approximately ten pages of text. Thiel, *Epistolae Romanorum pontificum genuinae*, vol. 1, 348–58.

99. Indeed, in the opening pages of *The Growth of the Papal Government* Ullmann argues that the Church in the Middle Ages was able to assert itself over secular leaders by arguing that kings and emperors needed the sacraments for their salvation. Though he does not credit Gelasius with the position, Ullmann has essentially reduced the entirety of the medieval church/state debate to the Gelasian position in the *Ad Anastasium*. Ullmann, *The Growth of the Papal Government in the Middle Ages: A Study in the Ideological Relation of Clerical to Lay Power*, 3rd ed. (London: Methuen, 1970).

100. Gelasius, *Ep.* 12.2–3.

101. In his letter to the Roman senator Faustus (who spearheaded Theoderic's embassy to Anastasius in 493/4), Gelasius makes a similar argument but roots his authority more directly in Peter's ability to bind and loose sin. Gelasius, *Ep.* 10.9.

102. Janet Nelson, "Gelasius' I's Doctrine of Responsibility: A Note," *Journal of Theological Studies* n.s. 18 (1967): 154–62; Ullmann, *The Growth of the Papal Government*, 20–21; P. H. D. Leupen, "The Sacred Authority of Pontiffs," in *Media Latinitas: Essays in Honor of L. J. Engles*, ed. Renée Nip et al. (Turnhout: Brepols, 1996), 245–48; Francis Dvornik, "Pope Gelasius and Emperor Anastasius I," *Byzantinische Zeitschrift* 44 (1951): 111–16. Jeffrey Richards was the first to argue that scholars were wasting their time trying to discern the functional difference between the two terms. Richards, *The Popes and the Papacy*, 21.

103. The quintessential late ancient Christian encomium for the divine sanction of imperial rule, of course, is Eusebius' *Life of Constantine*.

104. We see this, for example, in Aristotle's discussion of friendship in the *Nicomachean Ethics* (book 8.11), where Aristotle compares the king-subject relationship to the father-son relationship: "The friendship of a king for those who live under his rule depends on his superior ability to do good. He confers benefits upon his subjects since he is good and cares for them in order to promote their welfare, just as a shepherd cares for his sheep. Hence, Homer spoke of Agamemnon as 'shepherd of the people.' The friendship of a father for his children is of the same kind, but it differs in the magnitude of benefits bestowed."

105. Gelasius, *Ep.* 12.1–2

106. Ambrose may have been the first bishop to address an emperor as his "son"—he did so in his correspondence with the emperor Theodosius. We know, also, that Felix III (Gelasius' predecessor) employed this convention. As noted, it has long been presumed that Gelasius assisted Felix with his international diplomacy.

107. In some circumstances, especially following the reconquest in the sixth century, imperial approval was a prerequisite for a papal election.

108. These two possibilities, of course, are not mutually exclusive. In fact, they are likely mutually reinforcing factors.

109. "O my son, when the servants of Your Piety, the Illustrious Faustus Magister and Irenaeus, had returned to the city after fulfilling their public embassy, they said that Your Clemency had asked why I had not sent formal greetings to you after my election as Bishop of Rome. I must say that it was not my intention to avoid sending you a letter. However, because new representatives from the East made it known throughout the whole City that *on your orders* I was not allowed to see them, I decided that I ought to refrain from writing you because I was afraid that if I were to write I would be burdensome rather than dutiful to you." Gelasius, *Ep.* 12.1 (my emphasis).

110. Gelasius, *Ep.* 12.1.

111. Ibid.

112. As noted, Llewellyn has argued that Gelasius' well-known trouble with the senatorial families in Rome was related to the fact that he was not a Roman. Llewellyn, "The Roman Clergy," 254–58.

113. Dvornik interprets the passage in a straightforward fashion, arguing that Gelasius was not "yet" willing to break with contemporary understandings of the supreme rule of the emperor. Dvornik, "Pope Gelasius and Emperor Anastasius I," 112.

114. In *Ep.* 26.11 (a letter written to the bishops of Dardania) Gelasius notes that the emperor has intervened in the Acacian dispute under the mistaken assumption that he can justifiably do so. Gelasius then runs through a list of holy men from the past who resisted the unlawful usurpation of religious authority by secular leaders. Gelasius' list includes Nathan's rebuke of David, Ambrose's rebuke of Theodosius I, Leo's rebuke of Theodosius II, Pope Hilary's rebuke of the governor Philotheus, and Pope Simplicius' censure of the emperor Zeno.

115. Similarly, Gelasius concludes the letter with an acknowledgment that the Eastern Church regards the Apostolic See as "haughty and arrogant" (*Ep.* 12.11). He offers a series of clever responses to this charge, but the very fact that he must address the charge of arrogance, again, serves as a marker of the negative view of the See of Rome throughout the Eastern Church.

116. Gelasius, *Ep.* 12.9.

117. The five sees of the so-called Pentarchy were Rome, Constantinople, Alexandria, Antioch, and Jerusalem. See Chapter 4 for more on the development of the Pentarchy and its place in Justinian's legislation.

118. Ullmann, of course, interpreted Gelasius' assertions of papal preeminence as evidence of a universal Christian belief in the primacy of the Roman bishop. Wherever and whenever the Byzantine court failed to acknowledge that privilege, Ullman argues, we find evidence of latent paganism, most often manifest in Caesaro-papist rejection of the papacy. Ullmann, *The Growth of the Papal Government*, 9–13. Caspar similarly understood the primary obstacle to the ever-increasing momentum of papal ideology to be that of Byzantine Caesero-papism. Caspar, *Geschichte*, vol. 2, 33–39.

119. Gelasius, *Ep.* 12.9.

120. Gelasius, *Ep.* 7, 8, 11, 18, and 26. *Ep.* 11 is a letter to Gelasius by the bishops of Dardania, responding to his *Ep.* 7.

121. Gelasius, *Ep.* 18.4. Concerning the history and status of Thessalonica as a papal vicariate, I have benefited greatly from James Skedros, "Civic and Ecclesiastical Identity in Christian Thessaloniki" (public address, Harvard Divinity School, May 2007).

122. Gelasius, *Ep.* 18.4.

123. See especially *Ep.* 18.6 and 26.3–4.

124. Gelasius' argument of course relies on the Serdican privilege, the basic elements of which are explored in Chapter 1.

125. Gelasius, *Ep.* 26.3–4.

126. What *Epistle* 26 and 10 do more than anything is reveal the extent to which the Eastern Church had developed a series of sophisticated responses to the Roman condemnation of Acacius, which was in its eyes, as much as anything, a proxy for Roman ecclesiastical pretension. Far from yielding to papal claims to ecclesiastical authority or acknowledging the canonical claims of Roman jurisdiction, the Eastern Church had its own well-established canonical traditions for which it was able to mount reasoned arguments. Whatever the influence of imperial personalities, the Eastern Church was not without its own ecclesiological justifications or rhetorical craftsmanship.

127. It was Faustus who had reported to Gelasius that the emperor had been disappointed that he had not received Gelasius' announcement of his election. Gelasius, *Ep.* 12.1.

128. It is impossible to know whether Faustus would have received this letter while he was still in Constantinople, during some stage of his journey home, or after his return to Rome. The tone of the letter implicitly presumes that Gelasius expects Faustus to employ these arguments in future diplomatic efforts, but the bishop's structuring of the letter may be the result of a rhetorical posture rather than a realistic expectation that Faustus would advance Gelasius' case in future discussions.

129. Gelasius, *Ep.* 10.3.

130. Ibid.

131. Gelasius, *Ep.* 10.4.

132. Gelasius, *Ep.* 10.5.

133. Ibid.

134. It was customary for copies of the pope's official correspondence to be posted and/or read throughout the city.

135. A concerted effort to persuade the Eastern bishops might have involved a more comprehensive letter-writing campaign. I am not including *Ep.* 1 and 2 (a copy of *Ep.* 1), because they are believed to have been written on behalf of Pope Felix, when Gelasius served as his secretary. Thiel dates *Ep.* 1 and 2 to 489.

136. Gelasius, *Ep.* 3.16.

137. Gelasius, *Ep.* 27.4.

138. Ibid.

139. Gelasius, *Ep.* 27.9.

140. Ibid. *Ep.* 3.4 strikes a more personal posture of episcopal humility ("I am the least of all persons, even though I sit in this chair"), before moving to assertions of Roman privilege.

CHAPTER 4. THE PETRINE DISCOURSE
IN THEODERIC'S ITALY AND JUSTINIAN'S EMPIRE

1. By "secular" I simply mean to designate civil authority (imperial, senatorial, and Ostrogothic) as distinct from ecclesiastical authority.

2. For a balanced overview of the entire affair, see Thomas Noble, "Theodoric and the Papacy," in *Teoderico il Grande e i Goti d'Italia: Atti del XIII Congresso internazionale di studi sull'alto Medioevo* (Milan: Congresso Internazionale di Studi sull'alto Medioevo, 1992), 395–423.

3. For a discussion of the likelihood that Symmachus or his supporters purchased Theoderic's verdict, see Noble, "Theodoric and the Papacy," 405.

4. During his time in the city, Theoderic supported a series of games in the Coliseum and provided funds for rebuilding the city's defenses. See John Moorhead, *Theoderic in Italy* (Oxford: Clarendon, 1992), 60–65; and Wilhelm Ensslin, *Theoderich der Grosse*, 2nd ed. (Munich: F. Bruckmann, 1959), 107–13.

5. These charges are known through the so-called *Laurentian Fragment*, a rival papal biography (only partially extant) contained in the critical edition of the *LP*, 44–46.

6. According to the partisan *Laurentian Fragment* (46), Symmachus had stopped in Ariminum on his way to Ravenna, and while he was there he saw that the prostitutes with whom he had been accused of improper relations were also present. He took this to mean that Theoderic had summoned them and that the king was going to find him guilty. According to both Noble and Richards, Symmachus' flight was enough for Theoderic to believe that he was guilty of the charges against him, and it was for this reason that Theoderic ordered a further investigation into the matter. See Noble, "Theodoric and the Papacy," 407; and Jeffrey Richards, *The Popes and the Papacy in the Early Middle Ages: 476–752* (London: Routledge, 1979), 71.

7. See Noble, "Theodoric and the Papacy," 395–423, 407; Richards, *The Popes and the Papacy*, 71; and Ensslin, *Theoderich der Grosse*, 115. On Theoderic's efforts to avoid entangling himself in papal politics, see Noble, 404–9.

8. The *Laurentian Fragment* notes that the visitation was "sought by all." The *LP* (260–63) declares that the senators Festus and Probinus arranged the visitation.

9. MGH AA 12.423.4f. See also Ennodius, *Lib. pro Syn.* 60ff.; Symmachus, *Ep.* 12.7 (in Thiel) to the emperor Anastasius. See Moorhead, *Theoderic in Italy*, 118.

10. Our knowledge of the number of *tituli* churches at this time stems from a subscription list at the Roman Synod of 499, where the Roman presbyters are listed according to their attachment to their titular church. For the critical edition of the council's proceedings, see Mommsen, ed, *Acta Syn. A* cccxcviii, MGH AA xii (1894), 410–15. For the most current and thorough study of the titular churches, see Julia Hillner, "Families, Patronage, and the Titular Churches, c. 300–c. 600," in *Religion, Dynasty, and Patronage in Early Christian Rome: 300–900*, ed. Kate Cooper and Julia Hillner (Cambridge: Cambridge University Press, 2007), 225–61.

11. Theoderic's order is attested in two places, the *Laurentian Fragment* (46) and his *praeceptum* to the Senate, which has been published in MGH AA 12.392. Theoderic's

instruction to the Senate included the direction that the parishes of Rome be handed over to Symmachus. The entry in the *LP* for Symmachus is silent about the fact that Laurentius retained control for so long. See John Moorhead, "The Laurentian Schism: East and West in the Roman Church," *Church History* 47 (1978): 125–36, at 134, who argues that St. Peter's may well have been the only major basilica in the city open to Symmachus in 501.

12. See, for example, Charles Pietri, "Le Sénat, le peuple chrétien et le partis du Cirque à Rome sous le Pape Symmache," *Mélanges d'Archéologie et d'Histoire* 78 (1966): 123–39; and Moorhead, "The Laurentian Schism." It is worth noting, however, that there is little surviving evidence from the propaganda that was produced in this period that links the crisis to Eastern concerns, apart from a letter from the emperor Anastasius that endorsed Laurentius' claim. The letter has been transmitted as Symmachus, *Ep.* 10 (Thiel, 700).

13. Llewellyn notes that every candidate elected to the papal throne between 432 and 533 came from the rank of deacon, not priest, and speculates that this might well have led to collective resentment on the part of priests regarding the influence of deacons. Peter Llewellyn, "The Roman Clergy During the Laurentian Schism," *Ancient Society* 8 (1977): 245–75, at 248. On the origins and social makeup of the deaconal and priestly orders, one might consult vol. 1 of Pietri, *Roma christiana: Recherches sur l'église de Rome, son organisation, sa politique, son idéologie de Miltiade à Sixte III* (Rome: École Française de Rome, 1976).

14. Llewellyn, "The Roman Clergy," 249.

15. Peter A. B. Llewellyn, "The Roman Church During the Laurentian Schism: Priests and Senators," *Church History* 45 (1976): 417–27, esp. 423–27. He believes the priests of these churches formed a collective group or college and acted in unison. As a corrective, we should note that the priests of the titular churches in this period were appointed by the Roman bishop, who legally controlled their property (even if, in reality, it was the titular priests who managed it).

16. Hillner challenges Llewellyn's thesis that the senatorial patrons, not the bishop, controlled the endowments of these titular churches. See Hillner, "Families, Patronage, and the Titular Churches," esp. 248–61.

17. Llewellyn, "The Roman Church," 427.

18. Kristina Sessa, *The Formation of Papal Authority in Late Antique Italy: Roman Bishops and the Domestic Sphere* (Cambridge: Cambridge University Press, 2012), 213.

19. One of the more notable theories is that the debate centered on a dispute between the senatorial elites and the Roman bishop concerning the latter's administration of church property that had been endowed by the former. In this vein, Charles Pietri maintained that the senators objected to the ways that candidates for episcopal election were disposing of church properties to finance their own election campaigns. See Pietri, *Roma christiana*, 573. This theory has been challenged by Hillner, "Families, Patronage, and the Titular Churches."

20. As Noble rehearses with notable exactitude, our sources reveal only three historical circumstances that brought the Gothic court and the See of Rome together: the Laurentian/ Symmachian schism, the resolution of the Acacian schism in 519, and the

embassy of Pope John I, on behalf of Theoderic, to the imperial court in Constantinople in 525. See Noble, "Theodoric and the Papacy."

21. For example, Cassiodorus, who transmits a great deal of Theoderic's material, does not include a single letter to a Roman bishop. Similarly, Jordanes exhaustive Gothic history does not have any mention of Roman bishops. Jordanes, *Getica*, ed. Theodor Mommsen, MGH AA v. See Noble, "Theodoric and the Papacy," 398.

22. Noble, "Theodoric and the Papacy," 405.

23. Cooper and Hillner, "Introduction," in *Religion, Dynasty, and Patronage*, 1–18, esp. 4–6.

24. While one might claim any text is "partisan," what differentiates these particular papal documents from others is that they clearly, often explicitly, align themselves with either the Symmachian or the Laurentian faction and openly acknowledge their partisan interests.

25. W. T. Townsend, "The So-Called Symmachian Forgeries," *Journal of Religion* 13 (1933): 165–74, offers a summary of apocryphal myths produced in the early years of the controversy.

26. For an excellent summary of Duchesne's chronology that makes use of more recent investigations, see Kate Blair-Dixon, "Memory and Authority in Sixth-Century Rome: The *Liber Pontificalis* and the *Collectio Avellana*," in Cooper and Hillner, *Religion, Dynasty, and Patronage*, 59–76. Duchesne's chronology has been slightly revised by Herman Geertman, who argues that the surviving edition is the oldest (not the second oldest, as Duchesne believed) and was produced in 535. Geertman, ed., *Atti del colloquio internazionale "Il Liber Pontificalis" e la sotria materiale* (Rome: Papers of the Netherlands Institute in Rome, 2003).

27. See Duchesne, *LP*, xxx–xxxvii.

28. While the first edition may not be extant, its content is believed to be reflected in two surviving epitomes with their own emphases: the Felician, more concerned with issues of papal sovereignty and therefore more critical of secular leaders (including the Senate, Theoderic, and the emperor), and the Cononian, which emphasizes the details of papal patronage.

29. One of the key features of the *LP* in this regard is that it defends Chalcedonian orthodoxy against imperial attacks and preserves the Roman bishop's autonomy amid the nefarious meddling of Rome's aristocratic factions—a distinction in purpose that has fueled the diversity of scholarly interpretations of the schism.

30. It should not go unnoticed that the preface to the *LP* includes an apocryphal correspondence between Jerome and Damasus in which Jerome lauds the Petrine character of Damasus' governance of the Church. While one might argue that the text is thus "grounded" in the authority of Jerome and Damasus, it is equally important to note how those authorities appeal to the Petrine dimensions of the entire production.

31. See Moorhead, "The Laurentian Schism."

32. *LP*, 258–59.

33. *LP*, 44. See Noble, "Theodoric and the Papacy," 404 n. 30.

34. Scholars have identified a great number of these editorial omissions, especially those related to the Laurentian schism and to the biographies that correspond to the period of Justinian's reign (when the oldest surviving edition of the *LP* was produced). For example, Moorhead notes that the Roman synodal lists of 499, 501, and 502 contradict the *LP* in suggesting that the majority of the Roman clergy, both priests and deacons, supported Laurentius rather than Symmachus. For her part, Blair-Dixon demonstrates that the *Collectio Avellana* offers a very different portrayal of Vigilius, in that it emphasizes his rejection of Justinian's policy against the Three Chapters—an aspect of Vigilius' career completely ignored by the *LP*. See Moorhead, "The Laurentian Schism" and Blair-Dixon, "Memory and Authority."

35. *LP*, 261. The *LP* details the extent to which supporters of Symmachus suffered violence at the hands of pro-Laurentian mobs supported, first and foremost, by the aristocratic households of Festus and Probinus. That Rome had descended into violence is confirmed by Theoderic's open letter to the bishops meeting in synod in 502 and by the *Laurentian Fragment*, which describes it as a civil war. MGH AA 12.422.2–5 and 421.24 (ed. Mommsen); and *LP*, 46.

36. It is noteworthy that Symmachus and Gelasius are the only two popes whose generosity toward the poor is mentioned in the *LP*. In part, this mention simply attests to a late ancient Christian trope for piety. But it may also be the case for Symmachus, as it appears to have been for Gelasius, that generosity toward the poor offered a way for an otherwise unpopular pontiff to raise his profile and reputation. Symmachus' loyalty among the poor is attested by the sympathetic Ennodius, *Lib. pro Syn.* 61.

37. Joseph D. Alchermes, "Petrine Politics: Pope Symmachus and the Rotunda of St. Andrew's at the Old St. Peter's," *Catholic Historical Review* 81 (1995): 1–40.

38. Moorhead, "The Laurentian Schism," 135.

39. For a more detailed account of Symmachian building at St. Peter's, see Alchermes, "Petrine Politics," esp. 15f.

40. The Felician recension is especially critical.

41. See, for example, the harsh treatment that Theoderic receives in the biography of Pope John I (523–526), who was reduced by Theoderic to service as an envoy to the East. *LP*, 275–78.

42. The critical edition (along with a comprehensive introduction) is provided by Eckhard Wirbelauer, *Zwei Päpste in Rom: Der Konflict zwischen Laurentius und Symmachus (498–514)* (Munich: Tudov, 1993).

43. Wirbelauer, *Zwei Päpste in Rom*, 248–60.

44. Ibid., 284–300. Marcellinus is missing from several ancient papal lists, perhaps because editors omitted him due to the accusations that he had apostatized during the Diocletian persecution.

45. *Synodi sinuessanae gesta*, in Wirbelauer, *Zwei Päpste in Rom*, 300.

46. Wirbelauer, *Zwei Päpste in Rom*, 228–46.

47. Presented as a council, the *Constitutio* also includes a number of canons. Canon 4 maintains that the property of deceased priests should be turned over to the Roman Church—in other words, to its bishop. This would have been a direct challenge to the

independence of the *tituli* churches and their aristocratic sponsors, who were, for the most part, loyal to Laurentius. See Sessa, "Domestic Conversions"; Llewellyn, "The Roman Church," 420.

48. Wirbelauer, *Zwei Päpste in Rom*, 262–71. See Moorhead, *Theoderic in Italy*, 122–24; and Sessa, "Domestic Conversions."

49. See Sessa, "Domestic Conversions," 99; and Sessa, *The Formation of Papal Authority*, 230–46.

50. We must consider the possibility, in fact, that the fragment may have begun with a biography of Peter before moving on, eventually, to the portion of the text that survives.

51. A. Dufourcq, *Étude sur les gesta martyrum romains* (Paris: Fontemoing 1910), 287–321. See also Sessa, "Domestic Conversions," 87.

52. See Llewellyn, "The Roman Church," esp. 423–24. Interestingly, Pietri maintains that the same texts reflect a pro-episcopal position. Pietri, "Donateurs et pieux établissements d'après le légendier romain (Ve–VIIe s)," in *Hagiographie: Cultures et sociétés IV–XII siècle; Actes du Colloque organisé à Nanterre et à Paris 2–5 mai 1979* (Paris: Études Augustiniennes, 1981), 437–40.

53. See Llewellyn, "The Roman Church," 419.

54. Ibid., 420.

55. See Hillner, "Families, Patronage, and the Titular Churches."

56. H. K. Mann, "The Portraits of the Popes," *Papers of the British School at Rome* 9 (1920): 159–204, at 171. I discovered this reference in Moorhead, "The Laurentian Schism."

57. How forcefully John made that appeal is unknown, but he spent his final days as little more than a prisoner in Ravenna, where he died. The story derives primarily from the *Liber Pontificalis*, which, in addition to softening the pope's complicity in an embassy designed to protect the Arian communities of the East, includes a spectacular narrative about how all the citizens of Constantinople came out to greet the "vicar of St. Peter the apostle." *LP*, 275–78.

58. Technically, the Acacian schism came to an end during the reign of Justinian's uncle, Justin I, in March 519. But Justinian had already assumed the status of co-emperor by that time and is widely regarded as having played a major role in the healing of the schism.

59. Justinian joined his uncle as co-emperor in 518 and ruled by himself in 527–565, the longest reign of any Roman or Byzantine emperor. Not only did he rule over the largest territorial expanse of any late ancient emperor, but he, more than any other, was responsible for purging the Eastern Empire of latent forms of paganism and enforcing state-sponsored theological positions. Studies on the Justinianic period abound, but for an important contextual overview consult Michael Mass, ed., *The Cambridge Companion to the Age of Justinian* (Cambridge: Cambridge University Press, 2005).

60. The original *Corpus* has three parts: *Digest, Institutes,* and *Codex*. Paul Krueger, ed., *Corpus Juris Civilis*, 2 vols. (Berlin: Weidmann, 1929). A fourth part, known as the *Novellae*, or new laws, issued by Justinian himself, is often included. A critical edition of

the *Novellae* was published along with the rest of corpus. Rudolf Schoell and Wilhelm Kroll, eds. *Corpus juris civilis*, vol. 3, *Novellae* (Berlin: Weidmann, 1928).

61. *Novella* 6 provides the most explicit description of this. For a brief overview of Justinian's concept of diarchy, see John Meyendorff, "Justinian, the Empire, and the Church," *Dumbarton Oaks Papers* 22 (1969): 43–60.

62. For an overview of what is known about the production, translation, and reception of the *Novellae*, see Detlef Liebs, "Roman Law," in *The Cambridge Ancient History*, vol. 14, ed. Averil Cameron (Cambridge: Cambridge University Press, 1995), 251–52. The numerous inconsistencies in production and reception present the historian with not a few methodological problems. For an excellent overview of the challenges of using an earlier codex of Roman law, the Theodosian codex, see John Matthews, *Laying Down the Law: A Study of the Theodosian Code* (New Haven, Conn.: Yale University Press, 2000).

63. See, for example, *Codex* I.1.8.

64. A good example of this is ch. 1 of *Novella* 7, which lists the various regions of empire in an attempt to demonstrate that the law is binding throughout the civilized world. It is precisely this understanding of a worldwide, or "ecumenical," empire and an ecclesiastical division thereof that gave rise to the so-called Pentarchy, which served as the ecclesiological model for the Byzantine Church and, theoretically, continues to govern the Eastern Orthodox churches to the present. In brief, the Pentarchy refers to the division of the Christian world into five autonomous jurisdictions, each under the leadership of a patriarch. Canon 28 of the Council of Chalcedon (451) ranked the five sees, in order of preeminence, as Rome, Constantinople, Alexandria, Antioch, and Jerusalem. Despite continued papal objections, the principle and ranking were confirmed by Justinian's *Novella* 123. While neither the borders that separated the five patriarchates nor the number of autocephalous churches remained static in the Byzantine period, for many Christians around the world the original five sees have retained a measure of preeminence to the present day.

65. Rome is mentioned explicitly in *Novellae* 9, 42, 123, and 131. *Novellae* 5, 6, and 67 state explicitly that the legislation will be sent to all the patriarchs, but it does not list any of them. Interestingly, *Novella* 6 similarly says that it will be sent to each of the patriarchs. But, unlike the others, it lists several archbishops and imperial officials but does not include the bishop of Rome.

66. As early as 534, Justinian intended to organize the *Novellae* into an official collection. In 554, he again proposed an official collection along with translations that would be disseminated to the Western provinces. Neither plan seems to have come to fruition. Nevertheless, many private collections developed for the purpose of training legal students. Four of these survive, and it is from them that we possess most of our information about the *Novellae*. See Liebs, "Roman Law," 251–52.

67. I include *Novella* 133 among the number addressed to civil magistrates. The Greek text addresses this *Novella* to a number of imperial officials in Constantinople. The Latin translation, included in the critical edition by Schoell and Kroll, suggests that it was addressed to Patriarch Menas. *Novella* 58, which I also include as addressed to a civic

dignitary, states that the legislation has already been delivered to the "Ecumenical Patriarch" (the bishop of Constantinople). As the leader of the church in the imperial capital, the patriarch of Constantinople not only had the opportunity to influence some of Justinian's policies but, in return, would have been expected to enforce imperial edicts throughout the churches in his mega-jurisdiction, which at the time would have included Asia Minor, portions of modern-day Greece, and much of the eastern Balkans.

68. For example, *Novella* 7 took a law initially concerning only the Church of Constantinople and extended its reach throughout the empire. The law, which concerns property owned by the church, reportedly stems from the imperial reign of Leo I (457–474). *Novella* 79, which concerns the prosecution of monks, similarly acknowledges that the law originates from concerns in Constantinople, but intends that the new legislation be applicable throughout the empire.

69. For example, see *Novellae* 5, 6, and 67. For an excellent introduction to the way episcopal officials were co-opted into serving as imperial agents, see Claudia Rapp, *Holy Bishops in Late Antiquity* (Berkeley: University of California Press, 2005), esp. 203–8 and 274–90.

70. Meyendorff, perhaps anachronistically, identifies this *Novella* as a source for the Pentarchy model. See Meyendorff, "Justinian, the Empire, and the Church."

71. The Greek text of the second epilogue refers to them as archbishops, not patriarchs—just one reminder that the terminology for the leaders of the institutional Church remained inconsistent at this time.

72. Several of Justinian's policies and laws reflect his desire to establish a cooperative balance between church and state—a balance that many historians term "diarchy."

73. While *Novella* 6 seems in all ways consistent with Justinian's outlook, the emperor may not have wanted this legislation to spoil his solidarity with Pope John concerning the *Theopaschite Formula*, so the absence of Rome from the distribution list for *Novella* 6 might have been a deliberate attempt to conceal it from Roman eyes.

74. I would like to thank Ralph Mathisen, who encouraged me to pursue this question more fully than I had in a preliminary presentation of this material at the Byzantine Studies Conference in October 2008.

75. For example, in 546 and 547 Rome itself switched back and forth three times between imperial and Ostrogothic hands. The principal source for the imperial military expedition in Italy is Procopius, *De belli*, ed. J. Haury (Leipzig: Teubner, 1905–1913, rev. G. Wirth, 1976).

76. Schoell and Kroll date *Novella* 9 to April 535 and *Novella* 42 to August 536.

77. See Claire Sotinel, "Emperors and Popes in the Sixth Century: The Western View," in *The Cambridge Companion to the Age of Justinian*, ed. M. Maas (Cambridge: Cambridge University Press, 2005), 267–90. See also Jeffrey Richards' rich treatment of the pro-Gothic and pro-Eastern factions in the Senate and among the Roman clergy. Richards, *The Popes and the Papacy*, 100–135. See also Meyendorff, "Justinian, the Empire, and the Church."

78. Meyendorff briefly suggests the same thing. John Meyendorff, *Imperial Unity and Christian Divisions* (Crestwood, N.Y.: St. Vladimir's Seminary Press, 1989), 225.

79. Meyendorff offers an alternative thesis, that *Novella* 6 is equally concerned with promoting the Pentarchy and with asserting imperial authority in the Church. Meyendorff, *Imperial Unity*, 249.

80. See David Olster, "Justinian, Imperial Rhetoric, and the Church," *Byzantinoslavica* 50 (1989): 165–76.

81. While we might be able to argue that the *Novellae* of 535 and 536 are written with the expectation that Rome would soon be back within the borders of the empire, any such consideration in 519 would have been more idealistic than realistic.

82. The Pragmatic Sanction is included in the edition by Schoell and Kroll as "Appendix 7." Although Pope Vigilius is named as the person responsible for promulgating the Sanction in Italy, there is no discussion whatsoever of his actual authority.

83. Sotinel, "Emperors and Popes," 267–90. See also Robert Markus, "Carthage-Prima Justiniana-Ravenna: Aspects of Justinian's *Kirchenpolitik*," *Byzantion* 49 (1979): 277–306.

84. Concerning the history and status of Thessalonica as a papal vicariate, I have benefited greatly from James Skedros, "Civic and Ecclesiastical Identity in Christian Thessaloniki" (public address, Harvard Divinity School, May 2007).

85. For an overview of Roman landholdings in the western Balkans, see Richards, *The Popes and the Papacy*, esp. 317–18. The best survey of the competing claims for jurisdictional authority in the area is that of Brian Daley, "Position and Patronage in the Early Church: The Original Meaning of 'Primacy of Honour,'" *Journal of Theological Studies* n.s. 44 (1993): 529–53.

86. It is worth noting that Pope Vigilius was able to reassert his influence in Dacia/Illyria in 545, when Justinian reaffirmed the archdiocesan status of Justiniana Prima but made it a papal vicarage. See *Novella* 131.3.

87. Although the individual patriarchs are listed in ch. 3, ch. 22 does not list them.

88. It is worth mentioning, however, that a cleric condemned while traveling to Constantinople may choose to have his case heard in the capital by the city prefect (*Novella* 123.24). This exception seems to grant additional power to the See of Constantinople because of its unique proximity to the imperial court.

89. See Hamilton Hess, *The Early Development of Canon Law and the Council of Serdica*, rev. ed. (Oxford: Oxford University Press, 2002), esp. 69–90 and 125–29.

90. *Novella*, 131.2

91. Note that there was at this time still no tradition of an "apostolic founding" of the See of Constantinople. The tradition of Saint Andrew's supposed founding of the see did not proliferate until the seventh century.

92. Recall that Roman biographies of Peter recognized that the apostle had first been bishop of Antioch before moving to Rome and had sent his disciple Mark to form the See of Alexandria.

93. Whereas the first and second edicts (*Codex* I.1.5–6) simply inform the citizens of Constantinople that Justinian's formula has been approved by the Church, the third edict (*Codex* I.1.7), a letter to Patriarch Epiphanius, seeks the approval of the patriarch in a

more carefully nuanced fashion, even affirming that he is the head of the churches of these [Eastern] parts.

94. See especially Milton Anastos, "Justinian's Despotic Control over the Church as Illustrated by His Edicts on the Theopaschite Formula and His Letter to Pope John II," in *Mélanges Georges Ostrogorsky*, vol. 2 (Belgrade: Institute for Byzantine Studies, 1963–64), 1–11. See also Meyendorff, *Imperial Unity*, 226–27.

95. It is worth noting that the *LP* makes no mention of John's endorsement of the *Theopaschite Formula*.

96. *Codex* I.1.8.28–30.

97. Olster, "Justinian, Imperial Rhetoric, and the Church."

98. *caput est omnium sanctarum ecclesiarum. Codex* I.1.8.11.

99. *Ideoque omnes sacerdotes universali orientalis tractus et subicere et unire sedi vestrae sanctitatis properavimus. Codex* I.1.8.9.

100. *Codex* I.1.8.14.

101. Anastos, "Justinian's Despotic Control," 9.

102. *Codex* I.1.8.23.

103. Sotinel, "Emperors and Popes."

104. *Codex* I.1.8.1.

105. Justinian did not need papal approval to enforce the *Theopaschite Formula* in the East. He already had the support of the Eastern Church and Pope John could do little stop him, even if he had wanted to do so. But if Justinian was to insist on a controversial theological formula in the East, and if he felt that he needed papal support for an invasion of Italy, then it would have been necessary for the emperor to have papal support for the *Theopaschite Formula* as well. In other words, we can view Justinian's endorsement of the most elaborate affirmation of Roman ecclesiastical claims in *Codex* I.1.8 as the price he needed to pay to ensure papal approval, not only for the *Theopaschite Formula* but, perhaps more important, for the pending invasion of Italy. Justinian agreed to allow Pope John to claim, if only rhetorically, that it was he, the bishop of Rome, who was defining the theological formula because the emperor needed papal support for other initiatives.

106. *Codex*, I.1.1.

107. *Codex*, I.1.1.

108. *Theodosian Code* 16.1.2.

109. Note that there is no direct link between Damasus and Peter, simply that they continue to teach the Petrine faith.

110. The letter addresses John II of Constantinople as "holy archbishop and ecumenical patriarch." J. D. Mansi, ed., *Sacrorum conciliorum nova et amplissima collectio*, 31 vols. (Venice: Antonium Zatta, 1759–98), 8:1038. Before this, the title or variations of it were applied to other bishops. For example, at the Council of Ephesus in 449, Olympias of Evazensis referred to Dioscorus of Alexandria as "*sanctissimus pater noster et universalis archiepiscopus*." Mansi, 6:855. For a survey of the earliest uses of the title, see Siméon Vailhé, "Le titre de Patriarche Oecuménique avant saint Grégoire le Grand," *Echos d'Orient* 11 (1908): 66–67.

111. Mansi, 8:1042, 1058–59.

112. See, for example, André Tuilier, "Grégoire le grand et le titre de patriarche oecuménique," in *Grégoire le grand: [Colloque tenuà] Chantilly, centre culturel Les Fontaines, 15–19 septembre 1982; Actes*, ed. Jacques Fontaine, Robert Gillet, and Stan Pellistrandi (Paris: Centre National de la Recherche Scientifique, 1986), 69–82; Vailhé, "Le titre de Patriarche Oecouménique"; and Vailhé, "Saint Grégoire le Grand et le titre de Patriarche Oecouménique," *Echos d'Orient* 11 (1908): 161–71. See also George Demacopoulos, "Gregory the Great and the Sixth-Century Dispute over the Ecumenical Title," *Theological Studies* 70 (2009): 600–621.

113. Pope Hormisdas demanded that the restoration of communion be contingent on official condemnation of Patriarch Acacius and former emperors Zeno and Anastasius, including expunging their names from official Church records.

114. For more on the possible meaning of the title in its proper historical and theological context, see Demacopoulos, "Dispute over the Ecumenical Title," esp. 616–19.

115. *Novellae* 3, 5, 6, 7, 16, 42, 57, 67, and 79. The language of the title varies from law to law, and the Latin translations do not always conform to the Greek original.

116. *Novellae* 58 and 83.

117. Here, Epiphanius is identified as *sanctissimo et beatissimo archiepiscopo huius regiae urbis et oecumenico patriarchae* ("the very holy and blessed archbishop of this royal city and ecumenical patriarch").

118. Walter Ullmann's characterization of Justinian is representative. Ullmann, *The Growth of the Papal Government in the Middle Ages: A Study in the Ideological Relation of Clerical to Lay Power*, 3rd ed. (London: Methuen, 1970), 31–37.

119. Ibid.

120. See Meyendorff, *Imperial Unity*, 248–49.

121. As noted, nine of the twenty-one ecclesiastical *Novellae* were directed to the patriarch in Constantinople, which likely means he had himself been instrumental in the formulation of the legislation. And even though both the *Codex* and the *Novellae* contain certain affirmations of Roman ecclesiastical prestige, the same legislation repeatedly places Constantinople on equal or only slightly subordinate terms.

122. In other words, endorsing the title would not only ingratiate the patriarch to Justinian but also spread Justinian's influence in the Church. The emperor would learn from experience that it was easier to control a local bishop than a foreign one.

123. Note that John II's endorsement of the *Theopaschite Formula* occurs in the *Codex*, not the *Novellae*.

124. For example, monks, clerics, and bishops cannot be brought before secular judges (*Novellae* 79, 83, and 123); monks are subordinate to their local bishops (*Novella* 5); church property is protected by imperial law (*Novellae* 7 and 123); Paphlagonia is subordinate to Constantinople (*Novella* 29); and a foreign bishop may not enter Constantinople without permission of the patriarch (*Novella* 123.9).

125. See Francis Dvornik, *The Idea of Apostolicity in Byzantium and the Legend of the Apostle St. Andrew* (Cambridge, Mass.: Harvard University Press, 1958), esp. 97–98.

CHAPTER 5. RESTRAINT AND DESPERATION
IN GREGORY THE GREAT'S PETRINE APPEAL

1. Pope Pelagius II, Gregory's predecessor, is thought to have died from plague.

2. For a survey of the *Three Chapters* question in northern Italy and its impact on Roman influence in the area, see Robert Markus, *Gregory the Great and His World* (Cambridge: Cambridge University Press, 1997), 125–42.

3. Carole Straw, *Gregory the Great: Perfection in Imperfection* (Berkeley: University of California Press, 1991).

4. An earlier version of this section was delivered at the Oxford Patristics Conference in August 2007. It was subsequently published as George Demacopoulos, "Gregory the Great and the Appeal to Petrine Authority," *Studia Patristica* 48 (2010): 333–46.

5. On the significance of Gregory's *Book of Pastoral Rule*, see Demacopoulos, *Five Models of Spiritual Direction in the Early Church* (Notre Dame, Ind.: University of Notre Dame Press, 2007), 127–64. For the definitive statement on Gregory's authorship of the *Dialogues*, see Paul Meyvaert, "The Enigma of Gregory the Great's Dialogues: A Response to Francis Clark," *Journal of Ecclesiastical History* 39 (1988): 335–81. The current scholarly consensus on Gregory's commentary on the book of Kings is that it is inauthentic. Mark DelCogliano has recently published a defense of Gregory's authorship of a collection of homilies dedicated to the Song of Songs. DelCogliano, *Gregory the Great: On the Song of Songs (Translation and Introduction)* (Collegeville, Md.: Liturgical Press, 2012).

6. We should note that this particular emphasis in Gregory does not follow the trajectory identified by Pietri for the promotion of Petrine authority in the fourth and early fifth centuries. For Pietri, Petrine ideology and its association with the See of Rome flowed from artistic, liturgical, and missionary activity orchestrated by the Roman bishops; it was not theological. With Gregory, however, Peter does function as a theological resource but not as a theological resource for the promotion of papal or Petrine authority. Charles Pietri, *Roma christiana: Recherches sur l'église de Rome, son organisation, sa politique, son idéologie de Miltiade à Sixte III* (Rome: École Française de Rome, 1976), esp. 271–401 and 1413–1654.

7. Gregory, *Moralia* 1.1.1 and 3.21.41.

8. Gregory, *Moralia* 28.18.38.

9. Gregory, *Moralia* 28.11.27. For an assessment of Gregory's ideas and ideals concerning spiritual direction, see Demacopoulos, *Five Models*, 127–64.

10. For examples of Peter's humility, see Gregory, *Hom. Hiez.* 1.5.15 and 2.6.9. For his repentance, see *Hom. Hiez.* 1.4.7 and 1.8.2.

11. See, for example, Gregory, *Homiliae in Evangelia*, CCSL 141, 6.1 and 22.2.

12. For an overview of the scope and structure of the *Liber regulae pastoralis*, see *Gregory the Great, Book of Pastoral Rule*, trans. and intro. George Demacopoulos (Crestwood, N.Y.: St. Vladimir's Seminary Press, 2007), 9–26.

13. Gregory, *Liber regulae pastoralis* 2.6.

14. See, for example, what Conrad Leyser refers to as Gregory's rhetoric of vulnerability as a development of the ascetic emphasis on humility. Leyser, *Authority and Asceticism from Augustine to Gregory the Great* (Oxford: Oxford University Press, 2000).

15. Gregory, *Liber regulae pastoralis* 2.8.

16. Ibid.

17. Gregory, *Moralia* 3.20.

18. Gregory, *Moralia* 8.54.92.

19. Gregory, *Moralia* 29.22.42. See also *Hom. Hiez.* 2.6.9.

20. Gregory, *Moralia* 9.24.54, 14.49.57, and 27.26.50.

21. Gregory, *Hom. Evang.* 21.4.

22. Gregory, *Moralia* 29.22.42.

23. Gregory, *Hom. Hiez.* 2.6.9.

24. Ibid.

25. In fact, throughout the commentaries, Gregory typically lists Peter alongside other saintly figures Gregory chooses to extol for a particular virtue. Even in cases where Peter's leadership among the apostles is identified, the point is almost always that the scriptures offer many models for adhering to a Christian way of life. See, for example, *Hom. in Hiez.* 1.4.7 and 1.8.2.

26. Gregory, *Hom. in Evang.* 24.4.

27. The critical edition for Gregory's register is provided by D. Norberg, *Registrum Epistularum*, CCSL 140–140A. English readers will benefit from John Martyn's recent translation of the complete register. John Martyn, *The Letters of Gregory the Great*, 3 vols. (Toronto: Pontifical Institute of Medieval Studies, 2004).

28. A fully functioning administrative system in the Sicilian patrimony likely began during the tenure of Pope Pelagius I (556–561). Gregory personally contributed to the Sicilian landholdings when he disposed of his share of the family property upon taking his monastic vows in 574. According to Gregory of Tours, in a contemporary account, Pope Gregory also endowed six monasteries on this property in Sicily. Gregory of Tours, *History of the Franks* 10.1. See also John the Deacon, *Sancti Gregorii papae vita* 1.5–6, PL 75. For more on the Sicilian patrimony of the Roman Church, see Jeffrey Richards, *The Popes and the Papacy in the Early Middle Ages: 476–752* (London: Routledge, 1979), 307–22. See also Domnic Morneau, "Les patrimoines de l'Église romaine jusqu' à la mort de Grégoire le Grand," *Antiquité Tardive* 14 (2006): 79–93; and Vincenzo Recchia, *Gregorio Magno e la società agricola* (Rome: Studium, 1978).

29. Interestingly, there is no surviving textual record from a Sicilian Christian from this period. Our evidence is entirely one-sided, which, of course, poses no small challenge for the historian looking to recover Sicilian attitudes toward Rome.

30. While it is not entirely clear when the Sicilian patrimony was divided into two administrative units, it likely preceded Gregory. Gregory's contribution in this regard was to formalize a division in ecclesiastical organization of the island that mirrored the economic one. The Syracusan bishop was made the senior of the two. See Gregory, *Ep.* 2.50.

31. Concerning the Roman Church's involvement in estate management, see Kristina Sessa, *The Formation of Papal Authority in Late Antique Italy: Roman Bishops and the Domestic Sphere* (Cambridge: Cambridge University Press, 2012), esp. 90–126.

32. Even at this time, he title *rector* was a title of honor, not office.

33. See, for example, Pelagius I, *Ep.* 91, which ordered his agent to deprive the bishop of Tauromenium of the *pallium*. See Markus, *Gregory the Great*, 114 n. 23.

34. See, for example, *Ep.* 1.70, written to Peter, who was probably Gregory's most trusted servant. See also *Ep.* 13.35.

35. As Sessa pointed out, Pope Pelagius I (bishop of Rome, 556–561) had required the bishop Eleutherius of Syracuse to swear an oath regarding the administration of his private household (the issue concerned how a bishop could juggle a private household with his episcopal responsibilities), but Gregory was the first to include the swearing of an oath at Peter's tomb. Pelagius, *Ep.* 25, 33, and 44. See Kristina Sessa, "Domestic Emergencies: Pelagius (556–561) and the Challenge of Managing the *domus dei* in Post-Gothic War Italy," paper presented at the Oxford Patristics Conference, August 2011.

36. For example, several Sicilian bishops do not seem to have shared Gregory's views concerning clerical celibacy. See Gregory, *Ep.* 1.42, 4.34. See also Demacopoulos, *Five Models*, 144–53.

37. One exception that proves the rule is Gregory's initial instruction to his first rector for the Sicilian patrimony, Peter, which emboldened him that he would become a "true soldier of St. Peter" if he was able to perform his duty successfully. Gregory, *Ep.* appendix 1.

38. Richards, *The Popes and the Papacy*, 342–62.

39. *Ep.* 1.18. *Ep.* 1.42 instructs Peter to send lapsed priests to monasteries until they have completed their penances.

40. The four bishops were Agatho of Lipari, Victor of Palermo, Leo of Catana, and Gregory of Agrigentum. See Gregory, *Ep.* 1.70 and 2.15. A fifth, Felix of Messina, received a strongly worded rebuke for having sent expensive gifts to Rome. Gregory told him such behavior would not be tolerated; Felix should also be happy to know, however, that the gifts were sold and the money given to the poor of Rome. See *Ep.* 1.64.

41. Gregory, *Ep.* 2.29.

42. Ibid.

43. Richards, *The Popes and the Papacy*, 352. Martyn's comments are sprinkled throughout the notes of his translation of Gregory's letters. For his part, Robert Markus seems to have presumed that the Sicilian Church was thoroughly Roman before Gregory's election—that Gregory simply continued the tradition and did so effectively. See Markus, *Gregory the Great*, 112–17.

44. *Ep.* 2.5.

45. With Maximian's election, Gregory recalled Peter and transferred the role of vicar to Maximian. Employing an archbishop as vicar likely granted the pope greater leverage than the subdeacon Peter afforded for the pontiff's ambitious plan for reform.

46. Gregory, *Ep.* 5.20.

47. By July 595, the noblemen in Syracuse had informed Gregory that the populace was split between two candidates. See *Ep.* 5.54. One of them, Agatho, is identified as having the majority of support among the clergy and people. The other candidate is unnamed; perhaps it is Trajan, the man Gregory identified in the previous letter. Gregory asks that Agatho be sent to Rome so that he may be examined before his election. Nothing else appears in the correspondence until October, when a standard letter is sent to the newly elevated John (Gregory's preferred candidate), announcing that the pope has granted him use of the *pallium*. See *Ep.* 6.18.

48. Richards (*The Popes and the Papacy*, 352) notes that Paul of Triocala was deposed by Gregory. He provides no evidence or further discussion, except that he was replaced by a Gregorian candidate, Peter. Gregory's *Ep.* 3.49 to Theodore, bishop of Lilybaeum, mentions that the former bishop Paul is doing penance in a monastery in Theodore's see, and Gregory wants to make sure he remains there. Perhaps this is the Paul in question, but there is no indication that Paul is from the See of Triocala. What is more, Martyn argues (*The Letters of Gregory the Great*, vol. 1, 268 n. 154) that Paul's see is unknown and likely a great distance away.

49. Martyn argues (*The Letters of Gregory the Great*, vol. 2, 471 n. 103) that Agatho was reinstated to his see following successful completion of his penance, and that Gregory's *Ep.* 7.19, which mentions an unnamed bishop of Lipari, refers to Agatho. Richards (*The Popes and the Papacy*, 352), on the other hand, believes Gregory successfully deposed Agatho. If Martyn is correct that Agatho again became bishop of Lipari (cf. *Ep.* 7.19), what does that say about Gregory's ability to depose bishops and replace them with his own men?

50. Indeed, the only time he appears in the correspondence is in a letter addressed to him affirming that he should get a share of the revenue from the See of Agrigentum because he has been serving as episcopal visitor. According to John the Deacon, Peter of Triocala was a subdeacon in the Roman Church before his election. Given the lack of corroborating evidence, the fact that John was writing two hundred years later, and the very real possibility that he has confused this Peter with another subdeacon by the same name (the rector of the Sicilian patrimony that later served as interlocutor for the *Dialogues*), I submit that we do not know anything for certain about Peter of Triocala.

51. *Ep.* 4.12 relates the case of a man being forcibly married to a slave girl. Gregory instructs Maximian to investigate and punish the guilty party. He also tells him to criticize Felix, in whose see this outrage has taken place, and to warn Felix that if he hears about a similar situation in the future the Roman see will launch canonical proceedings against him. There is no further mention of Felix in the correspondence. Nor is there any additional mention of the see until Donus receives the *pallium* two years later. See Richards, *The Popes and the Papacy*, 352.

52. This is evinced by a comparison of *Ep.* 3.59 and 9.181.

53. For example, when Gregory wrote to his rector Cyprian concerning the vacancy in the See of Lilybaeum, he did not advocate for any candidate. The eventual bishop, Decius, was a member of the local clergy. See Gregory, *Ep.* 5.23 and 6.13.

54. See Gregory, *Ep.* 9.25 and 10.1.

55. *Ep.* 13.14 and 13.15 give additional details of the election. Gregory employs an otherwise unknown as visitor (Barbarus, the bishop of Carinae; even the see is not otherwise mentioned, although Norberg's index says it is the modern Hiccara, near Palermo). Interestingly, Gregory is determined that the candidate be a member of the clergy from the see but does nothing to promote a specific candidate. *Ep.* 13.15 indicates that at least a portion of the electorate had been pushing for a layman, to which Gregory responds that they will be excommunicated if they continue to do so. This is perhaps Gregory's strongest threat to the Sicilian Church in his correspondence.

56. See *Ep.* 13.12.

57. See Richards, *The Popes and the Papacy*, 353–56.

58. Richards (*The Popes and the Papacy*) argues that Urbicus had been too "Roman," so why would the pontiff promote another Roman candidate? On Gregory's criticism of the newly elected John, see *Ep.* 13.41.

59. John the Deacon, *Sancti Gregorii papae vita* 3.7, PL 75.

60. Even though Donus was elected with Gregory's blessing and received a *pallium*, Gregory criticized him for misuse of his position for financial profit. See Gregory, *Ep.* 8.3. This further calls into question the accuracy of the claim by John the Deacon that Donus was a Gregorian from Rome (which Richards and Martyn take for granted) and how much Gregory really supported Donus' candidacy or how much Donus supported the Gregorian ideals.

61. Norberg does not assign this letter a specific location within the register but instead lists it as appendix 1. Martyn determines to list the letter as *Ep.* 1.38a.

62. Gregory, *Ep.* appendix 1.

63. Gregory, *Ep.* 7.19.

64. Ibid.

65. The Feast of St. Peter, June 29, was a commemoration of his martyrdom, but Gregory here interprets martyrdom as a birth (*natalis*).

66. Gregory, *Ep.* 9.15.

67. Gregory, *Ep.* 9.31.

68. Gregory, *Ep.* 8.33.

69. Walter Ullmann, not surprisingly, sees Gregory's efforts among the Angli as a wholesale repudiation of the Byzantine Empire and an attempt to look elsewhere for the security of papal prestige. That thesis was sufficiently critiqued by Robert Markus. See Ullmann, *The Growth of the Papal Government*, 36–37; Markus, "Gregory the Great's Europe," *Royal Historical Society* 31 (1981): 21–36, at 30–31. See also Richards, *The Popes and the Papacy*, 26–27; and George Demacopoulos, "Gregory the Great and the Pagan Shrines of Kent," *Journal of Late Antiquity* 1 (2008): 375–91.

70. For an example of Gregory's overly optimistic expectation that he could persuade Theodelinda by the force of his theology, see *Ep.* 4.2 to Constantius, bishop of Milan. It had been one of the great achievements of Gregory's predecessors that the metropolitans of Milan had finally relented to the papal view concerning the *Three Chapters*. See Markus, *Gregory the Great*, 133–42.

71. See Gregory, *Ep.* 4.2 for Constantius' role in transmitting the letter to Theodelinda. For the circumstances of Constantius' sojourn in Genoa, see Markus, *Gregory the Great*, 133–42.

72. Gregory, *Ep.* 4.4.

73. Ibid.

74. See especially *Ep.* 4.37.

75. See Gregory, *Ep.* 4.37 for recognition of Constantius' successful approach. See also Markus, *Gregory the Great*, 133–42.

76. Gregory, *Ep.* 4.33.

77. Ibid.

78. In *Ep.* 4.37, Gregory goes so far as to congratulate Constantius for having withheld Gregory's initial epistle, recognizing the need for a letter that would be more effective with the queen.

79. Gregory, *Ep.* 5.60.

80. Gregory, *Ep.* 6.6.

81. *Ep.* 6.5.

82. Ibid.

83. Future letters to Brunhilde would contain other Petrine appeals, but none as direct as this one. For example, in *Ep.* 9.214, Gregory writes a letter of recommendation for a certain Hilary and concludes the letter with the request "and may your Excellency be rewarded by St. Peter, prince of the apostles, whom you venerate with Christian piety, in granting us what we ask."

84. Concerning his view that the relics of Peter possessed miraculous power, see *Ep.* 1.25, 1.29, 6.58, 8.33, and 13.43.

85. According to Thomas Noble, Symmachus was the first bishop of Rome to distribute a relic of St. Peter (he sent one to the Burgundian king, Sigismund). Gregory, however, first developed the distribution of relics as repeatable and deliberate acts of diplomacy. Thomas Noble, "Review: Michele Maccarrone on the Medieval Papacy," *Catholic Historical Review* 80 (1994): 518–33, at 527.

86. *Ep.* 1.25 (the exiled patriarch of Antioch), 1.29 (a member of the Constantinopolitan court), 1.30 (also a member of the royal court), 3.33 (a patrician in Gaul), 3.47 (an African bishop), 6.58 (Brunhilde), 6.6 (Childebert), 7.23 (the emperor's sister), 7.25 (a Constantinopolitan physician), 8.33 (a Sicilian official), 9.229b (Reccared), 11.43 (a patrician in Gaul), 12.2 (three African noblewomen), 12.14 (the bishop of Istria), and 13.43 (the patriarch of Alexandria). On a few occasions, the gift was accompanied by other relics of other saints, such as St. Paul (*Ep.* 6.58) and St. John the Baptist (*Ep.* 9.229b), or a fragment of the Cross of Christ (*Ep.* 9.229b). Concerning Gregory's distribution of the relics of St. Peter to members of the royal elite, see Grazia Rapisarda, "I doni nell'epistolario di Gregorio Magno," in *Gregorio Magno e il suo tempo* (Rome: Institutum Patristicum Augustinianum, 1991), vol. 2, 285–300.

87. Gregory, *Ep.* 4.30. Gregory seems to have been uncomfortable with the idea of partitioning the actual bones of a saint, which was already a common practice in the East,

although he was willing to allow the translation of relics from one place to another. See *Ep.* 14.7.

88. Gregory, *Ep.* 6.6.

89. Gregory, *Ep.* 9.229b.

90. Gregory, *Ep.* 6.58.

91. Ibid.

92. Concerning Gregory's estimation of the limits of Merovingian commitment to Christianity, see Demacopoulos, "Gregory the Great and the Pagan Shrines of Kent," 375–91, esp. 378–82.

93. Although various Eastern clerics began to refer to the patriarch of Constantinople as the "Ecumenical Patriarch" as early as 518, a Constantinopolitan patriarch first employed the title for himself in the year 588, when John IV wrote to Gregory's predecessor, Pelagius II. Pelagius, likely assisted by Gregory, viewed the title as an unwarranted assertion of Constantinopolitan authority and began the papal diplomatic effort to suppress the title.

94. Demacopoulos, "Gregory the Great and the Sixth-Century Dispute over the Ecumenical Title," *Theological Studies* 70 (2009): 600–621.

95. Gregory, *Ep.* 5.44.

96. Ibid.

97. Gregory, *Ep.* 5.37.

98. Ibid.

99. As noted in Chapter 2, in the years after the Council of Chalcedon, Pope Leo I exploited the belief that Constantinople was not an apostolic see when he wrote to both patriarch and emperor to defend his rejection of the council's Canon 28. See Brian Daley, "Position and Patronage in the Early Church: The Original Meaning of 'Primacy of Honour'," *Journal of Theological Studies* 44 (1993): 548–49; and Francis Dvornik, *The Idea of Apostolicity in Byzantium and the Legend of the Apostle St. Andrew* (Cambridge, Mass.: Harvard University Press, 1958), esp. 97–98.

100. Indeed, it would seem that one of Gregory's most rhetorically striking arguments in his initial barrage against John's use of the title was that the See of Constantinople had produced so many heretics. In short, Gregory asks, can the patriarch of Constantinople have universal authority if so many of its leaders have not only succumbed to heresy but have actually been the originators of heresy?

101. Gregory, *Ep.* 5.41.

102. Gregory, *Ep.* 7.24.

103. Gregory, *Ep.* 6.61.

104. Gregory, *Ep.* 7.24. Gregory had previously suggested to Maurice (*Ep.* 5.39) that John's use of the title was a "sign of the coming of the antichrist." But his letter to the patriarch of Antioch, which insists that the title is "born of the antichrist," is a stronger condemnation, reflecting a rhetorical escalation.

105. Gregory, *Ep.* 7.24.

106. None of Eulogius' letters survive.

107. Gregory, *Ep.* 7.37.

108. Another example of Gregory's acknowledgment of the apostolic credentials of other sees is *Ep.* 5.42.

109. Gregory, *Ep.* 7.37.

110. See, for example, Gregory, *Ep.* 8.28, 10.14, and 10.21.

111. In *Ep.* 9.157 Gregory even suggests that the synod may have been designed for the explicit purpose of doing so.

112. Gregory, *Ep.* 9.157.

113. Ibid.

114. Ibid.

115. See Gregory, *Ep.* 6.15, 6.16, and 6.17.

116. Gregory, *Ep.* 9.157.

117. Averil Cameron, *Christianity and the Rhetoric of Empire: The Development of Christian Discourse* (Berkeley: University of California Press, 1994).

118. The letters span roughly four years (August 593 to June 597) and cover a range of topics. Gregory, *Ep.* 3.61, 5.30, 5.36, 5.37, 6.16, 6.64, 7.6, and 7.30. Gregory knew Maurice well, having served as papal *apocrisiarus* in Constantinople in the 580s. In fact, he served as godfather to the emperor's oldest son, Theodosius.

119. Gregory, *Ep.* 3.61. See Demacopoulos, "Gregory the Great and a Post-Imperial Discourse," in *Power and Authority in Eastern Christian Experience*, ed. N Soumakis (New York: Theotokos Press, 2011), 120–37. It is worth noting that Gregory's rejection of the law stands in sharp contrast to Gelasius' response to a similar law. Cf. Gelasius, *Ep.* 14.14.

120. For example, in *Ep.* 5.30 Gregory thanks Maurice for his donations to the poor of Rome and uses the occasion to assert that the emperor's piety presages a long and prosperous rule. But even in the act of thanking the emperor, Gregory subtly undermines Maurice's temporal and spiritual self-determination by ascribing a personal role in Maurice's future success. In appreciation for Maurice's gift, the pontiff notes: "all of us with tearful prayers ask that almighty God, who has stung the heart of your Clemency so that you would [send these gifts], should preserve the empire of our Lordship safely, in the constancy of His love and extend your victories in all nations with the help of His majesty." The emperor's temporal successes, and the successes of his armies, in Gregory's account, are the result of a combination of divine grace, imperial piety, and priestly prayer. Imperial success is thus doubly dependent on pious action and the support of faithful priests.

121. This is a reference to Cicero, and an exceptionally rare example of Gregory using a direct quote from a pre-Christian author.

122. Gregory, *Ep.* 5.37.

123. Although it has long been a historiographical commonplace to speak of the papacy from the fifth century onward as a synthesis, or balance, between *christianitas* and *romanitas*—in other words, a relationship or fusion between Christian and Roman identity, which marks papal rhetoric and self-promotion—most studies have not emphasized the extent to which the imperial discourse, the discourse of imperial rights and obligations, was appropriated and transformed by the bishops of Rome. And while I have maintained throughout this chapter that Gregory's use of Petrine privilege and his promotion of papal

authority were more nuanced, more sophisticated, and more collegial than most other late-ancient popes, there is no doubt that he too re-inscribed the Petrine narrative through the media of imperial signs and symbols.

124. The Latin word *princeps* conveys both a princely referent (in a dynastic or imperial sense) and an authoritative referent (as in the source or origin of something). In theological language, *princeps* is often used as the Latin translation of the Greek *arche*.

125. Three times in the *Res gestae* the emperor Augustus refers to himself as the *princeps*, meaning here the "first citizen" (13; 30.1; 32.3). In the sixth century, the first line of Justinian's *Institutes* refers to the emperor as *princeps Romanus*. For more on Augustus' usage of the term, see John Percy Vyvian, Dacre Balsdon, and Miriam T Griffin, "Princeps," in *The Oxford Classical Dictionary*, ed. S. Hornblower and A. Spawforth, 3rd rev. ed. (Oxford: Oxford University Press, 2003), 1246–47; and Ronald Syme, *The Roman Revolution* (Oxford: Oxford University Press, 1939), 313–30. I would like to thank Matthew Briel, who first introduced me to this connection.

126. Demacopoulos, "Sixth-Century Dispute."

127. It is important to note that as much as Gregory wants to inject his own influence into imperial decision making, especially as it relates to the political situation in Italy, he is in no way suggesting that the Church (whether generally or his office specifically) is the supreme secular authority. We should not read into Gregory's statements an anachronistic papal government model that would develop in the later Middle Ages. Indeed, Gregory wants and expects the court to be the dominant secular authority. But he hopes that the court will act in a certain way, and he dangles the possibility of secular success as a prize for the specific model of deference to the Church and its leaders.

POSTSCRIPT: THE *LIFE OF ST. GREGORY OF AGRIGENTUM* AS A SEVENTH-CENTURY PETRINE CRITIQUE OF THE PAPACY

1. Archaeological and textual evidence suggests that the monastery was in existence by the early seventh century. See Jeffrey Richards, *The Popes and the Papacy in the Early Middle Ages: 476–752* (London: Routledge, 1979), 276–77. He speculates that the increased presence of Greek monasteries in Rome in the seventh century was the result of a combination of factors, including Justinian's reconquest of Italy in the sixth century and a steady stream of Eastern refuges who sought shelter from the Arab expansion in the East in the seventh century.

2. There is considerable debate over the dating, provenance, and authorship of the *vita*. Morcelli the initial editor of the *vita*, presumed that the subject of the life was the same Gregory of Agrigentum who is identified briefly in the letters of Pope Gregory. Morcelli also speculated that the author's disparaging remarks about the unnamed pope derived from a series of anti-Gregory pamphlets that circulated in Rome following the pope's death and, as a consequence, confirmed Morcelli's belief that the composition of the *vita* and its subject should be dated to the early seventh century. Morcelli, *PG* 98: 550–715. Albrecht Berger, who provided a critical edition and German translation of the

text in 1995, however, maintained that the life could not have been written before the mid-eighth century, that its subject was a different Gregory of Agrigentum than the bishop identified in Pope Gregory's epistles, and that this second Gregory could not have been in a Greek-speaking monastery in Rome before the mid-seventh century. Albrecht Berger, ed., *Leontios Presbyteros von Rom: Das Leben des heiligen Gregorios von Agrigent* (Berlin: Akademie, 1995). Some confirmation of this view can be found in Jean-Marie Sansterre's Ph.D. dissertation, "Les moines grecs et orientaux à Rome" (Brussels, 1980), who argues that there were no Greek monasteries in Rome until 649. More recently, John Martyn has provided an English translation and commentary based primarily on Berger's edition and has revived the original view that the subject of the *vita* was the contemporary of Pope Gregory I and that the *vita* was composed in Rome in the early seventh century. It is not my intent to explore the arguments of dating in detail; I will simply note that I believe Martyn's careful use of Pope Gregory's letters has effectively dismantled each of Berger's assertions and that the *vita* and its hero both belong in the late sixth/early seventh century. John R. C. Martyn, *A Translation of Abbot Leontios' Life of St. Gregory, Bishop of Agrigento* (Lewiston, N.Y.: Edward Mellen, 2004).

3. *Vita* 35. Despite the fact that Gregory lacks sufficient clerical qualifications to speak at such a council, he is reported to have amazed the entire assembly by his articulation of the faith and his "possession of the Holy Spirit."

4. *Vita* 38.

5. Whether or not the *vita* is accurate in its portrayal of the bishop being involved in the election is an entirely different matter. There is no record in Gregory's correspondence for his involvement in Bishop Gregory's election. For our purposes, it does not matter if the *vita* offers an accurate historical account; what is of significance is the literary portrayal of Pope Gregory.

6. *Vita* 62. According to ch. 69, Gregory spends two years and four months in prison before he is finally brought to trial. Part of the delay is the wait for the Eastern delegation.

7. Morcelli rejects the *vita*'s suggestion that Pope Gregory would have thrown Bishop Gregory into a prison, arguing instead that he would have been sent to a monastery. See Martyn's translation of Morcelli's note. Martyn, *A Translation*, 41–42. For a more recent study of Gregory's practice, see Julia Hillner, "Gregory the Great's 'Prisons': Monastic Confinement in Early Byzantine Italy," *Journal of Early Christian Studies* 19 (2011): 433–71.

8. See my discussion of this matter in Chapter 5.

9. *Vita* 40. All translations from the Greek are Martyn's.

10. *Vita* 62.

11. Ibid.

12. See especially George Demacopoulos, *Five Models of Spiritual Direction in the Early Church* (Notre Dame, Ind.: University of Notre Dame Press, 2007), 127–64.

13. *Vita* 63.

14. What is more, during Bishop Gregory's first trial in Sicily, he actually asks that the case be heard in Rome.

15. It is worth noting that when Pope Gregory writes to the emperor requesting that he send someone to the trial, he is portrayed as being entirely subject to the emperor. Indeed, throughout the text, the emperor stands second to the hero in deference.

16. *Vita* 67.

17. Moreover, when the Eastern delegation wants to have Bishop Gregory removed from the prison (ch. 69) he refuses to be released without the pope's permission.

18. *Vita* 67.

19. See Demacopoulos, *Five Models*, 165–66.

CONCLUSION: THE INVENTION OF PETER

1. Averil Cameron, *Christianity and the Rhetoric of Empire: The Development of Christian Discourse* (Berkeley: University of California Press, 1994), 2.

APPENDIX I: POPE GELASIUS TO AUGUSTUS ANASTASIUS

From the Thiel edition. Epistle 12. My thanks are due to Leilani Briel and George Demacopoulos who read drafts of these translations. I am especially indebted to Mattias Gassman who provided innumerable corrections and suggestions to my translation of Gelasius' convoluted Latin.

1. 1 Cor. 9:16.

2. Literally: "submit your neck."

3. 2 Tim. 2.19.

4. Prov. 27.6.

5. Song of Songs 6.8.

6. James 2.10.

7. Sirach 19.1.

8. A reference to Peter's confession that Jesus is "the Messiah, the Son of the Living God" in Mt. 16.16.

9. 1 Tim. 1.5.

10. Rom. 1.32.

11. Remembrance in the prayers of the church.

12. I.e., Acacius.

13. Cf. Philippians 2.6.

APPENDIX II: TRACT VI

1. Avellana Collection, Epistle 100. I use the text of Thiel, Tract VI here. Numbering is also according to Thiel. Günther's numbers do not agree.

2. Cf. 1 Cor. 6.16 ff.

3. *Affectus.*

4. John 8.7.

5. Mt. 7.3.

6. That is, Jesus. Cf. Heb. 4.14.

7. 1 Cor. 10.21.

8. "et sicut ait ille: *voluntatem habere te mentiendi, artem fingendi non habere.*" Though it has a proverbial ring, this accusative and infinitive construction reads like a direct quote. It appears to be an uncollected fragment of Cicero unknown outside Jerome's *Epistula adversus Rufinum* 5.63–65 (CCSL 79). For the Jerome *testimonium*, see Harald Hagendahl, *Latin Fathers and the Classics: A Study on the Apologists, Jerome and Other Christian Writers* (Göteborg, 1958), 171 and Pierre Lardet, *L'Apologie de Jérôme contre Rufin: Un commentaire* (*VC supplements XV*) (Leiden, 1993), 256, who notes Cicero's proclivity for coupling *mentiri* and *fingere.* At the turn of the century Eduard von Wölfflin, who was working on the *Thesaurus Linguae Latinae*, read Gelasius carefully looking for classical references, noted that *sicut ait ille*, when no other prose authority was mentioned, referred to Cicero, and suggested that this passage here might refer to a now lost speech of Cicero, though he did not know the parallel with Jerome. "Der Papst Gelasius als Latinist," *Archiv für lateinische Lexikographie und Grammatik* XII (Leipzig, 1902), 1–10.

9. Prehistoric king of the Arcadians, believed by Romans to have been a contemporary of Aeneas (twelfth-century B.C.E.)— four centuries before Romulus established Rome (776). See *Aeneid* book 8.

10. *Ab urbe condita* books 11–20, now lost.

11. Western emperor, 467–472 C.E.

12. Pun on *sacrum* and *exsecramentum.*

13. Reading *resticulo* here with Günther rather than *amiculo* with Thiel.

14. Castor and Pollux.

15. That is, it is easier to ship in grain during the summer than in winter, and this suffices for the city.

16. Cicero *De domo sua ad pontifices* 127.

17. Juvenal 6.285.

18. The rites of the Lupercalia.

19. Augustulus set aside the Roman *imperium* in 476.

BIBLIOGRAPHY

PRIMARY SOURCES

The Apostolic Fathers. Vol. 1: *I Clement. II Clement. Ignatius. Polycarp. Didache.* Trans. Bart Ehrman. Loeb Classical Library. Cambridge, Mass.: Harvard University Press, 2003.

Aristotle. *Nichomachean Ethics.* Ed. Ingrid Bywater. Reprint Oxford: Oxford University Press, 1986.

Athanasius. *Apologia Contra Arianos.* Ed. Jan M. Szymusiak. SC 56.

Codex Vercellensis (Acts of Peter). In *Acta apostolorum apocrypha*, vol. 1, ed. R. A. Lipsius and M. Bonnet. 45–103. Leipzig, 1891–1903.

Collectio Avellana. Epistulae imperatorum pontificum aliorum inde ab a. CCCLXVII usque ad a. DLIII datae Avellana quae dicitur collectio. Ed. Otto Günther. CSEL 35.

Corpus Juris Civilis. Vol. 3: *Novellae.* Ed. Rudolf Schoell and Wilhelm Kroll. Berlin: Weidmann, 1928.

Cyprian. *Epistulae.* Ed. Wilhelm Hartel. CSEL 3.

Damasus. *Epigrammata.* Ed. Antonio Ferrua. Vatican City: Bibliotheca Apostolica Vaticana, 1942.

Ennodius. *Opera.* Ed. Wilhelm Hartel. CSEL 6.

Epistulae Theodericianae variae. Ed. Theodore Mommsen. MGH AA 12.

Eusebius. *Church History.* Ed. Gustave Bardy. SC 31, 41, 55, 73.

———. *Life of Constantine.* Ed. Friedhelm Winkelmann. GCS Eusebius 1/1.

Gelasius. *Corpus.* In *Epistolae Romanorum pontificum genuinae*, ed. Andreas Thiel, vol. 1: 285–613. Braunsberg, 1868.

Gregory I. *Book of Pastoral Rule [Liber regulae pastoralis].* Ed. Floribert Rommel. SC 381–82.

———. *Book of Pastoral Rule.* Trans. and intro. George Demacopoulos. Crestwood, N.Y.: St. Vladimir's Seminary Press, 2007.

———. *Epistulae.* Ed. Dag Norberg. CCSL 140, 140A.

———. *Epistulae.* In *The Letters of Gregory the Great*, trans. John R. C. Martyn. 3 vols. Toronto: Pontifical Institute of Medieval Studies, 2004.

———. *Homilies on the Gospels [Homiliae in Evangelia].* Ed. R. Étaix. CCSL 141.

———. *Homilies on the Prophet Ezekiel [Homilae in Hiezechihelem].* Ed. Marcus Adriaen. CCSL 142.

———. *Morals on the Book of Job [Moralia in Job]*. Ed. Marcus Adriaen. CCSL 143, 143A, 143B.

Gregory of Nyssa. *Life of Macrina*. Ed. P. Marval. SC 178.

Gregory of Tours. *History of the Franks*. Ed. Rudolf Buchner. Berlin, 1955.

Innocent I. *Epistulae*. Ed. J. P. Migne. PL 20.

Irenaeus. *Against Heresies*. Ed. Adelin Rousseau and Louis Doutreleau. SC 100, 152–53, 210–11, 263–64, 293–94.

John Chrysostom. *Homilies on Matthew*. Ed. J. P. Migne. PG 58.

John the Deacon. *Sancti Gregorii papae vita*. Ed. J. P. Migne. PL 75.

Leo I. *Epistulae*. Ed. J. P. Migne. PL 54.

———. *Epistulae*. In *Acta Conciliorum Oecumenicorum I–IV*, ed. Eduard Schwartz. Berlin: De Gruyter, 1927–32.

———. *Epistulae* in *S. Leonis Magni Epistulae*. Ed. Carlo Silva-Tarouca. Rome: Universitatis Gregorianae, 1932–35.

———. *Sermones*. Ed. Antonius Chavasse. CCL 138–138a.

Leontius. *Leontios Presbyteros von Rom: Das Leben des heiligen Gregorios von Agrigent*. Ed. Albrecht Berger. Berlin: Akademie, 1995.

———. *A Translation of Abbot Leontios' Life of St. Gregory, Bishop of Agrigento*. Trans. John R. C. Martyn. Lewiston, N.Y.: Edward Mellen, 2004.

Liber Pontificalis. Ed. Louis Duchesne. 3 vols. 2nd ed. Paris: E. de Boccard, 1955.

Paulinus of Nola. *Epistulae*. Ed. Wilhelm Hartel. CSEL 29.

Procopius. *De Bellis*. Ed. Jacob Haury. Leipzig: Teubner, 1905–13. Rev. ed. G. Wirth, 1976.

Prosper of Aquitaine. *Epitome Chronicon*. Ed. Theodore Mommsen. MGH AA 9.

Die Pseudoklementinen. Ed. Bernhard Rehm. Vol. 1, *Homilien*, GCS 42; vol. 2, *Rekognitionen in Rufins Übersetzung*, GCS 51. Berlin: Akademie Verlag, 1992, 1994.

Res gestae divi Augusti: Text, Translation, and Commentary. Ed. and trans. Alison Cooley. Cambridge: Cambridge University Press, 2009.

Sacrorum conciliorum nova et amplissima collectio. 31 vols. Ed. J. D. Mansi. Venice: Antonium Zatta, 1759–98.

Seneca. *Dialogi*. Ed. L. D. Reynolds. Oxford: Oxford University Press, 1977.

Siricius. *Letter to Himerius of Terragona*. Ed. J. P. Migne. PL 13.

Sozomen. *Ecclesiastical History*. Ed. J. Bidez. Paris: Éditions du Cerf, 1983.

SECONDARY SOURCES

Alchermes, Joseph Donalla. "'Cura pro mortuis' and 'Cultus Martyrum': Commemoration in Rome from the Second Through the Sixth Century." Ph.D. dissertation, New York University, 1989.

———. "Petrine Politics: Pope Symmachus and the Rotunda of St. Andrew's at the Old St. Peter's." *Catholic Historical Review* 81 (1995): 1–40.

Amory, Patrick. *People and Identity in Ostrogothic Italy, 489–554*. Cambridge: Cambridge University Press, 1997.

Anastos, Milton. "Justinian's Despotic Control over the Church as Illustrated by His Edicts on the Theopaschite Formula and His Letter to Pope John II." In *Mélanges Georges Ostrogorsky*, vol. 2. 1–11. Belgrade: Institute for Byzantine Studies, 1963–64.

Armitage, J. M. *A Twofold Solidarity: Leo the Great's Theology of Redemption*. Strathfield: St. Paul's, 2005.

Bannister, Turpin. "The Constantinian Basilica of St. Peter at Rome." *Journal of the Society of Architectural Historians* 27 (1968): 3–32.

Bauckham, Richard J. "The Martyrdom of Peter in Early Christian Literature." In *Aufstieg und Niedergang der römischen Welt*, vol. 26. 539–95. Berlin: Fe Gruyter, 1992.

Baynes, Norman. Review of Erich Caspar, *Geschichte des Papsttums*." *English Historical Review* 47 (1932): 293–98.

Bénevot, Maurice. "Primatus Petro datur." *Journal of Theological Studies* n.s. 5 (1954): 19–35.

Binder, Gerhard. "Kommunikative Elemente im römischen Staatskult am Ende der Republik: Das Beispiel des Lupercalia des Jahres 44." In *Religiöse Kommunikation: Formen und Praxis von der Neuzeit*, ed. Gerhard Binder and Konrad Ehlich. 225–41. Trier: Wissenschaftlicher Verlag Trier, 1997.

Blair-Dixon, Kate. "Memory and Authority in Sixth-Century Rome: The *Liber Pontificalis* and the *Collectio Avellana*." In *Religion, Dynasty, and Patronage in Early Christian Rome: 300–900*, ed. Kate Cooper and Julia Hillner. 59–76. Cambridge: Cambridge University Press, 2007.

Bowes, Kimberly. *Private Worship, Public Values, and Religious Change in Late Antiquity*. Cambridge: Cambridge University Press, 2008.

Brooks, E. C. "The 'Epistola Clementis': A Petrine Infusion at Rome, c. AD 385." In *Studia Patristica*, vol. 15, pt. 1. 212–16. Berlin: Akademie Verlag, 1984.

Brown, Peter. *Power and Persuasion in Late Antiquity*. Madison: University of Wisconsin Press, 1992.

Cameron, Alan. *The Last Pagans of Rome*. New York: Oxford University Press, 2010.

Cameron, Averil. *Christianity and the Rhetoric of Empire: The Development of Christian Discourse*. Berkeley: University of California Press, 1994.

Caspar, Erich. *Geschichte des Papsttums*. 2 vols. Tubingen: J.C.B. Mohr, 1930–33.

———. "Kleine Beiträge zur älteren Papstgeschichte: IV. Zur Interpretation der Kanones III–V von Sardica." *Zeitschrift für Kirchengeschichte* 47 (1928): 164–77.

Chadwick, Henry. "St. Peter and St. Paul in Rome: The Problem of the 'Memoria Apostolorum ad Catacombs.'" *Journal of Theological Studies* n.s. 8 (1957): 39–51.

Clark, Elizabeth. *History, Theory, Text: Historians and the Linguistic Turn*. Cambridge, Mass.: Harvard University Press, 2004.

Clayton, Paul. *Theodoret of Cyrus: Antiochene Christology from the Council of Ephesus (431) to the Council of Chalcedon (451)*. Oxford: Oxford University Press, 2007.

Cooper, Kate. "The Martyr, the *Matrona*, and the Bishop: The Matron Lucina and the Politics of Martyr Cult in Fifth- and Sixth-Century Rome." *Early Medieval Europe* 8 (1999): 297–317.

Cooper, Kate, and Julia Hillner. "Introduction." In *Religion, Dynasty, and Patronage in Early Christian Rome: 300–900*, ed. Kate Cooper and Julia Hillner. 1–18. Cambridge: Cambridge University Press, 2007.

———, eds. *Religion, Dynasty, and Patronage in Early Christian Rome, 300–900*. Cambridge: Cambridge University Press, 2007.

Costambeys, Marios. "Burial Topography and the Power of the Church in Fifth- and Sixth-Century Rome." *Papers of the British School at Rome* 69 (2001): 169–89.

———. "Property and Ideology of the Papacy in the Early Middle Ages." *Early Modern Europe* 9 (2000): 367–96.

Costambeys, Marios, and Conrad Leyser. "To Be the Neighbor of St. Stephen: Patronage, Martyr Cult, and Roman Monasteries, c. 600–c. 900." In *Religion, Dynasty, and Patronage in Early Christian Rome, 300–900*, ed. Kate Cooper and Julia Hillner. 262–87. Cambridge: Cambridge University Press, 2007.

Daley, Brian. "Position and Patronage in the Early Church: The Original Meaning of 'Primacy of Honour'." *Journal of Theological Studies* 44 (1993): 529–53.

Demacopoulos, George. *Five Models of Spiritual Direction in the Early Church*. Notre Dame, Ind.: University of Notre Dame Press, 2007.

———. "Gregory the Great and the Appeal to Petrine Authority." In *Studia Patristica*, vol. 48, ed. Jane Baun et al. 333–46. Leuven: Peters, 2010.

———. "Gregory the Great and the Pagan Shrines of Kent." *Journal of Late Antiquity* 1 (2008): 375–91.

———. "Gregory the Great and a Post-Imperial Discourse." In *Power and Authority in Eastern Christian Experience*, ed. Fevronia K. Soumakis. 120–37. New York: Theotokos Press, 2011.

———. "Gregory the Great and the Sixth-Century Dispute over the Ecumenical Title." *Theological Studies* 70 (2009): 600–621.

De Rossi, Giovanni. *Roma sotteranea cristiana, descritta ed illustrate*. 3 vols. Rome: Cromolitografia Pontifica, 1864–77.

Dufourcq, Albert. *Étude sur les gesta maryrum romains*. 4 vols. Paris: A. Fontemoing, 1900–1910.

Dunn, Geoffrey. "Roman Primacy in the Correspondence Between Innocent I and John Chrysostom." In *Giovanni Crisostomo: Oriente e Occidente tra IV e V secolo*. 687–98. Rome: Institutum Patristicum Augustinianum, 2005.

Dunn, James. Review of Otto Zweirlien, *Petrus in Rom*. *Review of Biblical Literature* (2010): n.p.

Dvornik, Francis. *The Idea of Apostolicity in Byzantium and the Legend of the Apostle St. Andrew*. Cambridge, Mass.: Harvard University Press, 1958.

———. "Pope Gelasius and Emperor Anastasius I." *Byzantinische Zeitschrift* 44 (1951): 111–16.

Edwards, M. J. "The Clementina: A Christian Response to the Pagan Novel." *Classical Quarterly* 42 (1992): 459–74.

Elliot, James Keith, *The Apocryphal New Testament: A Collection of Apocryphal Christian Literature in an English Translation*. Oxford: Clarendon, 1993.

Elliot, John. "Peter, First Epistle of." In *Anchor Bible Dictionary*, vol. 5, ed. David Freedman. 269–78. New York: Doubleday, 2001.

Ensslin, Wilhelm. *Theoderich der Grosse*. 2nd ed. Munich: F. Bruckmann, 1959.

Geertman, Herman ed. *Atti del colloquio internazionale "Il Liber Pontificalis" e la sotria material*. Rome: Papers of the Netherlands Institute in Rome, 2003.

Goulder, Michael. "Did Peter Ever Go to Rome?" *Scottish Journal of Theology* 57 (2004): 377–96.

Green, Bernard. *The Soteriology of Leo the Great*. Oxford: Oxford University Press, 2008.

Greenslade, S. L. "The Illyrican Churches and the Vicariate of Thessalonica 375–395." *Journal of Theological Studies* n.s. 46 (1945): 17–30.

Grey, Patrick. *The Defense of Chalcedon in the East (451–553)*. Leiden: Brill, 1979.

Grig, Lucy. "Portraits, Pontiffs, and the Christianization of Fourth-Century Rome." *Papers of the British School at Rome* 72 (2004): 203–30.

Hansen, D. U. "Die Metamorphose des Heiligen: Clemens und die Clementina." In *Groningen Colloquia on the Novel*, ed. Heinz Hofmann, vol. 8. 119–29. Groningen: Egbert Forsten, 1997.

Harries, Jill. *Cicero and the Jurists: From Citizens' Law to the Lawful State*. London: Duckworth, 2006.

Hefele, Charles. *A History of the Councils of the Church*. Vol. 2, *326–429*. Edinburgh: T & T Clark, 1896; reprint New York: AMS Press, 1972.

———, *A History of the Councils of the Church*. Vol. 3, *431–451*. Edinburgh: T & T Clark, 1883.

Hess, Hamilton. *The Early Development of Canon Law and the Council of Serdica*. Rev. ed. Oxford: Oxford University Press, 2002.

Hilhorst, Anton. "The Text of the Actus Vercellenses." In *The Apocryphal Acts of Peter: Magic, Miracles, and Gnosticism*, ed. Jan Bremmer. 148–60. Leuven: Peeters, 1998.

Hillner, Julia. "Families, Patronage, and the Titular Churches of Rome, c. 300–c. 600." In *Religion, Dynasty and Patronage in Early Christian Rome: 300–900*, ed. Kate Cooper and Julia Hillner. 225–61. Cambridge: Cambridge University Press, 2007.

———. "Gregory the Great's 'Prisons': Monastic Confinement in Early Byzantine Italy." *Journal of Early Christian Studies* 19 (2011): 433–71.

Holleman, W. J. *Pope Gelasius I and the Lupercalia*. Amsterdam: Hakkert, 1974.

Huskinson, J. M. *Concordia Apostolorum: Christian Propaganda at Rome in the Fourth and Fifth Centuries; A Study of Early Christian Iconography and Iconology*. Oxford: B.A.R., 1982.

Jalland, Trevor. *The Church and the Papacy: An Historical Study, Being Eight Lectures Delivered before the University of Oxford, in the Year 1942, on the Foundation of the Rev. John Bampton, Canon of Salisbury*. London: SPCK, 1946.

———. *The Life and Times of St. Leo the Great*. New York: Macmillan, 1941.

Jones, Hannah. "Agnes and Constantia: Domesticity and Cult Patronage in the *Passion of Agnes*." In *Religion, Dynasty, and Patronage*, ed. Kate Cooper and Julia Hillner. 115–39. Cambridge: Cambridge University Press, 2007.

Kajanto, Iiro. *Onomastic Studies in the Early Christian Inscriptions of Rome and Carthage*. Helsinki: Institutum Romanum Finlandiae, 1963.

Kelly, J. N. D. *The Oxford Dictionary of Popes*. Oxford: Oxford University Press, 1986.

Klauck, Hans-Josef. *The Apocryphal Acts of the Apostles: An Introduction*. Trans. Brian McNeil. Waco, Tex.: Baylor University Press, 2008.

Knock, O. B. "Im Namen des Petrus und Paulus: Der Brief des Clemens Romanus." *Aufstieg und Niedergang der römischen Welt*, vol. 2, 27. Berlin: Walter de Gruyter, 1995.

Krautheimer, Richard. *Rome: Profile of a City, 312–1308*. Princeton, N.J.: Princeton University Press, 1980.

Krautheimer, Richard, et al. *Corpus basilicarum christianarum Romae*. Vol. 1. Vatican City: Pontificio Istituto di Archeologia Cristiana, 1937–77.

Krueger, Paul, ed. *Corpus Juris Civilis*. 2 vols. Berlin: Weidmann, 1929.

Lalleman, P. J. "The Relations Between the Acts of John and the Acts of Peter." In *The Apocryphal Acts of Peter: Magic, Miracles, and Gnosticism*, ed. J. N. Bremmer, 161–77. Leuven: Peeters, 1998.

Lampe, Peter. *Christians at Rome in the First Two Centuries: From Paul to Valentinus*. Trans. Michael Steinhauser. London: Continuum, 2003.

Leupen, P. H. D. "The Sacred Authority of Pontiffs." In *Media Latinitas: Essays in Honor of L. J. Engles*, ed. Renée Nip et al. 245–58. Turnhout: Brepols, 1996.

Leyser, Conrad. *Authority and Asceticism from Augustine to Gregory the Great*. Oxford: Oxford University Press, 2000.

Liebs, Detlef. "Roman Law." In *The Cambridge Ancient History*, vol. 14, ed. Averil Cameron. 251–52. Cambridge: Cambridge University Press, 1995.

Lindmann, Andreas. *Die Clemensbriefe*. Tubingen: Mohr Siebeck, 1992.

Lipsius, Richard A. *Die Quellen der römischen Petrus-sage kritisch untersucht*. Kiel: Schwers, 1872.

Lonstrup, Gitte. "Constructing Myths: The Foundation of *Roma Christiana* on 29 June." Trans. Lene Ostermark-Johansen. *Analecta Romana* 33 (2008): 27–64.

Llewellyn, Peter A. B. "The Roman Church During the Laurentian Schism: Priests and Senators." *Church History* 45 (1976): 417–27.

———. "The Roman Church in the Seventh Century." *Journal of Ecclesiastical History* 25 (1974): 363–80.

———. "The Roman Clergy During the Laurentian Schism (498–506): A Preliminary Analysis." *Ancient Society* 8 (1977): 245–75.

Maccarone, Michele. "Sedes Apostolica-Vicarius Petri: La perpetuità del primato di Pietro nella sede e nel vescovo di Roma (secoli III–VIII)." In *Il primato del vescovo di Roma nel primo millennio: Atti del Symposium storico-teologico (Roma, 9–13 ottobre 1989)*. 275–362. Vatican City: Libreria editrice vaticana, 1991.

Mann, H. K. "The Portraits of the Popes." *Papers of the British School at Rome* 9 (1920): 159–204.

Marazzi, Federico. *Patrimonia Sanctae Romanae Ecclesiae nel Lazio (secoli IV–X)*. Rome: Istituto Storico Italiano per il Medio Evo, 1998.

Markus, Robert. "Carthage-Prima Justiniana-Ravenna: Aspects of Justinian's *Kirchenpolitik*." *Byzantion* 49 (1979): 277–306.

———. *Gregory the Great and His World*. Cambridge: Cambridge University Press, 1997.

———. "Gregory the Great's Europe." *Royal Historical Society* 31 (1981): 21–36.

Martimort, A. G. "Vingtcinq ans de travaux et de recherches sur la mort de saint Pierre et de sa sépulture." *Bulletin de Littérature Ecclésiastique* 3 (1972): 89–98.

Martyn, John R. C. *A Translation of Abbot Leontios' Life of St. Gregory, Bishop of Agrigento*. Lewiston, N.Y.: Edward Mellen, 2004.

Mass, Michael, ed. *The Cambridge Companion to the Age of Justinian*. Cambridge: Cambridge University Press, 2005.

Mathisen, Ralph. *Ecclesiastical Factionalism and Religious Controversy in Fifth-Century Gaul*. Washington, D.C.: Catholic University Press, 1989.

Matthews, John. *Laying Down the Law: A Study of the Theodosian Code*. New Haven, Conn.: Yale University Press, 2000.

McLynn, Neil. "Crying Wolf: The Pope and the Lupercalia." *Journal of Roman Studies* 98 (2008): 161–75.

McShane, Philip. *La Romanitas et le Pape Léon le Grand: l'apport culturel des institutions imperials à la formation des structures ecclésiastiques*. Montreal: Tournai, 1979.

Merdinger, Jane. *Rome and the African Church in the Time of Augustine*. New Haven, Conn.: Yale University Press, 1997.

Meyendorff, John. *Imperial Unity and Christian Divisions*. Crestwood, N.Y.: St. Vladimir's Seminary Press, 1989.

———. "Justinian, the Empire, and the Church." *Dumbarton Oaks Papers* 22 (1969): 43–60.

Meyvaert, Paul. "The Enigma of Gregory the Great's Dialogues: A Response to Francis Clark." *Journal of Ecclesiastical History* 39 (1988): 335–81.

Minnerath, Roland. "La tradition doctrinale de la primauté pétrinienne au premier millenaire." In *Il primato del succesore di Pietro*. Rome: Città del Vaticano, 1998.

Mohlberg, Leo. "Historisch-kritische Bemerkungen zum Ursprung der sogennanten 'Memoria Apostolorum' an der Appischen Straße." In *Colligere fragmenta: Festschrift Alban Dold zum 70 Geburstag am 7.7.52*, ed. Bonifatius Fischer and Virgil Fiala. 52–74. Beuron: Beuroner Kunstverlag, 1952.

Moorhead, John. "The Laurentian Schism: East and West in the Roman Church." *Church History* 47 (1978): 125–36.

———. *Theoderic in Italy*. Oxford: Clarendon, 1992.

Morneau, Dominic. "Les patrimoines de l'Église romaine jusqu' à la mort de Grégoire le Grand." *Antiquité Tardive* 14 (2006): 79–93.

Moss, Candida. *Ancient Christian Martyrdom: Diverse Practices, Theologies, and Traditions*. New Haven, Conn.: Yale University Press, 2012.

Neil, Bronwen, *Leo the Great*. London: Routledge, 2009.

Nelson, Janet. "Gelasius' I's Doctrine of Responsibility: A Note," *Journal of Theological Studies* n.s. 18 (1967): 154–62.

Noble, Thomas. "Review: Michele Maccarrone on the Medieval Papacy." *Catholic Historical Review* 80 (1994): 518–33.

———. "Theodoric and the Papacy." In *Teoderico il Grande e i Goti d'Italia: Atti del XIII Congresso internazionale di studi sull'alto Medioevo*. 395–423. Milan: Congresso internazionale di studi sull'alto Medioevo, 1992.

North, J. A. "Caesar at the Lupercalia." *Journal of Roman Studies* 98 (2008): 144–60.

Oakley, Francis. "Walter Ullmann's Vision of Medieval Politics." *Past and Present* 60 (1973): 3–48.

Olster, David. "Justinian, Imperial Rhetoric, and the Church." *Byzantinoslavica* 50 (1989): 165–76.

Pietri, Charles. "Aristocratie et société cléricale dans l'Italie chrétienne au temps d'Odoacre et de Théodoric." *Mélanges des Écoles Françaises de Rome et d'Athènes* 93 (1981): 417–67.

———. "*Concordia apostolorum et renovatio urbis*: Culte des martyrs et propagande pontificale." *Mélanges d'Archéologie et d'Histoire de l'École Française de Rome* 73 (1961): 275–322.

———. "Donateurs et pieux établissements d'après le légendier romain (Ve–VIIe s)." In *Hagiographie: Cultures et sociétés IV–XII siècle; Actes du Colloque organisé à Nanterre et à Paris 2–5 mai 1979*. 435–53. Paris: Études Augustiniennes, 1981.

———. "Le Sénat, le peuple chrétien et le partis du Cirque à Rome sous le Pape Symmache." *Mélanges d'Archéologie et d'Histoire* 78 (1966): 123–39.

———. *Roma christiana: Recherches sur l'église de Rome, son organisation, sa politique, son idéologie de Miltiade à Sixte III*. Rome: École Française de Rome, 1976.

Pouderon, Bernard. "Flavius Clemens et le proto-Clément juif du roman pseudo-clémentin." *Apocrypha* 7 (1996): 63–79.

Pietri, Luci. "Évergetisme chrétien et foundations privées dans l'Italie de l'antiquité tardive," in *Humana Sapit*. Ed. J.-M. Carrié and Rita Lizzi. Brepols: Turnhout, 2002.

Pratscher, Wilhelm. *Der Herrenbruder Jakobus und die Jakobustradition*. Göttingen: Vandenhoeck & Ruprecht, 1987.

Rapisarda, Grazia. "I doni nell'epistolario di Gregorio Magno." In *Gregorio Magno e il suo tempo*, vol. 2, 285–300. Rome: Institutum Patristicum Augustinianum, 1991.

Rapp, Claudia. *Holy Bishops in Late Antiquity*. Berkeley: University of California Press, 2005.

Recchia, Vincenzo. *Gregorio Magno e la società Agricola*. Rome: Studium, 1978.

Reed, Annette Yoshiko, "Heresiology and the (Jewish-)Christian Novel: Narrativized Polemics in the Pseudo-Clementine Homilies." In *Heresy and Identity in Late Antiquity*, ed. Eduard Iricinschi and Holger Zellentin. 273–98. Tübingen: Mohr Siebeck, 2008.

Richards, Jeffrey. *The Popes and the Papacy in the Early Middle Ages: 476–752*. London: Routledge and Kegan Paul, 1979.

Sághy, Marianne. "*Scinditur in partes populous*: Damasus and the Martyrs of Rome." *Early Medieval History* 9 (2000): 273–87.

Salzman, Michelle. *On Roman Time: The Codex Calendar of 354 and the Rhythms of Urban Life in Late Antiquity.* Berkeley: University of California Press, 1990.

———"Leo's Liturgical Topography: Contestations for Space in Fifth Century Rome," *Journal of Roman Studies* (forthcoming).

Schor, Adam. *Theodoret's People: Social Networks and Religious Conflict in Late Roman Syria.* Berkeley: University of California Press, 2011.

Sessa, Kristina. "Domestic Conversions: Household and Bishops in the Late Antique 'Papal Legends'." In *Religion, Dynasty, and Patronage in Early Christian Rome: 300–900*, ed. Kate Cooper and Julia Hillner. 79–114.Cambridge: Cambridge University Press, 2007.

———. "Domestic Emergencies: Pelagius (556–561) and the Challenge of Managing the *domus dei* in Post-Gothic War Italy." Paper delivered at Oxford Patristics Conference, August 2011.

———. *The Formation of Papal Authority in Late Antique Italy: Roman Bishops and the Domestic Sphere.* Cambridge: Cambridge University Press, 2012.

Skedros, James. "Civic and Ecclesiastical Identity in Christian Thessaloniki." Public address, Harvard Divinity School, Cambridge, Massachusetts, May 2007.

Sotinel, Claire. "Emperors and Popes in the Sixth Century: The Western View." In *The Cambridge Companion to the Age of Justinian*, ed. Michael Maas. 267–90. Cambridge: Cambridge University Press, 2005.

Straw, Carole. *Gregory the Great: Perfection in Imperfection.* Berkeley: University of California Press, 1991.

Syme, Ronald. *The Roman Revolution.* Oxford: Oxford University Press, 1939.

Taylor, Justin. "The Early Papacy at Work: Gelasius I (492–6)." *Journal of Religious History* 8 (1975): 317–32.

Thomas, Christine. "The 'Prehistory' of the *Acts of Peter.*" In *The Apocryphal Acts of the Apostles*, ed. François Bovon. 39–62. Cambridge, Mass.: Harvard University Press, 1999.

Townsend, W. T. "The So-Called Symmachian Forgeries." *Journal of Religion* 12 (1933): 165–74.

Trout, Dennis. "Damasus and the Invention of Early Christian Rome." *Journal of Medieval and Early Modern Studies* 33 (2003): 517–36.

Tuilier, André. "Grégoire le grand et le titre de patriarche oecuménique." In *Grégoire le grand: [Colloque tenu à] Chantilly, Centre culturel Les Fontaines, 15–19 Septembre 1982; Actes*, ed. Jacques Fontaine, Robert Gillet, and Stan Pellistrandi. 69–82. Paris: CNRS, 1986.

Turner, C. H. "The Latin Acts of Peter." *Journal of Theological Studies* 32 (1931): 119–33.

Uhalde, Kevin. "Pope Leo I on Power and Failure." *Catholic Historical Review* 95 (2009): 671–88.

———. "The Sinful Subject: Doing Penance in Rome." In *Studia Patristica*, vol. 44, ed. Jane Baun et al. 405–14. Leuven: Peeters, 2010.

Ullmann, Walter. *Gelasius I (492–496): Das Papsttum an der Wende der Spätantike zum Mittelalter.* Stuttgart: Anton Hiersemann, 1981.

———. *The Growth of the Papal Government in the Middle Ages: A Study in the Ideological Relation of Clerical to Lay Power.* 3rd ed. London: Methuen, 1970.

———. "Leo the First and the Theme of Papal Primacy." *Journal of Theological Studies* n.s. 11 (1960): 25–51.

———. *A Short History of the Papacy in the Middle Ages.* 2nd ed. London: Routledge, 2003.

———. "Significance of the Epistola Clementis in the Pseudo-Clementines." *Journal of Theological Studies* n.s. 11 (1960): 295–317.

Vailhé, Siméon. "Le titre de Patriarche Oecouménique avant saint Grégoire le Grand." *Echos d'Orient* 11 (1908): 65–69.

———. "Saint Grégoire le Grand et le titre de Patriarche oecouménique," *Echos d'Orient* 11 (1908): 161–71.

van der Horst, Pieter. Review of Otto Zwierlein, *Petrus in Rom. Bryn Mawr Classical Review* (2010). n.p.

Veyne, Paul. *Bread and Circuses: Historical Sociology and Political Pluralism.* Trans. Brian Pearce. London: Penguin, 1990.

Vouaux, Léon, *Les Actes de Pierre.* Paris: Letouzey, 1922.

Vyvian, John Percy, Dacre Balsdon, and Miriam T. Griffin. "Princeps." In *The Oxford Classical Dictionary*, ed. Simon Hornblower and Antony Spawforth. 1246–47. 3rd rev. ed. Oxford: Oxford University Press, 2003.

Wessel, Susan. *Leo the Great and the Spiritual Rebuilding of a Universal Rome.* Leiden: Brill, 2008.

White, Lynn. "The Byzantinization of Sicily." *American Historical Review* 42 (1936): 1–21.

Wirbelauer, Eckhard. *Zwei Päpste in Rom: Der Konflict zwischen Laurentius und Symmachus (498–514).* Munich: Tudov, 1993.

Zwierlein, Otto. *Petrus in Rom: Die literarischen Zeugnisse.* Berlin: De Gruyter, 2010.

ACKNOWLEDGMENTS

One of the great privileges of teaching at Fordham University is the opportunity to instruct (and learn from) a talented group of doctoral students. This book originates from a question I fielded during a doctoral seminar several years ago. At the time, I was unable to articulate an answer that I thought was satisfactory, so I promised to provide a more suitable response. I soon discovered, however, that a simple answer would not be forthcoming and determined that I would make a more serious investigation into the matter. Along the way, I have benefited from a number of graduate research assistants who surely spent far more time thinking about the late ancient papacy than they had ever expected upon enrollment. In particular, I would like to thank Jon Stanfill, Lindsey Mercer, John Garza, Allan Georgia, Malik Muhammed, and especially Matthew Briel. The two appendices to this volume, which are the first published English translations of these important Gelasian texts, are the work of Mr. Briel and well reflect his advanced skills.

Although the completion of this project took longer than I had initially anticipated, I was able to finish earlier than I would have otherwise because of a very generous research fellowship awarded by the Carpenter Foundation. That, combined with a Fordham Faculty Fellowship, enabled an entire year of sabbatical research during calendar year 2011. Revisions to the text were made possible by a Faculty Research Grant during Summer 2012.

As my research progressed, I benefited immensely from generous and inspiring colleagues. Among my colleagues at Fordham, I especially wish to thank Michael Peppard and Larry Welborn, who offered quick and insightful answers to every query I put to them. Beyond Fordham, I have benefited immensely from my conversations with other scholars of the early papacy, especially Kristina Sessa and Kevin Uhalde. I must thank both of them, along with James Skedros, Michelle Salzman, and Ashley Purpura, for generously sharing research prior to publication. I would like to thank Michael Peppard for his careful review of Chapter 1 and I owe a special debt of gratitude to Kristina Sessa and to Ben Dunning, each of whom read the entire manuscript and offered critical suggestions for revision. Any shortcomings that remain are, of course, my own. I would also like to express my appreciation to Peter Kaufman, Stephen Shoemaker, and Aristotle Papanikolaou, friends for many years, who continue to offer generous counsel whenever it is sought.

I am delighted to have this book published in the Divinations series at the University of Pennsylvania Press. Derek Krueger, a long-time friend and one of the series editors, encouraged me to submit the project and offered many kindnesses along the way. The senior humanities editor, Jerry Singerman, has been a delight throughout the process. I must also acknowledge my appreciation for the two anonymous readers who offered important critiques, affirmations, and suggestions for improvement. I hope that they will find their insights pursued in the pages that follow.

Finally, I would like to note that this book is dedicated to my parents, Terry and Mary Lynn Demacopoulos, and to my in-laws, Rev. John and Margaret Orfanakos, for their love, generosity, and example.